Advanced
QuickBASIC 4.0

Advanced
QuickBASIC 4.0

Murray Lesser

BANTAM BOOKS
TORONTO · NEW YORK · LONDON · SYDNEY · AUCKLAND

ADVANCED QUICKBASIC 4.0
A Bantam Book / April 1988

ISBN 0–553–34546–X

Published simultaneously in the United States and Canada

PRINTED IN THE UNITED STATES OF AMERICA

B   0   9   8   7   6   5   4   3   2   1

In memory of

Robert M. Lesser

Contents

Contents

Contents

Preface

Although it is theoretically possible to program any computable problem using any complete programming language, most applications are easier to program in some languages than in others. Programming languages are designed (or have evolved) to emphasize particular capabilities. A language is "best" to use for an application when there is a good match between application requirements and the emphasized capabilities of the language. In my opinion, modern *compiled* BASIC, extended with assembly-language procedures, is the best language to use for applications requiring a great deal of string manipulation, and is more convenient than most others for data-processing applications involving "random" files.

Unfortunately, most programmers know BASIC only in its *interpreted* implementation. Microsoft interpreted BASIC became the *lingua franca* of the microcomputer world when Bill Gates and Paul Allen (the founders of Microsoft) wrote their first primitive BASIC interpreter for the MITS Altair (the first commercially available microcomputer) in 1975. The language has been greatly extended since then. Support has been added for disk files, graphics, sound generation, and other specialized input/output devices. The programming capabilities have been modernized to include most of the "structured programming" concepts.

However, interpreted BASIC suffers from many ills: program execution is usually painfully slow, large programs are difficult to write and debug (and even more difficult to read or modify later), and program size is severely limited. In spite of these drawbacks, the use of interpreted BASIC has flourished because it offers "instant gratification" to the programmer. As soon as the program has been written, execution can be attempted with essentially no added effort.

Compiled BASIC doesn't suffer from the ills of interpreted BASIC. Programs written for the compiler not only perform better, but are easier to write, easier to debug, and easier to modify — albeit the approach to program design and implementation must be more structured than with the interpreter. But, using a compiler correctly entails additional compiling and linking processes between completing the text of the source code and producing an executable file. Compiled BASIC did not offer instant gratification until the advent of the Microsoft QuickBASIC compiler version 2.0 for the IBM PC family and close compatibles.

The new version 4.0 of QuickBASIC permits text editing, rapid incremental compiling, and then running the executable program — in a continuous (menu-driven) operation without leaving what Microsoft calls its "development environment." Most of *Learning and Using Microsoft QuickBASIC*, the tutorial supplied with version 4.0, is devoted to the canned development environment. However, the more versatile version 4.0 conventional compiler lets the serious programmer construct better-performing programs using less memory space.

This book covers what the QuickBASIC manuals leave out. It shows you how to extend the BASIC language with your own assembled subroutines, how to augment the compiler-furnished libraries with your own searchable libraries of assembled and compiled procedures, and how to design complex programs for easy implementation and debugging outside of the development environment.

— Murray L. Lesser

Chapter 1
Introduction

This book is a do-it-yourself text on extending the BASIC language by using the Microsoft QuickBASIC compiler version 4.0 in its efficient "separate compilation" mode. The book is written for those with some prior knowledge, but who are not professional programmers. I have assumed that you are moderately proficient at writing programs with the IBM BASICA or Microsoft GW-BASIC interpreter, or have even used QuickBASIC under its "development environment," but have had little or no experience using a true compiler.

If you have ever attempted to use an assembled subroutine with an interpreted BASIC program, you will be surprised how much easier it is with the fully compiled implementation. This ease of linking compiled BASIC programs to searchable libraries of assembled subroutines and functions is the basis for "extending" the language to specialize it for any particular need not covered in Microsoft's implementation.

You can use my illustrative assembled routines as is, without having any knowledge of how to write simple assembly-language programs. But if you can write your own, the ones in this book are merely examples. You can build on the techniques shown to meet your own programming needs.

Conventions Used in the Text

Basic is a much-used word in this book. When it is written in all upper-case letters, it refers to the language; otherwise it has the usual English meaning. BASIC with no modifier is used for topics common to both the compiler and interpreter implementations. I use BASICA as a generic term for specific references to interpreted BASIC, and QBASIC when the topic is restricted to the QuickBASIC compiler. I use "compiled BASIC" when discussing topics common to QBASIC and earlier Microsoft 16-bit BASIC compilers.

Examples of BASIC commands, both in the text and in the listing comments, use a notation similar to that used in the Microsoft manuals, with a few important exceptions. These exceptions allow the same conventions to be used in the text as appear in the listings and in the "prompt" messages on the display screen when the program is running.

I use *angle brackets* (greater-than and less-than symbols) surrounding what Microsoft calls *placeholders* for mandatory information you must supply, rather than the italicized words used by Microsoft. If the text within the angle brackets is in lowercase (e.g., <text>), this refers to a variable name or file name you must furnish. If the material is in upper case (e.g., <LF>), this refers to an ASCII control character. (<LF> stands for "Line Feed" and is obtained from the IBM keyboard with the key combination Ctrl-Enter.)

Another exception is the use of single square brackets ([]) to surround optional statement entries, rather than the double square brackets used in the Microsoft manual. An ellipsis [...] within the square brackets indicates that the structure previously shown may be replicated as necessary.

QBASIC *keywords* (called "reserved words" in the BASIC manual), as used in functions and statements, are shown all in uppercase (e.g., OPEN, CLOSE). Keyword usage is not optional except when enclosed in square brackets. However, since the compiler itself is case-insensitive, you can use either upper- or lowercase, or mixed, characters for keywords when writing your programs.

Names of programs, and of variables and files used within programs, are also shown as all capital letters in the text and in the listings, although the system is case-insensitive to such names.

Many words in computer terminology have a generic meaning as well as a specific meaning within a particular language. I use lowercase to distinguish generic terms from equivalent BASIC keywords (e.g., open, close).

Several terms used in the text, dealing with computer system and architecture matters, may be outside the vocabulary of many BASIC programmers. These are defined, although not necessarily at the point of first usage. Definitions are marked in the Index by page numbers in italics.

Superscript numbers in the text refer to notes,[1] which will be found at the end of each chapter. Especially important information (compiler idiosyncrasies, corrections to QBASIC manual errors, and other potential booby traps) is marked with the symbol *N.B.* and is shown indented in the text.

Program listings are the essence of any book on language usage. The ones in this book were designed to be read, and are a necessary adjunct to the text. The line numbers (including the following colon) shown in the listings are for discussion purposes and should not appear in any transcriptions you make. Text references to groups of line numbers (e.g., lines 11–21, listing 2-1) are inclusive.

An important part of learning any new language system is running experiments. Most figures show either short listings of experimental programs you might run, or are copies of the display during the running of some of the experiments or full programs I have furnished.

Versions, Bugs, and Idiosyncrasies

It is extremely doubtful that any program requiring more than two pages to list the source code is entirely bug free. While reputable software houses make every effort to test their programs, it is impossible to test a major program completely, since this would require using every possible combination of inputs. Thus, all major system programs (compilers, assemblers, and operating systems) contain bugs. All reputable software publishers depend on their users to find and report the *subtle* bugs (those value-dependent in a nonobvious fashion) that have not been discovered during normal testing.

N.B.   While every attempt has been made to test the programs and routines shown in the listings in this book, neither the author nor the publisher make any warranties concerning them and neither assumes any responsibility or liability of any kind for errors or the consequences of any such errors.

New program versions serve two purposes: one is to fix the "known" bugs at the time of the version release. The other purpose is to enhance the previous version by adding more capabilities. Unfortunately, enhancements introduce new bugs. Versions that contain major enhancements are likely to contain major bugs.

QuickBASIC version 2.0, the first with a built-in development environment, was no exception to this rule. Six months later, a bug-fix version 2.01 was distributed (free) to all registered owners of version 2.0. Three months later, version 3.0 was released (not free). This fixed most of the bugs (that I know about) remaining in version 2.01. While there were some additions to the language itself, version 3.0's major enhancement was an improved "source-code debugger."

Source-code debuggers may be of interest to those programmers who write a complete complex program first and wonder why it doesn't work afterward. However, no debugger is of much help if you don't know enough about the location of your trouble to know what to look at. And if you do know that much, there are easier ways to find the problem. A neatly prepared listing of a well-structured program and some temporary debugging code are still the best debugging tools if your complex program is implemented and tested in small stages.[2]

QuickBASIC version 4.0 appeared six months after version 3.0. Its major enhancements are a significant change in the way the development environment operates — both as it appears to the user and in its internals — and a significant improvement in the way the BASIC support system (in separately compiled programs) manages available memory during run time. The remaining enhancements are changes to the assembly-language interface and more changes to the BASIC language itself. Due to the latter changes, some programs written for earlier versions of QuickBASIC must be modified before they can be recompiled under version 4.0.[3]

Since major enhancements generate major bugs, there are two new ones in version 4.0. One appears only when running the QuickBASIC development environment on diskette-only systems. The other major bug is only apparent when you run either the development environment (QB.EXE) or any program separately compiled from the stand-alone compiler (BC.EXE) on an IBM PC or PC-XT with an IBM mono adapter installed as the primary display. External "fixes" for both of these bugs are described in the "System Setup" section in the next chapter.

New releases come rather frequently in the microcomputer world, and there may have been additional releases of QuickBASIC by the time you read this book. Always read both the README.DOC and the UP-DATE.DOC files that come with the distribution diskettes of your compiler for the latest information on errors and fixes for both the manual and the compiler.

Of course, not all reported bugs are really bugs; they are what I call "idiosyncrasies" of the program — the result of deliberate design decisions made by the program implementer. The "problem" is an idiosyncrasy that produces results differing from what the person reporting the bug expects. There are several idiosyncrasies in QBASIC that I find annoying. I will tell you about them at the appropriate time.

As of this writing, the most recent version of the Disk Operating System (DOS) used with IBM PCs and compatibles is 3.3. Although, in theory, any QBASIC program will run under any version of DOS later than 2.0, this may not be true in practice — depending on the statements used in the program. For example, SHELL does not always work properly under DOS versions earlier than 3.0. Two of the programs shown in later chapters require DOS version 3.2, or later, to run as written.

Hardware/Software Requirements

QuickBASIC is not a generic MS-DOS compiler. It, and the programs compiled by it, make direct calls on the IBM PC ROM BIOS interfaces for many functions, rather than using the slower and less powerful DOS interfaces. (I have followed the same philosophy in my assembled subroutines.) As a consequence of this design decision, the compiler and compiled programs will run only on systems that adhere to the IBM BIOS interfaces — members of the IBM PC family and close compatibles.

According to its manual, QuickBASIC requires a minimum installed memory of 320 kilobytes (K). This figure is a bit misleading. It is the minimum memory for using the QuickBASIC development environment to compose, compile and run moderately sized programs all in memory, providing you are not using too many DOS options or memory-consuming "terminate and stay resident" (TSR) programs. You can compile and run much larger programs in the same installed memory if you ignore the development environment and use only the separate compiler, BC.EXE.

You will need an assembler to use the assembly-language routines. QuickBASIC version 4.0 uses slightly different interfaces to assembled subroutines and functions than did its predecessors, matched to the "simplified segment definition" procedure introduced with the Microsoft Macro Assembler (MASM) version 5.0 (as shown in the assembly-language listings in this book). If you are using an earlier version of MASM, you must supply the equivalent detailed segment definitions as discussed in Chapter 11.

You will also need a good screen editor. Although the QBASIC development environment includes a screen editor (which can be used in its "document" mode for writing assembly source code), I find it frustrating to use. The built-in editor is menu-driven, with "dialog boxes" designed for use with a mouse, but awkward to use from the keyboard.[4] It also lacks many of the niceties that make a programmer's text editor convenient to use.

Most compilers and assemblers that run under DOS require the *source code* (your original program text) to be formatted as a DOS sequential file (sometimes called an "ASCII file"). That is, each line of code must end with the <CR><LF> control characters, in that order. Many word-processing text editors (particularly the "what you see is what you get" type) do not produce ASCII files unless coerced to do so.

My primary computer system is a 640K IBM PC-XT, with one 360K internal diskette drive, one 720K (3.5-inch) external diskette drive, and one 10Mb hard disk. It has two display adapters installed: an enhanced graphics adapter (EGA) driving an enhanced color display (ECD) as the primary display, and a mono adapter driving a mono display as the secondary. Printed output is through an asynchronous communications adapter driving a Qume Sprint 5/45 daisy-wheel printer. "Normal" printer output is rerouted from LPT1 output to the COM1 output, using the installed device driver described in Appendix A. The manuscript for this book was written and printed on this system. The programs were also written and tested on this machine.

My backup computer system is an early (1982 vintage) IBM PC, with two diskette drives, which has been updated to current specs with a new ROM BIOS and a current-design 8088 microprocessor. This 640K system has only the mono adapter and display. The attached printer is an IBM

Proprinter XL, driven from the LPT1 port on the mono adapter. Most of the programs were also tested on this system.

All the hardware in these systems (with the exception of the Qume printer) carries IBM nameplates. I mention this point because some third-party substitutes do not use the same BIOS interfaces. If your hardware requires a special installed device driver or a "terminate and stay resident" program to be operable on a PC or compatible, some of the routines in this book may not work as expected.

For Your Library

No single text on computer usage can be self-contained. I am assuming that you have the three manuals distributed with QuickBASIC version 4.0, so I do not repeat much of the detailed information contained in those books.

If you need to learn assembly-language programming, one of the better texts on the subject was written by David J. Bradley,[5] a member of the original IBM PC design team. This book was recommended to me by a programmer in Boca Raton, primarily because the examples are full program listings, not merely the program fragments found in many texts.

If you are interested in the design philosophy of the 8086/8088 microprocessor chips (the "brains" of most PCs), you should read Stephen Morse's book.[6] Morse is the architect of the 8086/8088.

The primary programmer's reference for the PC-DOS operating system is the IBM *Disk Operating System Technical Reference*. If you are using an MS-DOS system on a compatible, the equivalent reference is Microsoft's *MS-DOS Programmer's Reference*. Make sure you get the reference manual corresponding to the version of DOS you are using.

Programmer/owners of IBM machines will find the *Technical Reference* manual for their machine very useful. All IBM hardware *Technical Reference* manuals have the same title, but there is a separate edition for each machine type. There is also a multivolume addendum for the options and adapters, along with updates for the later devices. The hardware Technical Reference manuals (for all systems except members of the Personal System/2 family) contain ROM BIOS listings and are the best available information on the BIOS interfaces.[7] Telephone IBM at 800-426-7282 and ask to be put on the mailing list for the *Technical Directory*, which lists the titles and prices of the IBM PC technical documentation that is available for general sale.

If you are using a compatible, you may or may not be able to find equivalent publications for your machine. Try the dealer you bought it from.

There are several general references on using DOS and BIOS interfaces. The best one I have read is Peter Norton's *Programmer's Guide.*[8]

Programming Style

Programming is not a science. It is not even a branch of mathematics. Programming is an art form, somewhat akin to writing essays. Programming, like essay writing, deals with constructing an unambiguous written exposition of a logical train of thought. Fortunately for programmers, it is easier to write an unambiguous description of a logical train of thought intelligible to machines, than one intelligible to people. Unfortunately for programmers, it is necessary that the program source code also be intelligible to people — or at least to other programmers.

As with every other art form, "style" is an important element in the difference between good programs and bad programs. There are two facets to programming style. The obvious one is the manner in which the program is designed and implemented. Every programmer adopts certain "comfortable" constructs and uses them over and over in similar circumstances. One can almost tell, when reading the ROM BIOS listings in the various IBM *Technical Reference* manuals, when different programmers were at work. One will clear a register with a SUB statement; another will use a XOR statement. The two have an equivalent effect, and the assembled instructions take up the same space and the same number of clock cycles to execute. The choice is a matter of programming style.

But programming language development (and standardization) follows fads. New ways of doing the same thing, only some of which offer genuine convenience, are continually being added to the languages. I consider it poor programming style to confuse readers with new programming "jargon" when the familiar forms provide the same service just as conveniently. For example, I never use the specialized GOTO substitutes (such as "EXIT FOR") that have been added to QuickBASIC; a real GOTO with an explicit label makes the program much easier for the reader to understand, and often provides better performance.

The other facet to programming style is the way the program appears when listed. Six months after you have written that marvelous well-debugged program, you will want to revise it. Unless you can understand what the program does (and how it does it) from the program listing, you will have very little chance of making a revision without introducing a flock of new bugs.

The major requirements for source-code legibility, other than the program itself be well-structured, are that:

- The variable names be properly chosen to have meaning.
- The program listing be neatly arranged on the sheets of paper.
- The program have proper comments.

Although nonprogrammers might need a manual, properly commented source- code is all the documentation another programmer should need to understand what the program does and how it does it. Most high-level-language programmers could learn a lesson in commenting from reading the source- code written by expert assembly-language programmers (see those ROM BIOS listings, or the source-code for IN-TRPT.ASM, on one of your QBASIC 4.0 distribution diskettes).

A minor aspect of programming style is the character "case" the program is written in. Both the QBASIC compiler and the assembler are case-insensitive (except inside of quoted strings). Thus, it is a programmer's choice whether to use the old-fashioned all uppercase, the C-inspired all lowercase, or the Pascal-induced mixed case. I happen to prefer all uppercase for the actual code with normal mixed-case text for comments, because I am more interested in having the comments easy to read at a glance than I am the code. This is the style used in the listings. However, I have used all lowercase text in the little demonstration programs shown as figures.

Notes

1. Notes contain bibliographic references, bits of history, and additional information not altogether required. With the excep-

tion of the references, the notes are written to stand alone. Unless you are a compulsive footnote reader, they can be left until you arrive at the "Notes" section of each chapter.

2. Although I never use a debugger when developing my own programs, I use two to study other people's programs when the source-code is not available. I use the Microsoft symbolic debugger SYMDEB (distributed with MASM 4.0) or the IBM Personally Developed Software interrupt chaser PCWATCH to study the internal structure of operating systems and language processors.

3. Although it is sometimes necessary to modify old programs to fit new versions of a compiler, it is probably good programming practice to use only the latest version of any language processor.

4. Computer rodents are not useful with text editors; when I am typing text, I do not want to take my hands off the keyboard.

5. David J. Bradley, *Assembly Language Programming for the IBM Personal Computer*, Prentice-Hall, Englewood Cliffs, N.J., 1984.

6. Stephen P. Morse, *The 8086/8088 Primer*, 2nd edition, Haydn Book Company, Rochelle Park, N.J., 1982.

7. The ROM BIOS programming interfaces for all IBM models are described in the *IBM Personal System/2 and Personal Computer BIOS Interface Technical Reference.*

8. *The Peter Norton Programmer's Guide to the IBM PC*, Microsoft Press, Redmond, Wash., 1985.

Chapter 2

QuickBASIC Basics

There are several important differences in usage between programs written to be compiled under QuickBASIC and equivalent programs intended to be run under its nearest interpreted sibling, BASICA version 3.3. Many of these stem from essential differences between the way a compiler processes source code and the way an interpreter does. Others stem from actual differences in the way the language was defined in the two implementations.

In this chapter some of the basic differences between using the two implementations are illustrated by an introduction to the "separately compiled" mode of compiler operation. I will introduce other major differences in the topics covered in the rest of the book.

Fundamentals of Compiling

Using any high-level language requires a translation of the symbols of that language to the symbols causing the machine to perform the desired sequence of elementary operations. In BASICA the only "translation" done before run time is during program entry. Each BASICA keyword is converted to an equivalent single-byte identifier, and each numeric constant and line number is converted to its internal representation. All variable names, string constants, comments, and any blank spaces for legibility remain in the program as written.

During run time, each statement is translated (compiled) into machine language when it is ready to be executed. The locations (in memory) of the data corresponding to named variables are found each time they are needed, by searching a variable-name list. Once executed, the translation is thrown away. BASICA has little knowledge of where it has been, and none of where it is going, during run time.

BASICA can use, at most, only 64K to hold the compressed source code, the name list and values of all the variables used, the file buffers, and the stack. Most experienced BASICA programmers pack as many statements on a line as possible and use as few comments as they can get away with, in an attempt to deal with this limitation. Part of the interpreter mythology is that such efforts at producing nonreadable programs also decrease program running time. Probably the hardest thing for an experienced BASICA programmer to learn when moving to compiled BASIC is that using these "tricks" doesn't make any difference in the size or running time of the final program, but does make the compiled program much more difficult to write, debug, or modify later.

In compiled BASIC, available memory is the only restriction on the size of the code portion of the executable program. The 64K (maximum) DGROUP is used only for constant and variable data storage, BASIC's file buffers, and the stack. In addition, QBASIC can store many array types in any available memory, even *outside* the 64K area.

When you compile a BASIC program with BC.EXE, the statements are translated only once, during *compile time*. The compiler reads and processes the source file (<filename>.BAS)[1] and writes the *object* file (<filename>.OBJ) to the default drive. There are no comments or variable names, and very few label names, in the object code. All decisions relative to data storage and order of code execution are made during compile time.

An object file is not executable until it has been *linked*. Linking selects the called-for subroutines from the searchable libraries and resolves all the address cross-references in any linked-together modules.[2] The <filename>.EXE file produced by the linker is an executable file, ready to be loaded into memory and executed by the DOS command processor.

As I will show later, the compiler does a moderate amount of code optimization. Among other things, allowable arithmetic operations between constants in a statement are done at compile time, and duplication of common subexpressions within a block of statements is eliminated. Thus, it is unlikely that arithmetic expressions will be evaluated in the sequence they would have been in BASICA (nominally left to right as written).

The development environment, QB.EXE, operates in a manner somewhat between compiling and interpreting. To oversimplify a little, each line is "compiled" and checked for syntax errors at the time you press the Enter key. Data is stored in known locations, rather than in a list structure. There is no explicit link time. At execution time, the precompiled lines are executed in a manner similar to the way an interpreter would, except it is not necessary to recompile each line as it is found, nor to search for variables by name. There is no code optimization when running under the development environment, so the order of code execution may not be the same as when running the same program after it has been separately compiled. Some errors that are caught by BC during compile time are not found by the development environment until run time. Arithmetic results between the two versions may not agree, and pathological uses of defined functions may produce different side effects.

BC compiles most integer arithmetic and execution-flow control statements into in-line machine code, and makes library calls for all other BASIC functions. Programs can be compiled to link to either of two compiler-furnished libraries.

The default case is to link to the shorter library, BRUN40.LIB, which sets up linkages to the BASIC library functions through programmed interrupts to the *run-time module*, BRUN40.EXE. The initializer portion of programs so compiled will load the run-time module into memory before execution begins. The BRUN40.EXE file must be in the default directory or in a directory shown on the DOS environment PATH list while running a program using it. The run-time module contains *all* the QBASIC support functions and will be memory resident in its entirety.

You can compile your program to link to the long library, BCOM40.LIB, by appending the /o switch to the BC call command. The BCOM40.LIB is searched at link time and only those support routines actually required by the program are linked to it. Programs compiled to be linked to the long library will usually take up less memory space at run time, and the total elapsed time to run the program will be less because it is not necessary to load BRUN40.EXE before the program starts, or to reload COMMAND.COM after it finishes.

You might be wondering why anyone would use the default separate-compile mode when the /o mode results in a program that is both faster and takes up less memory space. The default compile mode is useful during program development because of the shorter linking time. It should be used for the final executable program if disk space is a limiting factor or (sometimes) when the program contains SHELL statements.

System Setup for Compilation

The details of setting up your system for using QBASIC in the preferred "separately compiled" mode depend on whether you have an all-diskette system or have both diskette and hard disk drives. The first operation, of course, is to make backup copies of the compiler distribution diskettes. Put the originals in a safe place, in case of emergency, and use the backup copies to make your program-implementing "working" files.

Using an All-Diskette System

One of the problems with using QBASIC 4.0 and MASM 5.0, particularly with the later versions of DOS, is that all the system programs have grown so large that it is very inconvenient to set up an all-diskette system using 360K (5.25-inch) diskettes, particularly if you don't have enough installed memory to use a virtual disk. I have found it relatively convenient to use a separate *boot* diskette, putting the QuickBASIC files on their own diskettes. If you are not content with the QB built-in text editor, you can put your text editor on the boot diskette.

Format your boot diskette with the /v/s switches and add the necessary CONFIG.SYS and AUTOEXEC.BAT files. Figure 2-1 shows a sample CONFIG.SYS file for a diskette-only system containing at least 512K of installed memory. I have found that setting BUFFERS=4 is sufficient for optimum performance when reading and writing sequential files with no subdirectories involved. If you are using DOS 3.2 or earlier, this will insure enough DOS buffers; if you are using DOS 3.3 or later, this will prevent wasting valuable memory space with too many buffers. Of course, if any program you run regularly requires more file buffers, you

```
BUFFERS=4
DEVICE=A:\VDISK.SYS 100 kbytes, 512 byte sectors, 32 directory entries
```

Figure 2 - 1
Sample CONFIG.SYS file for 512K diskette-only system

can increase this number, but too many file buffers *decrease* performance and unneeded file buffers take up space better used elsewhere.

If you are running DOS 3.3 on a PC or XT compatible (one with an 8088/8086 microprocessor), you should add a STACKS=0,0 command to your CONFIG.SYS file to avoid cluttering up memory space with unneeded stack frames.

You will note there is no FILES= statement in Figure 2-1. I have never needed more than the default five files open simultaneously. However, some programs you write or use may require more. An excess in the number of allowable simultaneously open files does not cause performance degradation, but it does use up space.

VDISK.SYS is the device driver (furnished with DOS versions 3.0 and later) to install a *virtual* (memory-mapped) disk, which is invaluable in speeding up the process of program development. As a further bonus, if you always use a virtual disk as the default drive, it lessens the probability of inadvertently erasing a wanted file. However, since the virtual disk goes away every time you shut off the power (or reboot the system), you must remember to copy files to a real diskette if you want to keep them.

The virtual disk installation variables shown in Figure 2-1 were chosen for a 512K installed memory and DOS 3.3 to allow an available memory (as shown by CHKDSK) of about 370,000 bytes for compiling and linking — if no additional DOS options and no TSR programs are installed. If your available memory falls below about 350,000 bytes, decrease the size of the virtual disk accordingly. Eliminate the virtual disk entirely if it contains less than 64K. (See the chapter on "Configuring Your System" in the *Disk Operating System* manual for further information on using the CONFIG.SYS file.)

```
ECHO OFF
PATH A:\;B:\
SET LIB=B:\
SET INCLUDE=B:\
DATE
TIME
C:
CLS
```

Figure 2 - 2
Sample AUTOEXEC.BAT file for 512K diskette-only system

Figure 2-2 shows a sample AUTOEXEC.BAT file to be associated with the CONFIG.SYS file previously shown. This command list will be run automatically every time you boot your system.

The commands in AUTOEXEC.BAT set the PATH, LIB, and IN-CLUDE environment variables to work with the compiler and linker, then ask for the date and time (not necessary if you have a self-installing real-time clock), and leave the system with the screen clear and the virtual disk as the default drive. The LIB environment tells the linker where to look for searchable libraries if they are not found in the default directory.

N.B.   You *must* use the most recent version of Microsoft LINK.EXE that you have — either the version furnished with the QBASIC compiler or a later version furnished with another Microsoft language.

The INCLUDE environment string is not used by QuickBASIC, but is used by the assembler and many other language compilers to find "include" files. A compiled utility, shown in Chapter 8, corrects this deficiency in QBASIC.

If you do not have enough memory to specify a virtual disk in the CONFIG.SYS file, delete the references to the B drive in the PATH command, set the LIB environment string to the A drive, do not use the IN-CLUDE environment string, and set B (rather than C) as the default drive in the next-to-last command.

N.B.   If you are running on an IBM PC or XT system with an IBM mono adapter as the primary display device, the QBASIC 4.0 development environment or a program compiled under BC version 4.0 may produce a strange cursor on return to DOS.

The basic problem is with a bug in the ROM BIOS of those machines. However, the implementers of previous versions of QBASIC knew about the bug and programmed around it. If you experience a cursor problem on your system, substitute the DOS command "MODE MONO" for the CLS command in Figure 2-2 and add the DOS file MODE.COM to your boot diskette.

Your second working diskette should contain the development environment, QB.EXE, and the help file, QB.HLP (if you use it). This diskette must also carry a copy of COMMAND.COM.[3] (If you are using the QB editor and do not require MODE.COM on your boot diskette, you may be able to put your system boot files on this QB diskette — particularly if you sacrifice the QB.HLP file.) This diskette should be run from the A drive.

N.B.   When you call QB from the DOS command line, it looks through the directories in your PATH environment string, hunting for a file named QB.INI. If it doesn't find QB.INI, it goes about its business using the default "view" options. However, if QB version 4.0 finds a directory name in the PATH environment string with no diskette in the drive *before* it finds QB.INI, it will die with a "string space corrupt" message.

The "fix" is to add a QB.INI file to your QB diskette — even if you don't really need it. Pick up the "View, Options" menu and then exit it immediately with the Enter key. When you leave the QB environment, copy the newly written QB.INI file from the default drive to the A drive.

Your third working diskette should contain the executable files necessary to separately compile and link programs, and to prepare private searchable libraries: COMMAND.COM, BRUN40.EXE, BC.EXE, LINK.EXE, and LIB.EXE. If you write assembled COM programs, you might also put EXE2BIN.EXE on this diskette.[4] This diskette will also be run from the A drive, as there is no reason to have QB.EXE and BC.EXE on the system at the same time.

```
BUFFERS=6
DEVICE=C:\VDISK.SYS 179 kbytes, 512 byte sectors
```

Figure 2 - 3
Sample CONFIG.SYS file for 640K hard disk system

Your fourth working diskette should contain the necessary libraries and any "include" files. Start with BCOM40.LIB, BRUN40.LIB, and BQLB40.LIB. You will later add your private searchable subroutine and function library, your private "include" files, and (if you wish) a "Quick" library that can be used with the QB development environment. This diskette is used in the B drive.

Your fifth working diskette is a utility diskette containing MASM, often-used DOS utilities, and the utilites you write. Since it may be run from either drive, it should contain copies of COMMAND.COM and BRUN40.EXE, as well as any other programs you might need.

If you don't have enough memory for a virtual diskette, you will also need a "scratch" default disk for program writing, compiling and linking. This diskette, used in drive B, should carry your "include" files and any "Quick" library you use. When you link your object files, LINK will tell you it can't find a library file. Insert the "library" diskette in the A drive and reply with "A:."

Using a System with a Hard Disk

Life is much easier with a hard disk. Figure 2-3 shows a sample CON-FIG.SYS file for a 640K hard disk system. The BUFFER number has been increased by two, to compensate for the fact that subdirectories are usually used with a hard disk. If you fancy subsubdirectories, etc., increase the BUFFER number by two more for each additional level of directory you indulge in. Note that the size of the virtual disk has been increased to 179K, equivalent to a single-sided, 9-sector data diskette. If you have only 512K installed memory, use the VDISK installation variables shown in Figure 2-1.

```
ECHO OFF
PATH C:\;C:\WORD;C:\PROG
SET LIB=C:\LIB
SET INCLUDE=C:\HEADER
DATE
TIME
D:
CLS
```

Figure 2 - 4
Sample AUTOEXEC.BAT file fo 640K hard disk system

A corresponding AUTOEXEC.BAT file is shown in Figure 2-4. This assumes that the programs you normally use (including DOS utilities) are in the C drive root directory; both compilers, the assembler, the linker, the library manager, EXE2BIN, and BRUN40.EXE are in the PROG subdirectory; the text editor is in the WORD subdirectory; the libraries are in the LIB subdirectory; and all "include" files are in the HEADER subdirectory. The default virtual drive is now drive D, since the hard disk is drive C. If you have two hard disks installed, the virtual drive will be drive E.

A Trial Run

HELLO.BAS (Listing 2-1) is an expanded version of Kernighan and Ritchie's now-classic "hello" program.[5] I have elaborated on the original "hello" somewhat to illustrate some style factors and some characteristics of QBASIC. Remember that the pseudo line numbers, including the following colons, are for discussion only; they should not be included in your transcription.

N.B.   All listings in this book have been written with my text editor. You cannot write source code as shown with the built-in QB editor unless you use it in "document" mode. You can write equivalent-operating programs in the development environment mode, but the pseudo line numbers will not agree. The

```
 1:  '                    ***   HELLO.BAS   ***
 2:
 3:  '        A demonstration program
 4:  '        Written by M. L. Lesser, 8/13/86
 5:  '        Recompiled with Microsoft BC (QuickBASIC version 4.0)
 6:
 7:  ' Setup (nonexecutable statements):
 8:      DEFSTR T
 9:      DIM TEXT.1, TEXT.2, TEXT.3                'Variable "declarations"
10:
11:  ' Main program:
12:      LET TEXT.1 = "hello, world"
13:      LET TEXT.2 = " maximum available bytes " + "in string space"
14:      LET TEXT.3 = " maximum available bytes " _
15:                          + "for free space"
16:      PRINT: PRINT TAB(10);
17:      CALL SHOW(TEXT.1)
18:      PRINT
19:      PRINT FRE("");
20:      CALL SHOW(TEXT.2)
21:      PRINT FRE(-1);
22:      CALL SHOW(TEXT.3)
23:  END
24:
25:  '  Compiled subroutine:
26:  SUB SHOW(T) STATIC
27:      PRINT T
28:  END SUB
29:
30:  '  End of source code
```

Listing 2 - 1

development environment does not allow you to add compiled subroutines or declared functions at arbitrary locations in the source code; it will also throw in unnecessary DECLARE statements at the beginning of the code.

Lines 1–5 of Listing 2-1 are the prologue. The minimum information to be shown in a prologue includes the name of the program, the purpose of the program, the name of the programmer, when the program was written, and the compiler version used. If HELLO required special calling conventions, they would also be described in the prologue.

Lines 7–9 are the nonexecutable instructions to the compiler regarding how to treat variables when it finds them later in the source code. Nonexecutable statements do not generate code, but some assign memory addresses associated with variable names. These take effect as soon as they are seen during the initial compiler scan of the source code and cannot be bypassed by a GOTO. The nonexecutable statements in QBASIC are: COMMON, CONST, DATA, DECLARE, DEF<typ>, DIM (for static arrays), OPTION BASE, REM (I use the apostrophe version), SHARED, STATIC, the "TYPE...END TYPE" blocks, and the metacommands.

Since the DIM statement (line 9) lists only simple variables, the only effect it has in this program is to cause the compiler to assign data space for the variables when the DIM statement is encountered, rather than waiting until the variable names first appear in an executable statement. I will show uses for this convention in later programs. A period is the only useful separator (for legibility) that can be used within a variable name in a BASIC program.

The string variables TEXT.2 and TEXT.3 (lines 13–14) are set up using an identical string constant within each assignment statement, so you can experiment with the effects of the compiler /s switch. The underscore in line 14 is the compiled BASIC *continuation symbol*. It causes the following physical line to be concatenated to the current line at the underscore location, and any information following the underscore is lost. Although I use the underscore for increasing the readability of the source code, it also permits using logical lines (concatenated physical lines) of unlimited length. (The QB development environment does not recognize the underscore except in a newly loaded program written with another editor; physical lines written in the environment are limited to 256 bytes.)

The FRE function (lines 19 and 21) is not the same as in BASICA. FRE with any string or numeric argument *except* -1 or -2 forces garbage collection in string space (DGROUP) and then returns the amount of remaining free string space. FRE(-1) forces garbage collection everywhere in available memory; it returns the total amount of free space left in the system — including any in string space. FRE(-2) shows the amount of never-used stack space. FRE(-2) is not very useful except possibly during program implementation; it might give you an idea of whether or not to increase the available stack space (with a CLEAR statement) if you are using recursive procedures.

Lines 25–28 are the source code for a compiled subroutine, accessed with the CALL statement (lines 17, 20, and 22) rather than with the GOSUB statement. Called subroutines are discussed in the next two chapters.

```
                hello, world
    50076    maximum available bytes in string space
    193180    maximum available bytes for free space
```

Figure 2 - 5
Running HELLO.BAS in the QB development environment

Figure 2-5 is a copy of my screen after loading the previously written source code for HELLO.BAS into the development environment from the default drive with the command:

```
                QB HELLO
```

and running it by pressing the F5 key.

N.B.   Be careful if you call the QB development environment specifying a source file with a path to a subdirectory that is not on the default drive, or attempt to load such a file after you have arrived in the development environment. When you leave the development environment, the directory path specified in the call is left as the current directory of that drive. The default directory will not be changed.[6]

Since there are two ways to separately compile a QBASIC program, we will try HELLO.BAS both ways. First, compile for the run-time module with the command:

```
                BC HELLO;
```

After compilation is complete, link HELLO with the command:

```
                LINK HELLO;
```

Linking will take a little less than ten seconds on an all-diskette system when the object code is on a virtual disk; most of the time is taken up

Compile mode	String space	Free Space
BC HELLO;	57,014 bytes	344,262 bytes
BC HELLO/O;	61,350 bytes	394,598 bytes

Figure 2-6
Results of running separately compiled HELLO

with reading from the diskettes. If you check the default directory, you should find the three files HELLO.BAS, HELLO.OBJ, and HELLO.EXE. You might run the newly compiled and linked HELLO before you do anything else.

Now recompile HELLO.BAS to link to BCOM40.LIB, but change the name of the object file to HELLOO.OBJ during compilation with the command:

```
BC HELLO/O,HELLOO;
```

Link HELLOO as before. Linking to the longer BCOM40.LIB will take about fifty seconds on an all-diskette system, with a large amount of drive action as the linker searches the library for the required BASIC functions.

The data shown in Figure 2-6 were obtained when I ran HELLO and HELLOO on my system. The data from running HELLO are more directly comparable to the data in Figure 2-5, since the development environment includes a copy of BRUN40.EXE in its innards. Even so, the separately compiled version has almost 7,000 more bytes available in string space than does the version run under QB. Comparing the total free space between the two runs shows that the separately compiled program will run in a memory having about 151,000 fewer bytes than is required for running the same little program under the development environment.

The stand-alone program (compiled with the /o switch) has about 4,000 more bytes of string space, and uses about 50,000 fewer bytes to run in, than does the version compiled for the run-time module. The penalties for this extra memory space at run time are the longer link time and the requirement for more disk storage space for the executable file. However, no single stand-alone executable file will take up more disk space than will the equivalent default-mode executable file plus the run-time module. Thus, the disk-space savings is "real" only if there are enough executable files using the same run-time module.

You may decrease the executable file size slightly by "packing" during link time. Microsoft linkers (version 3.0 and later) have a built-in EXEPACK mode, called with the linker /e switch. Try linking HEL-LOO.OBJ (changing the name of the executable file) with

```
LINK HELLOO,HELLOE/E;
```

and notice the slight decrease in the size of the executable file between HELLOO and HELLOE. Running HELLOE will produce the same results as running HELLOO.

A side effect of producing a packed executable file is that the file cannot be disassembled with DEBUG or any of its siblings. SYMDEB warns you when you are dealing with a packed file; DEBUG just shows you erroneous information.

The Compiler Switches

I have mentioned a few of the compiler switches in passing, but here is a complete summary of the switches that can be used with the BC separate compiler. To use any compiler switch, enter it on the command line following the name of the program to be compiled.

/A   The /a switch produces pseudo assembly-language source code, but only if you also specify a compiler listing file. Using the /a switch is demonstrated in the optimization experiment in the following section.

/AH   The /ah switch allows dynamic arrays of numerics, fixed-length strings, or records to exceed 64K each — providing that enough "total space" is available. I cannot discuss it since I have never used it.

/C: This switch allows changing the default buffer size for communication send/receive programs written in QBASIC. I have never used it.

/D   This is the "debug" compile mode switch. While it provides additional run-time checking, it is not useful in a well-designed and well-tested program. It adds both size and running time to the executable code.

/E,/X   These are the error-trap enable switches. The /e switch is usually used; the /x switch is necessary when trapping errors in compiled subroutines. Error trapping is discussed in Chapter 5.

/MBF   The /mbf switch can be used if you have recompiled an old program, written for a previous version of QBASIC, that uses existing random records containing floating-point numbers. I see no need for this, as it is better practice to modify either the program to fit the old standard numeric representation or the files to fit the new standard. See the discussion of techniques for modifying files in Appendix B of the *Learning and Using Microsoft QuickBASIC* manual.

/O   The /o switch causes the program being compiled to link to the long library, BCOM40.LIB.

/R   Normally, BASIC stores array elements in memory in "column major" order, as does its ancestor FORTRAN. If you compile with the /r switch, QBASIC will store array elements in "row major" order, as do Pascal and C. In general, you should not use the /r switch. Array-element storage order and its importance for assembled subroutines are discussed in Chapter 4.

/S   If your source code contains many quoted strings and you do not have enough memory to compile the program, using the /s switch might save enough symbol space to allow the program to compile as written. You may pay for this in decreased string space.

```
defint a-z
let a = 5: b = 25
let c = 4 * a * 3 + b
let d = b + 12 * a
```

Figure 2 - 7

OPTI.BAS — Compiler optimization demonstration

/V,/W   These are the "event-trap" enable switches. They are of most use in writing video-game programs. I have never used them, as I prefer "event polling" where feasible. Event polling is discussed in Chapter 5.

/ZI,/ZD   These options are useful only when compiling and linking for use with a trace debugger, and are not discussed in this book.

An Optimization Exercise

Figure 2-7 is a small demonstration program designed solely to give you a feel of what the compiler optimizer does and how you can either aid or defeat the optimization by the way you write your programs. While the program in Figure 2-7 will execute, it does nothing useful. It was written to be compiled with the /a switch; the optimization (or lack thereof) is shown by examining the pseudo assembly code.

The interesting thing about this little program is that the last two statements are logically equivalent (c will be equal to d), although they are expressed differently.

Compile OPTI.BAS with the command:

```
BC OPTI/A,,;
```

The extra pair of commas generates a "listing file." The /a switch causes a symbolic representation of the compiler output in pseudo as-

```
0030    0006
0030    **              I00002:  mov   A%,0005h   [Store A]
0036    **                       mov   B%,0019h   [Store B]
003C    **                       mov   ax,000Ch   [ 4 * 3 ]
003F    **                       imul  A%         [     * A ]
0043    **                       add   ax,B%      [     + B ]
0047    **                       mov   C%,ax      [Store C]
004A    **                       mov   D%,ax      [Store D]
004D    **                       call  B$CENP
0052    000E
```

Note: Comments in square brackets added

Figure 2 - 8
Excerpt from compiler listing file, OPTI.LST

sembly language to be included in that file. Figure 2-8 is an excerpt from that listing file.

A short lesson in reading these "assembly" listing files: they represent the "machine" code in the module that will be executed during run time. The full listing file shows each block of source code that is compiled as a unit, followed by the assembly code to execute that block. All the code shown in Figure 2-8 was compiled in one block from the source-code in Figure 2-7. I have eliminated the repetition of the source-code statements and have added some notes in the square brackets.

All numbers are in hex. The first column of numbers is the relative address in the module-code segment that contains the machine-language instruction shown. The second column of numbers (where given) is the number of bytes in data space that have been assigned by the compiler up to that point. Your code in QBASIC compiled modules starts at relative address 0030h; the earlier addresses and the initial 6 bytes of data storage are used by the initializer.

The label "I00002" was supplied by the compiler. Each capitalized (with type-designation suffix) symbol represents the data-space location storing that variable. Thus, the instructions in code-segment addresses 0030 and 0036 store the values of a and b in their allotted memory words. There is no multiplication of four times three in the running code. The multiplication was done during compile time, producing the literal 12 (0Ch) used in the instruction at address 003C. The result of the run-time

```
0030 0006
0030  **              I00002: mov   A%,0005h
0036  **                      mov   B%,0019h
003C  **                      mov   ax,000Ch
003F  **                      imul  A%
0043  **                      add   ax,B%
0047  **                      mov   C%,ax
004A 000C
004A  **              I00003: mov   ax,000Ch
004D  **                      imul  A%
0051  **                      add   ax,B%
0055  **                      mov   D%,ax
0058  **                      call  B$CENP
005D 000E
```

Figure 2 - 9
Exerpt from compiler listing file, NO_OPTI.LST

multiplication is stored in the data address corresponding to c (instruction address 0047) and also in the data address corresponding to d (004A) without recomputing the last source-code statement. The CALL in instruction 004D is a compiler-supplied END statement.

Now convert OPTI.BAS to NO_OPTI.BAS (not shown) by inserting the label a: in front of the last line, and compiling as before. Figure 2-9 is an equivalent excerpt from NO_OPTI.LST. The now-labeled last statement in the source code was not compiled in the same block with the previous statements; it caused a new block to be started, identified by the compiler-furnished label "I00003." The compiler did not eliminate the duplicated subexpression; the value of d is recomputed. The compiler assumes all line numbers or line labels are *entry points* (targets of RESUMEs, GOTOs, or GOSUBs), so you cannot assume a labeled statement will be executed immediately following the preceding one in the source code.

Unnecessary labels may well increase the size and running time of the final executable code. However, sometimes readability of source code is aided, with no penalty, by adding a real label to a statement that the compiler considers to have an implicit label. These locations are described in Chapter 5.

There are no checks for integer arithmetic overflow in either demonstration program. I leave it as an exercise for the reader to determine the effects of compiling OPTI.BAS with the /d switch.

When It Won't Compile

If you didn't make any mistakes in transcribing my source code, you have seen the encouraging message "0 Severe Error(s)" when each separate compilation is complete. But what do you do when you are compiling a program of your own and the number of "Severe Error(s)" reported is not zero? How do you find the mistake(s) in your source code?

The compiler will flash its error findings on the display screen as they come along. It will show you a copy of each line where it *discovered* an error, along with an error message. Unfortunately, the marked error lines are somewhat difficult to locate in a long source file because the compiler doesn't identify them with pseudo line numbers. Also, if you have a lot of errors, the messages will scroll off the screen. So how do you tell where these compile-time syntax errors occur?

The easy way is to recompile with the command:

```
BC <filename>,,;
```

to produce a listing file showing the complete source code without including pseudo assembly code. This <filename>.LST file will contain the error messages flagging the statements where the compiler discovered an error. You can compare this listing file with the listing of your original text-editor-produced source code, making it is easy to locate the offending statements.

The key word in the preceding paragraphs is "discovered." The compiler cannot find a syntax error in your source code until it comes across something that shouldn't be in that location, or until it can't find something it expected before it ran into an entirely different situation. For example, if you forget to put the NEXT statement at the end of a FOR...NEXT loop, the compiler is not likely to find out about it until the source code ends. Thus, the "FOR without NEXT" error message will be marking the last line of code. You have to use your ingenuity, with the message as a strong hint, to find the actual source of the error.

Multiple error messages can be very misleading. BC attempts to continue the compilation by making an internal compensation for the error it found and restarting itself from the assumed recovery point. If BC guesses wrong, it will "discover" a flock of errors that really aren't there. It is best to handle multiple error messages by fixing the cause of the first one, leaving the others alone unless you are sure of them. Then attempt recompiling. If you are lucky, one fix will take care of several reported errors.

N.B.   The only problem with BC's usually excellent internal error recovery is that you can probably link and then run the object file so produced if you don't notice that the error(s) occurred. Of course, the results you would get might be surprising.

Getting the program to compile without errors does not insure that it will run without any run-time errors. And even if it does run, that does not insure that it is producing the correct results. As is shown in following chapters, proper design and implementation of a complex program allows that program to be built and tested in relatively small stages, each stage being erected on the foundation of carefully tested and debugged code. Thus, the inevitable bugs introduced during program development are likely to be localized to the code just added and might be relatively easy to find.

Notes

1. Microsoft BASIC compilers provide the default file extension BAS when loading a source file. If the source file has any other extension, it must be included in the call to the compiler.
2. A *module* of object code is a separate file produced either by compiling or assembling a file of source code. The linking process is discussed in detail in Chapter 11.
3. If you are operating a diskette-only system, whenever you use the compiler in development environment mode, or run a compiled program that was linked to the BRUN40.LIB library or that uses dynamic fixed-length-element arrays or the SHELL command, you must have a copy of COMMAND.COM on the diskette in the A drive.

4. EXE2BIN.EXE is not distributed with DOS 3.3. It is distributed with the version 3.3 *DOS Technical Reference* manual.
5. Brian W. Kernighan and Dennis M. Ritchie, *The C Programming Language*, Prentice-Hall, Englewood Cliffs, N.J., 1978, p. 5.
6. The *current directory* of any drive is the directory displayed as a result of using the DOS "DIR <d>:" command, where <d> is the drive letter corresponding to any installed drive. The *default directory* is the one displayed as a result of the "DIR" command with no drive specification. The default directory is the current directory of the *default drive*.

Chapter 3

Procedures with Simple Variables

The QBASIC language is easily extended with subroutines and functions contained in individual modules, written either in assembly language and assembled, or in QuickBASIC and compiled, depending on the capability being provided and the taste of the programmer. After the module has been written and tested, it is made available for use in programs requiring the capability by adding the module to a "private" searchable library. During link time, only those modules actually used by the program will be included in the executable code.

The methods used to write subroutine or function modules and to construct a private searchable library are introduced in this chapter. The first section is a rapid review of the concepts of QBASIC functions and subroutines, and of the method of passing variables between the main program and these constructs. The concepts are illustrated by example in the following sections.

The example shown is the skeleton of a utility to list QBASIC source code in a format equivalent to that used for the listings in this book. The main module of the program is compiled and then linked to a second module containing a separately compiled function and a third module containing a set of assembled subroutines. Both supporting modules are linked from a searchable library; neither is specified explicitly at link time.

Functions and Subroutines

Defined and declared functions, assembled and compiled called subroutines, and GOSUB subroutines are all used for programming convenience. Which programming substructure to use for a particular need is largely a matter of programming style, although each has its particular advantages and disadvantages.

The terminology dealing with functions and subroutines can get very confusing. In an attempt to bring a little order into this computational chaos, I will try to use the following terms in a consistent manner. The term *substructure* is used as a generic for all forms of programmed functions or subroutines. The more formal generic term *procedure* is applied only to those functions and subroutines that *may* be compiled or assembled in a separate module and combined in a searchable library for later use.

Strictly speaking, the characteristic that distinguishes a *function* from a *subroutine* is that a function returns a value after being performed, while a subroutine merely performs a process. In BASIC a function cannot be used except in a statement doing something with the returned value. Examples are: "PRINT <function>" and "LET <variable> = <function>."

When not-so-strictly speaking, one frequently describes a subroutine as returning a value. However, this value is "returned" as one of the named variables used as arguments in the statement that CALLs the subroutine.

QBASIC provides three types of functions. The intrinsic BASIC functions are built into the language. The traditional BASIC programmed functions are defined by using the "DEF FN" statement. I will refer to these as *defined functions*. In addition to the single-line defined functions permitted by BASICA, QBASIC allows multiline defined functions. The defining code for either must appear in the module of source code executing the function before the first time the function is used. Defined functions are identified by FN<name>, where <name> has a type definition corresponding to that of the value returned by the function.

The third form, the *declared* function, is a QBASIC 4.0 addition. Declared functions share many characteristics with called subroutines. In particular, they can be written in separate modules and loaded into searchable libraries.

The QBASIC manual distinguishes between three classes of subroutines, referred to as: "subprograms," "assembled subroutines," and "subroutines." The manual writers have used the somewhat misleading term *subprogram* to refer to compiled subroutines reached by the CALL statement. Now, from the standpoint of the calling program, subprograms and assembled subroutines have very much in common and few differences. So I will refer to both of these subroutine classes as *called subroutines* or simply *subroutines*.

Subroutines reached by the GOSUB statement ("subroutines" in the manual) have restricted usage in QBASIC programs due to scope limitations on labels (as discussed in Chapter 5). I refer to these as *GOSUB subroutines*.

Passing Variables in an Argument List

In BASIC, variables are passed to called subroutines and declared functions by *reference*. That is, the procedure is passed the *address* of the memory location carrying the first byte of the value of that variable. With the exception of SHARED variables, the variable addresses are passed by listing their names in an argument list.

For example, if you have a called subroutine named DUZIT that operates on the values of two variables and returns a result in the third, the subroutine call could be:

```
CALL DUZIT(FIRST,SECOND,THIRD)
```

where FIRST, SECOND, and THIRD are the names of the three variables whose addresses are passed to the subroutine.

The three variable names following the subroutine name, each separated by a comma and all contained within parentheses, constitute the *argument list*. While there is no requirement that all the variables named in an argument list have the same type definition, each variable must be of the type the subroutine expects to occupy that position in the list.

Constants (or expressions) can be passed to subroutines in the place of variables. Thus a later DUZIT call could be:

```
CALL DUZIT(256,MAYBE,ENOUGH)
```

Since variables are passed to procedures by reference, usually when a compiled called subroutine or declared function changes the value of a variable passed to it, that change will be reflected in the named variable in the calling program. There are times that you might wish to prevent such a change from occurring. You can force a variable named on the argument list to become an expression by enclosing it in its own set of parentheses.

Constants and expressions are also passed by reference, but the address passed is that of a temporary variable established by the compiler for the purpose. A "subroutine return" to a temporary variable does not change the value of any variable in the calling program.

If DUZIT were a compiled called subroutine, it would be defined by a block of code starting with the header

```
SUB DUZIT(X,Y,Z) STATIC
```

where (X,Y,Z) is the *formal parameter list* of the subroutine. Compiled called subroutine definitions are closed with the "END SUB" statement.

The keyword STATIC in a procedure header insures that previous values of local variables (those defined only within the procedure) retain their values between calls. If STATIC is omitted from the header, the local variables will be initialized to zero (null for strings) each time the procedure is called, except for those variables declared STATIC within the procedure itself. Defining a procedure with the keyword STATIC in its header will result in shorter, faster code.

The relationship between the variables named in an argument list (used to call a procedure) and those named in a formal parameter list (used to define that procedure) is very close: there must be the same number of variables in both, and the variables in corresponding positions in both lists must have the same type definitions. Errors in either type or number between the two lists can lead to all sorts of nasty unpredictable results.

Unless a subroutine has been *declared*, the compiler cannot make type- or number-mismatch checks for subroutines called from a separately compiled module, and doesn't make them when the called subroutine is in the same module. Subroutines can be declared (in each module where they are used) either by defining the subroutine or by using a "DECLARE SUB" statement. Subroutine declarations are effective in a module only after the declaration appears. It is unnecessary to declare called subroutines if argument-list checking is not required, unless you wish to use the dubious privilege of "calling" subroutines without the CALL statement.

Compiled declared functions are treated in a manner similar to compiled called subroutines. The defining header is

```
FUNCTION <name> (<parameter list>) STATIC
```

where <name> must be type defined to indicate the type of value that will be returned. There will be fewer mistakes in your function definitions and declarations if you use <name> with a type-defining suffix, rather than relying on the implicit DEF<typ> declarations currently in force. When <name> is used in a "function call," it need not include the suffix. The function definition is closed with the "END FUNCTION" statement.

Declared functions *must* be declared in the module using them, ahead of first use, so the compiler can identify <name> as belonging to a function, not to a variable. As with called subroutines, functions may be declared either with a formal "DECLARE FUNCTION" statement or by the function definition itself.

Variable Declarations

The term *variable* has an entirely different meaning in a computer language than it does in algebra. In computerese, a variable is a named entity having the three attributes: type, scope, and value.

BASIC has two variable categories. For *simple variables*, the name refers to a single entity. For *array variables*, the name refers to a related set of entities identified by the name and a *subscript* number (or numbers). All members of an array have the same type and scope but each has an individual value. Only simple variables are discussed in this chapter. The more complex subject of using array variables in procedures is treated in the next.

Variable names must begin with an alphabetic character and contain only alphanumeric characters or periods. Up to thirty-one characters are significant. In compiled BASIC, variable names do not appear in the executable code; the name has been replaced by a reference to the memory location holding the first byte of its value (for arithmetic variables) or of its descriptor (for string variables).

Declaring a variable reserves memory space for it. A variable is *declared* in BASIC when its name is used for the first time (in source-code listing sequence). Any variable that has not been *type defined* before naming it will be given the default type attribute of single-precision floating point (DEFSNG).

Since BASIC has no formal mechanism for declaring variables, any typographical error in a variable name declares a different variable. This is a common source of hard-to-find errors in BASIC programs. A preprocessor program to filter out such "nondeclared" variables is shown in Chapter 9.

A variable type can be defined implicitly with a DEF<typ> nonexecutable statement, or can be defined explicitly with a type symbol appended to the variable name *each time it is used*. Implicit type definitions take place as soon as they are scanned (in listing order) by the compiler, and replace any previous implicit declarations for the same alphabetic characters. The permissible type-defining symbols are: %, &, !, #, or $, for integer, long integer, single-precision floating point, double-precision floating point, or string variables, respectively. Explicit type definitions can also be made by using "AS <type>" in variable declaration statements (DIM, COMMON, SHARED, and STATIC).

Variable Scope

The *scope* of a variable name is that part of a program over which the name is "recognized" to have an associated value. Traditionally, all variables in BASIC were considered to be *global*; their scope was the entire program. Actually, this was never true. The scope of variables declared as formal parameters of defined functions has always been *local* to the function itself. In QBASIC, the only variables that are truly global in a module are those that have been declared SHARED in the main portion of the module. All others have either local or (what I call) *main* scope.

In compiled BASIC, variables declared in the main portion of a module do not have scope inside of a compiled called subroutine or declared function unless they are declared as SHARED either in the main program or within the procedure. Variables used within defined functions (*except* those declared in the formal parameter list or declared STATIC within multiline functions) have main scope. These main variables used in the function will have the value existing at the time the function is executed.

Variables declared within a called subroutine or declared function (even with the same name as outside) are *local* to that subroutine unless they were declared SHARED. For example, if you declare (by using the name) the variable NUMBER in the main part of the program and also declare NUMBER in a compiled called subroutine, unless NUMBER has been declared as SHARED, there is no relationship between the value of NUMBER in the main program and the value of NUMBER in the subroutine.

The exception to the preceding paragraph applies to variables declared in the parameter list of the procedure. These have the scope of the "replacing" variable named in the argument list.

A STATIC declaration within a procedure overrides a SHARED declaration in the main program, giving that variable name local scope within the procedure. SHARED and STATIC variable declarations within a procedure or multiline function are nonexecutable statements and must precede any executable statements in that substructure involving the variables named.

A variable in compiled BASIC has scope over only one module except for variables declared in an equivalent COMMON statement in each module. Since the only portions of a linked module that can be reached from the main module are called subroutines and declared functions, separately compiled modules must use COMMON SHARED declarations.

There are other named entities in QBASIC that have scope rules of their own. The scope of symbolic constants is discussed in the next chapter, labels in Chapter 5, and file identity numbers in Chapter 10.

Programmers whose experience is limited to interpreted BASIC haven't worried much about variable scope, because there have been very few chances to create scope bugs. It helps to run a few simple experiments to clarify the material in this section. A program for one such experiment is shown in Figure 3-1; the results of running it are shown in Figure 3-2.

I suggest you study the two figures until you understand why the results are as they are. You might try variations on the theme, until you fully understand scope limitations.

 the Wait—

```
defstr a-z
def fnfirst(a)
    let a = "new-a": b = "new-b"
    let fnfirst = "after running fnfirst"
end def

sub second(c) static
    let c = "new-c": d = "new-d"
    print "after running second"
end sub

let a = "old-a": b = "old-b"
let c = "old-c": d = "old-d"
print "before running the function"
print "a = " a, "b = " b
print fnfirst(b)
print "a = " a, "b = " b
print "before running the subroutine"
print "c = " c, "d = " d
call second(d)
print "c = " c, "d = " d
```

Figure 3 - 1
SCOPE.BAS, a local variable demonstration

```
before running the function
a = old-a      b = old-b
after running fnfirst
a = old-a      b = new-b
before running the subroutine
c = old-c      d = old-d
after running second
c = old-c      d = new-c
```

Figure 3 - 2
Running SCOPE.BAS

Separately Compiled Modules

You should write a separately compiled module if you intend to reuse that module in several different main programs (and it is not feasible to write it in assembly language), if you want the error-trapping restrictions confined to a separate module (as shown in Chapter 5), or if the main program is too large to be compiled as a single module. Except for error traps, all executable code in separately compiled modules must be within either called subroutine or declared function definitions.

When a module is compiled, the compiler does not "know" that the module may contain only nonmain procedures. Thus, each separately compiled module will contain a dummy main program. Besides the usual initializing code, the compiler inserts GOTOs *around* the compiled procedures and an END statement. If you were to compile and link a module containing only compiled subroutines and then attempt to run it, the only code that would be executed would be the dummy main code: the executable module would be loaded, the run-time module would be loaded (unless the module was compiled with the /o switch), and the "program" would END, giving you back the DOS prompt.

When a separately compiled procedure is used, execution will begin at the first executable statement following the procedure header statement and will return to the calling program at the "END SUB/FUNCTION" statement (or at an intervening "EXIT SUB/FUNCTION" statement). Although the dummy main instructions will not be executed, they will occupy a minimum of 80 bytes in the executable code of each linked compiled module.

TIME.BAS

TIME.BAS (Listing 3-1) is a module containing the compiled declared function TIMESTAMP, which returns a string variable. TIMESTAMP returns the conventional twelve-hour (AM/PM) representation of the time furnished by the system clock.

The prologue to the listing (lines 1–14) describes the subroutine, and the comments in the rest of the source code point out the decisions made when the subroutine is run. Details given in the listing comments are not repeated in the text.

```
 1:  '********************************************************************
 2:  '                            TIME.BAS                              *
 3:  '    TIMESTAMP$ is a declared function that returns the current time *
 4:  ' of day (given by the system clock) as an eight-byte string in    *
 5:  ' 12-hour form, either "hh:mm am" or "hh:mm pm".  The leading zero  *
 6:  ' will be replaced with a <SP> for times from 1:00 through 9:59, am or *
 7:  ' pm.                                                              *
 8:  '                                                                  *
 9:  '    Declare with: DECLARE FUNCTION TIMESTAMP$ ()                   *
10:  '                                                                  *
11:  '    Written as compiled subroutine by M. L. Lesser, October 1, 1986 *
12:  '        Rewritten as compiled declared function, November 2, 1987 *
13:  '            Compiled with Microsoft QuickBASIC (BC) version 4.0   *
14:  '********************************************************************
15:
16:  FUNCTION TIMESTAMP$ STATIC
17:      LET T$ = LEFT$(TIME$,5)                  'Read clock (hh:mm)
18:      IF VAL(T$) = 0 THEN                      'It is between midnight and 1 am
19:          LET T$ = "12" + RIGHT$(T$,3) + " am"
20:      ELSEIF VAL(T$) < 12 THEN                 'Between 1:00 am and noon
21:          LET T$ = RIGHT$(STR$(VAL(T$)),2) + RIGHT$(T$,3) + " am"
22:      ELSEIF VAL(T$) = 12 THEN                 'Between noon and 1:00 pm
23:          LET T$ = T$ + " pm"
24:      ELSE                                     'After 1:00 pm
25:          LET T$ = RIGHT$(STR$(VAL(T$) - 12),2) + RIGHT$(T$,3) + " pm"
26:      END IF
27:      LET TIMESTAMP = T$
28:  END FUNCTION
```

Listing 3 - 1

TIMESTAMP uses the built-in TIME$ function to read the system clock, and then converts the return to the desired notation with a single IF-block (lines 18–26). The IF-block is initiated by a statement in which IF is the first word on the line (other than a label) and THEN is the last (other than a comment). The whole IF-block (ending with "END IF") is treated by QBASIC as though it were the BASICA equivalent: a single IF...THEN...ELSE line with individual statements separated by colons where necessary.

The block of code following each THEN will be executed when the corresponding IF or ELSEIF <condition>[1] is the first in the IF-block to be evaluated to "true" (any nonzero number). Each executable block may have as many statements as required, usually written one to a line. The indentation shown is not essential; it is a matter of programming style used for source-code clarity. After any code block is executed, control is transferred to the implicit label on the first statement following the "END IF."

ELSEIF is a keyword that must be written as a single word. If you separate ELSEIF into two words (as would be necessary in BASICA), the compilation will fail with at least one "severe error." ELSEIF and THEN must be the first and last words on the line to maintain the IF-block structure.

The IF...ELSEIF...ELSE structure is useful when you need to perform only one of a set of transformations, depending on the values of one or more entities. You will note that not all of the conditions tested in TIMESTAMP are mutually exclusive. The tests are performed in sequence until the first "true" condition is found. The block headed by ELSE is default code to be executed if no test condition is satisfied.

The IF-block performs a function similar to that of the "SELECT CASE" block. In general, most tasks that can be performed easily with "SELECT CASE" can be performed about as easily with an IF-block, but the reverse is not true. TIMESTAMP is a toss-up example; it is not difficult to write it in either form. You might try writing a SELECT CASE version.

If you were to compile and link TIME.BAS and then attempt to run it, you would find that you could not run TIME.EXE from the default directory without using a drive code in the command line. Why not? If you don't know, try it.

A Bit of Testing

Before you load any procedure into your private library, you should test it by designing and running an appropriate *test driver*. Fortunately, it is usually easier to test a limited-function procedure to a reasonable confidence level than it is to test an entire program.

As Kernighan and Plauger wrote: "When bugs occur, they usually arise at the 'boundaries' or extremes of program operation."[2] The essence of building and using a test driver is to determine which "boundaries" are important and how to test them.

Figure 3-3 shows TEST.BAS, a suitable driver for TIMESTAMP. Note that the function is declared before it is used. Separately compile both TEST.BAS and TIME.BAS, and link them together with the command:

```
LINK TEST TIME;
```

Then test TIMESTAMP at all of its "boundaries."

```
declare function timestamp$ ()
print chr$(34) timestamp chr$(34)
```

Figure 3 - 3
TEST.BAS, a test driver for the TIMESTAMP$ function

For TIMESTAMP, the "boundaries" are where execution shifts down the IF-ELSEIF chain. The easiest way to set up test conditions is to run TEST repeatedly for different clock times as set by using the DOS built-in TIME command. Start by setting your system clock to 00:59:45. Continue to rerun TEST until the time displayed changes from "12:59 AM" to "1:00 AM." Then use the TIME command to set the clock to 11:59:45 and repeat the test procedure. When you have run through the whole set of conditions to be tested in TIMESTAMP, and have demonstrated that all of them return the proper display, you have tested the module as well as can be expected.

Assembled Procedures

There are several advantages to using assembled procedures rather than separately compiled procedures to extend QBASIC when feasible. Assembled procedures are always faster and take up less memory space. In particular, subroutines to control the characteristics of the hardware — especially the peripheral devices — are very easy to write and are easier to use than the equivalent compiled program segments.

It is possible, although not always easy, to write procedures in assembly language to handle any type of BASIC variable. The only restriction is that assembled procedures dealing with string variables cannot change the string descriptor nor the length of the string value. However, I have never found it necessary to write an assembled procedure using floating-point variables. My hardware-control subroutines having arguments pass only integers.

The assembled module PRINT.ASM (Listing 3-2) is a typical (if simplified) module of hardware-control subroutines making use of direct calls on ROM BIOS interrupt functions. In discussing its structure, I am assuming that you have at least a reading familiarity with 8086/8088 assembly-language programming.

The Assembled Procedure Interface

The simplified segment definitions introduced in MASM 5.0 are matched to the segment definition requirements for QBASIC introduced with QBASIC 4.0. An example of using this scheme is shown in Listing 3-2. All QBASIC programs use the "medium" model designation (line 3), which produces the following consequences. The assembler will always supply a data segment having the name _DATA, and put it into DGROUP. (Since there is no ".DATA" directive in this module, the data segment will be empty.) The name of the code segment starting at the ".CODE" directive (line 35) will be <name>_TEXT, where <name> is the name of the file containing the module. The proper ASSUME and ENDS directives will be supplied by the assembler.[3]

All procedures in QBASIC are reached by a FAR CALL instruction, so an assembled procedure must be coded into a <name> PROC FAR, where <name> is the procedure name used in the BASIC calling statement. The FAR is supplied by MASM 5.0 if no distance is given with the PROC directive. Each name must be identified (for the library manager and linker) as a PUBLIC name, inside the CODE segment but outside of the PROC itself. I find it convenient to write the PUBLIC pseudo-op just prior to the PROC directive for each procedure in the module (lines 37–38).

The rules for naming procedures are similar to those for naming BASIC variables: the name must start with an alphabetic character and must contain only alphanumeric characters (compiled procedure names can also contain periods), with up to thirty-one characters being significant. When naming procedures, remember that you cannot have duplicate PUBLIC names in a library.

Variables are passed to the procedure by reference. The offset portion of the address in DGROUP containing the first byte of the variable value is pushed onto the stack by the calling program, in the order the names are given in the argument list. The stack is a last-in first-out device. Thus, the *last* address pushed will be the first address found following the

```
 1:          PAGE   ,105
 2:          TITLE  PRINT
 3:          .MODEL MEDIUM
 4: ;************************************************************************
 5: ;                          PRINT.ASM                                  *
 6: ;    A module of assembled elementary printer-control subroutines to be *
 7: ; linked to programs written for the Microsoft QuickBASIC compiler.    *
 8: ;    PSKIP will work with any printer driven from the LPT1 port (serial *
 9: ; printers by means of the installed device driver SERIAL.SYS).  PFORM *
10: ; requires that the printer support the form-feed <FF> symbol.         *
11: ; PAGELEN will operate correctly only with printers compatible with    *
12: ; IBM PC printers.  PROPRIN will operate correctly only with printers  *
13: ; compatible with the IBM Proprinter or Proprinter XL.                 *
14: ;               Written by M. L. Lesser, September 30, 1986            *
15: ;               Modified for Microsoft MASM 5.0, 10-22-87             *
16: ;************************************************************************
17:
18: ;    Macro definitions:  Send symbol to printer via INT 17:
19: PRINTER MACRO  SYMBOL                    ;;For first use within a PROC
20:         XOR    DX,DX                     ;;Specify LPT1 port
21:         PRINT  SYMBOL
22: ENDM
23:
24: PRINT   MACRO  SYMBOL          ;;For subsequent uses within a PROC
25:         MOV    AX,SYMBOL
26:         INT    17H
27: ENDM
28: ;    Symbol definitions used with PRINTER and PRINT macros:
29: LFEED   EQU    10                        ;<LF>
30: FFEED   EQU    12                        ;<FF>
31: CR      EQU    13                        ;<CR>
32: ESCAPE  EQU    27                        ;<ESC>
33: ;    End of macros and symbol definitions
34:
35: .CODE                                    ;Simplified segment definition
36:
37:         PUBLIC PSKIP
38: PSKIP   PROC
39: ;************************************************************************
40: ;    PSKIP(<n>) sends <n> <LF>s, followed by a <CR>, to the printer.  *
41: ;************************************************************************
42:         PUSH   BP                        ;Save BASIC's stack frame
43:         MOV    BP,SP                     ;Set subroutine stack frame
44:         MOV    BX,6[BP]                  ;Address of <n>
45:         MOV    CX,[BX]                   ;Value of <n> in CX
46:         CMP    CX,0                      ;Check for zero or negative <n>
47:         JLE    DONE                      ;Send only <CR> if <n> <= 0
48: AROUND: PRINTER LFEED                    ;Send <LF>s to printer
49:         LOOP   AROUND                    ;    until <n> have been sent
50: DONE:   PRINT  CR                        ;Transmit <CR>
51:         POP    BP                        ;Restore BASIC stack frame and
52:         RET    2                         ; delete argument from stack
53: PSKIP   ENDP
54:
55:         PUBLIC PFORM
56: PFORM   PROC
```

Listing 3 - 2 (continued)

```
57:    ;***********************************************************************
58:    ;     PFORM transmits a formfeed <FF>, followed by a <CR>.          *
59:    ;***********************************************************************
60:            PUSH    BP                      ;Safety precaution only
61:            PRINTER FFEED                   ;Send <FF>
62:            PRINT   CR                      ;followed by <CR>
63:            POP     BP
64:            RET
65:    PFORM   ENDP
66:
67:            PUBLIC  PAGELEN
68:    PAGELEN PROC
69:    ;***********************************************************************
70:    ;     PAGELEN(<n>) sets the form length to "<n> AND 127" lines       *
71:    ; (equivalent to "<n> mod 128" for positive <n>) and sets the current *
72:    ; position of the paper to "top of form."  The page length is set to 1 *
73:    ; line if (<n> AND 127) = 0.  PAGELEN will produce unpredictable      *
74:    ; results with printers not compatible with IBM PC printers.         *
75:    ;     PAGELEN(<n>) uses the command sequence <ESC> C n               *
76:    ;***********************************************************************
77:            PUSH    BP
78:            MOV     BP,SP
79:            PRINTER ESCAPE                  ;Transmit <ESC> symbol
80:            PRINT   'C'                     ;Transmit "C"
81:            MOV     BX,6[BP]
82:            MOV     AX,[BX]                 ;Value of <n>
83:            AND     AX,07FH                 ;<n> mod 128 for <n> positive
84:            OR      AL,AL                   ;Is <n> AND 7F > 0
85:            JNZ     OK                      ;Use positive value as given
86:            INC     AL                      ;Else force <n> = 1
87:    OK:     INT     17H                     ;Send to printer
88:            POP     BP
89:            RET     2
90:    PAGELEN ENDP
91:
92:            PUBLIC  PROPRIN
93:    PROPRIN PROC
94:    ;***********************************************************************
95:    ;     PROPRIN sets a member of the Proprinter family to 12-pitch NLQ  *
96:    ; typeface.  PROPRIN will produce unpredictable results with printers *
97:    ; not compatible with the IBM Proprinter or Proprinter XL.           *
98:    ;***********************************************************************
99:            PUSH    BP
100:   ;   Set 12 characters per inch (<ESC> ':'):
101:           PRINTER ESCAPE
102:           PRINT   ':'
103:   ;   Set NLQ (double strike) printing (<ESC> 'G'):
104:           PRINT   ESCAPE
105:           PRINT   'G'
106:           POP     BP
107:           RET
108:   PROPRIN ENDP
109:
110:           END
```

Listing 3 - 2

two words of the FAR RETurn address, which were automatically pushed as part of the FAR CALL instruction.

When the procedure is entered, the DS and SS segment registers will point to the origin of DGROUP, which contains all the data available to the program not stored in dynamic arrays.[4] The BP register will point to the stack frame associated with the calling program.

Before control is returned to the calling program, the procedure must assure that the DS, SS, BP, SP, SI, and DI registers have the same values they had when it was entered. The values in the remaining registers are "don't care" both on entry and before return. (The AX and DX registers are used for returning values from assembled declared functions. See the example in Chapter 5.)

It is conventional to make "PUSH BP" the first executable instruction in any assembled procedure (line 42) even if no variables are passed.[5] If variables are passed, the following instruction copies the contents of the SP register into the BP register, to establish the local stack frame of the procedure (line 43). If the contents of the DS, SI, or DI registers are to be changed during the procedure, the to-be-modified registers are then saved on the stack.

The DGROUP offset address of the *last* variable passed will be at stack offset [BP]+6. The offsets of the remaining variables follow in reverse order, each one located 2 bytes higher than its neighbor. The *first* variable named in the argument list will be at stack offset [BP]+4+2n, where n is the number of variables passed.

Only one variable was passed to PSKIP (line 44). Once you have the address of the variable in one of the index registers (BX or SI), it can be used to get the value (line 45).

When the active portion of the procedure is finished, any registers saved on the stack are popped in reverse order to which they were pushed. "POP BP" is the last instruction prior to the RET (lines 51–52).

In addition to restoring the required register values on completion, the procedure must also clean up the stack for passed variables by appending 2n as an operand for the RET instruction, where n is again the number of variables passed (line 52).

The module is closed with the usual END assembler directive (line 110). Since this is not a main module, there is no start-point operand for the END.

There is no "automatic" pass back of changed argument variables to the calling program except for string variables or variables passed in

COMMON regions. Examples of assembled subroutines "returning" integer variables, those having more than one variable in the argument list, and those dealing with string variables are shown in later chapters.

PRINT.ASM

PRINT.ASM (Listing 3-2) is an example of an assembled module containing simple printer-control subroutines. Since the listing comments describe the action of the program, the text is primarily devoted to those aspects of the program structure not already discussed.

The PAGE directive (line 1) is used to keep the assembler from folding each assembled line in PRINT.LST to a maximum 80-column width. I set my editor to write 72-column lines, so that source code (including pseudo line numbers) can be listed on 80-column printers. MASM puts 33 characters of assembled code in front of each source-code line, making a maximum line width of 105 columns in my assembler LST files. The wide-line display makes the portion of the file I am interested in easier to read with my text editor.

The TITLE directive (line 2) tells MASM to supply a title for each page header in the assembler listing file (<filename>.LST); it isn't required if you don't use assembly listing files.

The two macro definitions PRINTER and PRINT (lines 19–32) contain the code necessary to transmit a byte to the printer by calling on ROM BIOS INT 17H. PRINTER is used to transmit the first byte. It sets DX to zero, indicating output is to be made to the LPT1 port, before expanding PRINT. Unless DX is changed, subsequent printer bytes in the same subroutine are sent with PRINT.

The source code is assembled to an object file with the command:

```
MASM PRINT;
```

If you also want a listing file (PRINT.LST) showing the results of the assembly, use the command:

```
MASM PRINT,,;
```

I leave it as an exercise for the reader to devise a suitable test driver for the subroutines in the PRINT module.

Managing the Private Library

There are two ways to link procedures in separate modules to a main module. The hard way is to compile or assemble each separate module and link the corresponding object files to the main program object file with a command similar to:

```
LINK <program> <sub1> [<sub2>] [...];
```

Compiler inserted code in the <program>.OBJ file will force linking of the required modules from the appropriate compiler-furnished library. While this is the proper approach for test drivers or for linking the parts of programs too big to compile in one piece, it entails a horrendous amount of bookkeeping if used generally for all programs using separate procedure modules. Commercial program developers, who are juggling several different products made up of many intermingled modules, mechanize this dog work with a utility such as MAKE.EXE, furnished with the Microsoft MASM distribution diskettes.

The easy way to eliminate keeping track of which main source file requires what supplementary modules linked to it is to put all the generally reusable object modules into a private searchable library. Then, link all the modules required by the main program with the command:[6]

```
LINK <program>,,,<libname>
```

where <libname>.LIB is the appropriate procedure library file. The linker will search <libname> for modules containing PUBLIC names required to satisfy <program>'s external references, and only those modules will be linked. The corresponding compiler-furnished library will be linked *after* the private library, so any references made by the linked <libname> modules to modules in the compiler-furnished library will be satisfied.

Private libraries are constructed and managed with the LIB.EXE utility. We will call ours PQB.LIB, just to give it a name.

N.B. Do not confuse these LIB-managed libraries with "Quick" libraries constructed with the LINK utility. "Quick" libraries are private run-time modules that can be used with the QB develop-

```
PAGELEN..........print              PFORM............print
PROPRIN..........print              PSKIP............print
TIMESTAMP........time

time                Offset: 00000010H  Code and data size: 1fdH
   TIMESTAMP

print               Offset: 00000650H  Code and data size: 6aH
   PAGELEN          PFORM              PROPRIN          PSKIP
```

Figure 3 - 4
Sample library index file (PQB.IDX)

ment environment. They are discussed, along with other linker processes, in Chapter 11.

Start by compiling TIME.BAS for the default mode (no switches) and then assembling PRINT.ASM. Build the initial version of PQB.LIB with the command:

```
lib pqb+print+time,pqb.idx;
```

The LIB utility is case-sensitive; the module names in the index file, PQB.IDX, will be shown in the case used on the LIB command line.

The index file is the "table of contents" to the PQB library. A copy of the displayed just-built PQB.IDX file is shown in Figure 3-4. The top portion is a list of all the procedures in the library and the modules they come from, in alphabetic order by procedure name. The bottom portion is a list of the modules in the order they were loaded into the library, showing the procedures contained in each module and the amount of code and data space (in hex) occupied by that module when it is linked to a program.

Copy the PQB.LIB file to a directory listed in your LIB environment list. Also copy the LIB and IDX files to your procedure archive diskette, along with the source-code files for the two modules. Save the listings of the source code for both modules and the listing of the IDX file in your programmer's notebook where they will become part of your permanent program-development tool kit.

```
DECLARE FUNCTION TIMESTAMP$ ()
DECLARE SUB PSKIP (A%)
DECLARE SUB PFORM ()
DECLARE SUB PAGELEN (A%)
DECLARE SUB PROPRIN ()
```

Listing 3 - 5
Sample declaration $INCLUDE file (PQB.BI)

You will need to declare any library functions used in your programs, within the module using them. The easy way is to keep a header file, declaring all the procedures in the corresponding library, and "include" that header file in every source-code module you write. Unnecessary declarations take up space in the compiler's symbol table at compile time, but have no effect on the executable code.

The header file PQB.BI, declaring procedures in the two current library modules, is shown in Figure 3-5. Notice that all procedures have "prototype" formal parameter lists, with an empty list where no argument is required. These lists are used by the compiler for checking that the argument list on each procedure call contains the proper number of entries, each of the proper type.

I prepared my PQB.BI with my text editor and will append new declarations as the library is modified. Store yours in the directory named in your INCLUDE environment string and keep a listing of it in your programmer's notebook.

LIST.BAS

There is no LLIST statement in compiled BASIC. You can list your source code by using the built-in PRINT menu command in the QB development environment, but that utility has all the deficiencies of LLIST: the text lines are printed smack up against the left printer margin, listing continues on consecutive lines with no margins at the top and bottom of the page, and there are no page headers or page numbers.

LIST.BAS (Listing 3-3) is only the *skeleton* of a utility to list source code and other ASCII files, neatly. LIST is the first phase of an example of building a program piecemeal, testing each piece as you go.

Skeleton programs accept the normal input and produce the final output of the full program, but do not take care of the exception cases. This version of LIST will list all the source-code files illustrated in this book, but there are no user-friendly conveniences. LIST must be customized for different printers or different maximum line lengths by changing its source code, recompiling, and relinking. If LIST cannot find the file requested on the DOS command line, it will die with an error message. The added enhancements, removing these (and other) deficiencies, are built in later chapters.

The $INCLUDE metacommand to read in PQB.BI is shown in line 31. The metacommand is disguised as a comment and is followed by a colon. The complete name of the file to be"included" is then given, surrounded by apostrophes (single quotes). QBASIC can't find an include file unless either the complete path to its directory is given in a statement or the file is on the default drive.

The "printer characteristics" (lines 34–36) are coded as initialized variables. While symbolic constants could be used in this version, the final version of LIST requires the default printer characteristics to be coded as variables so the program can "customize" itself for the installed printer.

The PAGE.WIDTH constant (line 34), used in setting the print margins (line 62), indicates the maximum number of columns your printer can put on a page. The assumption is that printers having print lines limited to 8 inches will have the paper aligned to center the print line across the page; wide-line printers will have the pin feeds located to print the first column at the left edge of the paper after it has been burst.

The multiline defined function FNHEADER (lines 39–52) is used to print the page headers. The function is assigned a string value (line 43) used by the main program for displaying the page currently being listed. FNHEADER then resets the main variable COUNT to zero and prints the header. The local variable PAGE.NUM (line 40) could have been declared as a main variable since it isn't used elsewhere in the program. The local declaration is "insurance," to eliminate possible bugs introduced by additions to the program.

The code for defined functions *must* precede any use of the function, in source-code listing order, or the compiler will find a severe "Function not defined" error. The compiler supplies the GOTO around the function

```
 1:  '****************************************************************************
 2:  '                              LIST.BAS                                    *
 3:  '     LIST lists ASCII source-code files having a 72-column maximum        *
 4:  ' line length on an IBM Proprinter XL in 12-pitch NLQ mode, listing 55     *
 5:  ' lines per page with a header on each page and pseudo line numbers on     *
 6:  ' each line.  LIST can easily be customized for other printers.            *
 7:  '     To customize, set the printer characteristics as follows:            *
 8:  '          PAGE.WIDTH is the maximum number of characters per line, as      *
 9:  '               limited by pitch and either paper width or printer.         *
10:  '          PAGE.OFFSET is the number of <LF>s necessary to move from the    *
11:  '               paper "home" position (perforations at the tear-bar)        *
12:  '               to setting the first print line at the top of the next     *
13:  '               page.  Use "PAGE.OFFSET = 36" for the IBM Graphics          *
14:  '               printer and equivalents.                                    *
15:  '          PROPRINTER is an on/off switch.  Set "PROPRINTER = -1" if an     *
16:  '               IBM Proprinter is installed and you wish to print in        *
17:  '               12-pitch NLQ mode.  Set "PROPRINTER = 0" for all other     *
18:  '               configurations.                                            *
19:  '     To omit pseudo line numbers, comment out line 80.  This will          *
20:  ' increase the maximum allowable source text line length to 80             *
21:  ' columns.  If the printer allows, longer line lengths can be listed       *
22:  ' by changing the constants in lines 48, 50 and 62.                        *
23:  '               Written by M. L. Lesser, October 1, 1986                   *
24:  '     Rewritten for Microsoft BC (QuickBASIC version 4.0), 11/2/87         *
25:  '****************************************************************************
26:  '   Setup (nonexecutable statements):
27:      DEFINT A-Z
28:      DEFSTR F,H,R,T
29:      DIM COUNT, FILE, LINE.NUM, MARGIN, PAGE.WIDTH, PAGE.OFFSET
30:      DIM PROPRINTER, TEXT, TIME
31:  '   $INCLUDE: 'PQB.BI'                        'Declaration header
32:
33:  '   Printer characteristics:
34:      PAGE.WIDTH = 102                          '8.5-inch paper at 12 pitch
35:      PAGE.OFFSET = 0                           'No initial paper offset
36:      PROPRINTER = -1                           'Proprinter installed
37:
38:  '   Defined header function:
39:  DEF FNHEADER
40:      STATIC PAGE.NUM                           'Static local variable
41:
42:      LET PAGE.NUM = PAGE.NUM + 1
43:      LET FNHEADER = "Listing page" + STR$(PAGE.NUM)
44:      LET COUNT = 0                             'Reset page line count
45:      LPRINT                                            'Top blank line
46:      LPRINT TAB(MARGIN + 1);                           'First header line
47:      LPRINT "Listed on " DATE$;
48:      LPRINT TAB(80 + MARGIN - LEN(FILE)) FILE
49:      LPRINT TAB(MARGIN + 8) "at " TIME;                'Second header line
50:      LPRINT TAB(MARGIN + 73) "page" PAGE.NUM
51:      CALL PSKIP(3)                                     'Three more blanks
52:  END DEF
53:
54:  '   Main program:
55:      LET FILE = COMMAND$                       '<filespec> from command line
56:      IF INSTR(FILE,".") = 0 _                  'If no <ext> on <filespec>
```

Listing 3 - 3 (continued)

```
57:          THEN LET FILE = FILE + ".BAS"      '  add ".BAS"
58:       OPEN FILE FOR INPUT AS #1             'Error-abort if file not found
59:  '  Customize for printer and list first page header:
60:       LET TIME = TIMESTAMP$
61:       WIDTH LPRINT 255                       'Bug killer
62:       LET MARGIN = (PAGE.WIDTH - 80)/2
63:       IF PROPRINTER THEN CALL PROPRIN        'Set Proprinter for 12-pitch NLQ
64:       IF PAGE.OFFSET THEN                    'If using IBM Graphics printer
65:           CALL PSKIP(PAGE.OFFSET)            '  set print line at top of page
66:           CALL PAGELEN(66)                   '  and reset form-feed point
67:       END IF
68:       PRINT FNHEADER                         'First page header
69:  '  Read and list file:
70:       WHILE NOT EOF(1)                       'As long as there is any text left
71:           LINE INPUT #1, TEXT                'Read a line of text
72:           LET LINE.NUM = LINE.NUM + 1        'Update line number
73:           LET COUNT = COUNT + 1              'Update page line count
74:           IF LEFT$(TEXT,1) = CHR$(12) THEN        'If first byte is <FF>
75:               CALL PFORM                     '  eject page
76:               PRINT FNHEADER                 '  list new header
77:               LET TEXT = MID$(TEXT,2)        '  delete <FF>
78:           END IF
79:           LPRINT TAB(MARGIN + 1);
80:           LPRINT USING "#####:  "; LINE.NUM;
81:           CALL TABBER                        'Detab text line
82:           LPRINT TEXT                        '  and list it
83:           IF COUNT = 55 AND NOT EOF(1) THEN      'If 55 lines on page
84:               CALL PFORM                     '  Skip to top of next page
85:               PRINT FNHEADER                 '  and list new header
86:           END IF
87:  '  Emergency exit - responds only to Ctrl-C:
88:           IF INKEY$ = CHR$(3) THEN END
89:       WEND                                   'Continue until file listed
90:       CALL PFORM                             'Eject remainder of last page
91:       IF PAGE.OFFSET THEN                    'If Graphics printer
92:           CALL PSKIP(66 - PAGE.OFFSET)       '  skip to tear-bar
93:           CALL PAGELEN(66)                   '  and reset top of form
94:       END IF
95:  END                          'End of main program
96:
97:  '  Compiled subroutine to expand <HT>s to every eighth column:
98:  SUB TABBER STATIC
99:       SHARED TEXT
100:
101:       LET I = INSTR(TEXT,CHR$(9))           'Find first <HT>
102:       WHILE I <> 0                          'As long there are any <HT>s
103:           LET REST = MID$(TEXT,I+1)         'Unexpanded portion of TEXT
104:           LET TEXT = LEFT$(TEXT,I-1)        'Expanded portion of TEXT
105:           LET N = 8 - (I-1) MOD 8           'No. of <SP>s to insert for <HT>
106:           LET TEXT = TEXT + SPACE$(N) + REST
107:           LET I = INSTR(TEXT,CHR$(9))       'Any more to deal with?
108:       WEND                                  'Continue until done
109:  END SUB
110:  '  End of source code
```

Listing 3 - 3

definition; it "knows" you are defining a multiline function if the "DEF FN<name>" line does not include "= <expression>" (line 39). Multiline function definitions are closed by the statement "END DEF" (line 52).

The compiler furnishes the built-in string constant COMMAND$ (line 55), passing information entered on the DOS command line to the program. The value of COMMAND$ is the text following <progname> on the command line, not including any redirection symbols. COMMAND$ strips off the leading consecutive <SP> symbols (but not any <HT>s) and converts the rest of the command line to all uppercase.

The "WIDTH LPRINT 255" statement (line 61) is required in every program using the LPRINT instruction, and would be so required even if Microsoft removed the LPRINT bug from BASIC. The bug in LPRINT inserts a <CR><LF> symbol pair after the "WIDTH LPRINT" number of characters have been sent to the printer (the default value is 80) even if there are no more characters in the LPRINT statement. This introduces an unwanted blank line into the printed output when the normal "line end" symbol is transmitted. You really want the program to tell the user if it gets a line too long to print, rather than to surprise the user by automatically clobbering the output listing with additional lines. (One of the deficiencies in this version of LIST is that it *doesn't* tell you.) Inserting "WIDTH LPRINT 255" in any program before the first use (in execution order) of LPRINT deletes the automatic <CR><LF> insertion.

The test for a <FF> (line 74) is not particularly useful in this version of LIST. It will force pagination if your text editor will allow you to embed control symbols in the text and your language processor will accept them (QBASIC won't). It is a convenience for the final version, which will print wide assembler listing files with no added line numbers, using the assembler-supplied headers.

Line 88 is an emergency exit in case you wish to stop wasting paper because you didn't really want to list the file you named on the command line. Unless the program was compiled with the /d switch, QBASIC programs ignore the Ctrl-C and Ctrl-Break keys except when executing statements requesting normal input from the keyboard. If you did compile with the /d switch, QBASIC still ignores Ctrl-C when executing the remaining statements. The emergency exit shown in line 88 recognizes only Ctrl-C.

The END statement in line 95 is not necessary in this version, because the compiler will provide a GOTO around the remaining called subroutine code and an END at the end of the source code. However, it is good programming style to denote where the main program ends, and may be necessary with further additions.

LIST includes the compiled subroutine TABBER (lines 98–109), which expands embedded <HT> symbols with spaces to every eighth print column. (QBASIC expands tabs in PRINT, but not in LPRINT, statements.) It is usually easier to expand the source text than it is to set printer tab stops. This routine is also used in later versions for determining the maximum line length in the source text and setting the margins accordingly. The variable TEXT is declared SHARED (line 99), which makes it a global variable.

Even though the skeleton LIST is a very short program, it is best to implement and test it in two stages. The first stage consists of the code ending at line 78, followed by a single line of *debugging code*

```
lprint "here"
```

and ending with the exit code in lines 90–95. This first stage tests only the customizing code and the header function. After copying PQB.BI to the default directory, compile LIST with:

```
BC LIST;
```

and (after it compiles with no errors) link it to the required modules in the private library with:

```
LINK LIST,,,PQB
```

When you run this test version, you should get the header printed at the top of a new page, followed by three blank lines and the "here" line, after which the page should eject. The message "Listing page 1" should be displayed on your screen. But your printer has to be powered on to see these results.

If you are using a parallel printer and it is not turned on, you will get only the run-time error message "Device fault." If you are using a serial printer with the driver shown in Appendix A, the response depends on previous history due to the characteristics of the RS-232C interface. If the serial printer has *never* been turned on since system power-on, you will just wait — seeing nothing until you turn on the printer. If the printer has *ever* been turned on, you will see the "Listing page 1" display with no printing; the interface can't tell that the printer has been turned off, so it ships characters down the cable to be lost at the other end. You can stop this nonsense with a Ctrl-C, turn on the printer, and run the program again.

When the partial-LIST produces the right output, delete the line of debugging code and add the rest of the code shown in the listing. Test the entire program by listing itself. I carefully made the listing 110 lines, so you could demonstrate a not-too-subtle bug by deleting the "AND NOT EOF(1)" from line 83. Some "boundaries" to be tested depend on the number of inputs, not on their values.

Notes

1. I use the *placeholder* <condition> to indicate the test condition associated with IFs and WHILEs. The corresponding term used in the QBASIC manual is *booleanexpression*.
2. Brian W. Kernighan and P. J. Plauger, *Software Tools*, Addison-Wesley, Reading, Mass., 1976, p. 14.
3. The explicit segment definitions required by earlier versions of MASM are discussed in Chapter 11.
4. Dynamic arrays of variable-length strings (actually, arrays of string descriptors) are also stored in DGROUP.
5. Even though they are supposed to, not all ROM BIOS routines return the BP register unmodified.
6. The "link to private library" form of linker command will write a linker listing file, <program>.MAP, to the default directory. These usually unwanted files will vanish at session end if you are using a virtual disk. If you are using a real disk, you will have to erase the MAP files before you close the session.

Chapter 4

Using Array Variables

An array variable is a set of related elements, all having the same name, type, and scope, with each array element accessed by varying the value of one or more subscripts. Array variables in QuickBASIC can be declared in either of two modes: static or dynamic. These two modes have different performance characteristics and completely different storage allocation properties.

Many of the characteristics of programs containing array variables — including their use in compiled and assembled procedures — are demonstrated in this chapter, using variations on Jim Gilbreath's SIEVE benchmark.[1] A *benchmark* is a contrived program intended to demonstrate certain aspects of system behavior and may not be at all indicative of other (perhaps more important) system characteristics. SIEVE.BAS (Listing 4-1) is primarily sensitive to the way QBASIC accesses array elements and to the way it optimizes nested integer loops.

The benchmark results shown were obtained by running versions of SIEVE, compiled with QBASIC 4.0, on my IBM PC-XT (4.77 MHz 8088, no 8087). The actual values are not important. Comparisons between the numbers indicate the relative effects on performance and space requirements of different programming approaches to accomplishing the same task.

```
1:   '***************************************************************************
2:   '                          SIEVE.BAS                                     *
3:   '              Eratosthenes Sieve Prime Number Program                   *
4:   '     Transliterated from Jim Gilbreath's Pascal listing as shown in     *
5:   '      "A High-Level Language Benchmark," Byte, September 1981, p. 182    *
6:   '                  Copyright (C) 1981 Jim Gilbreath                       *
7:   '                 Used with the permission of Jim Gilbreath              *
8:   '                                                                        *
9:   '           Transliterated by M. L. Lesser, September 27, 1986           *
10:  '           Modified for Microsoft QBASIC BC version 4.0, 11/13/87       *
11:  '***************************************************************************
12:  ' Setup:
13:       '$STATIC
14:       DEFINT A-Z
15:       DEFSNG T
16:       CONST SPACE = 8190, TRUE = -1, FALSE = NOT TRUE
17:       DIM COUNT, I, ITER, K, PRIME, TIME.S, TIME.F
18:
19:       DIM FLAGS(SPACE)
20:
21:  ' Main program:
22:       PRINT "10 iterations"                          'Starting message
23:       LET TIME.S = TIMER                             'Starting time
24:       FOR ITER = 1 TO 10
25:           LET COUNT = 0                              'Initialize COUNT
26:  ' Initialize FLAGS array:
27:           FOR I = LBOUND(FLAGS) TO UBOUND(FLAGS)
28:               LET FLAGS(I) = TRUE
29:           NEXT I
30:  ' Run SIEVE code:
31:           FOR I = LBOUND(FLAGS) TO UBOUND(FLAGS)
32:               IF FLAGS(I) THEN             'TRUE marks location of prime
33:                   LET PRIME = I + I + 3    '  Value of the prime
34:                   LET K = I + PRIME        '  First multiple of prime
35:                   WHILE K <= UBOUND(FLAGS) ' Loop to kill multiples
36:                       LET FLAGS(K) = FALSE '     Nonprimes set FALSE
37:                       LET K = K + PRIME
38:                   WEND                     ' until all multiples set
39:                   LET COUNT = COUNT + 1    '  Another prime added to COUNT
40:               END IF
41:           NEXT I                           'Find next prime
42:       NEXT ITER                     'Run all ten cycles
43:       LET TIME.F = TIMER            'Final time
44:       PRINT COUNT "primes found"   'Ending message (1899)
45:       PRINT USING "Elapsed time is ###.# seconds"; TIME.F - TIME.S
46:       PRINT
47:       PRINT USING "###,### "; FRE("");
48:       PRINT "bytes free in string space"
49:       PRINT USING "###,### "; FRE(-1);
50:       PRINT "bytes free in memory"
51:  END
52:  ' End of source code
```

Listing 4 - 1

Declaring Array Variables

The individual elements of an array are specified by an array name and one or more subscripts, depending on the number of array dimensions. Arrays declared with only one subscript are one-dimension arrays, those with two subscripts are two-dimension arrays, etc.

Arrays should be declared by a DIM statement of the form

```
DIM [SHARED] <array>(<maxsub1>[,<maxsub2>][,...])
```

where <array> is the name of the array and <maxsub1>, <maxsub2>, etc., are the maximum subscript values for the first, second, etc., dimension of the array. For example, line 19 of Listing 4-1 dimensions FLAGS() as a one-dimension array having a maximum subscript value of 8,190. Since there is no "OPTION BASE 1" statement preceding the DIM statement, the minimum subscript value is 0. Hence, there are 8,191 elements in the array.

Line 19 is an example of "standard" BASIC array dimensioning. Starting with QBASIC 4.0, you may also use bounded array dimensioning, similar to that required in Pascal; both the lower and upper bounds of the dimension range can be supplied and either the lower or both can be negative numbers. The compiler considers standard array dimensioning as a special case of bounded dimensioning; the lower bound is given by the "OPTION BASE" statement and the dimension supplied is the upper bound.

The subscript values in DIM declarations may be constants or variables, depending on the array mode. All nonintegers will be rounded to integers when the declaration takes effect. The compiler does not catch invalid subscript values unless the array was dimensioned with integer constants. Invalid subscript dimensioning not caught by the compiler, such as rounding a floating-point constant in standard dimensioning to a negative integer, are run-time errors. Unlike most "Subscript out of range" errors, it is not necessary to compile with the /d switch for the run-time support to catch them.

Unfortunately, BASIC includes an implicit array variable declaration similar to its implicit simple variable declaration. If you haven't dimensioned the array properly before any use (in listing order) of a variable name with one or more subscripts, the compiler will assign enough memory space for an array having a maximum subscript of 10 for each dimension indicated. Inadvertent array dimensioning usually originates in typos, such as "PRINT CHRS(34)" when you really meant "PRINT CHR$(34)."

Implicit array dimensioning is not a "Severe error," but you will see the "Array not Dimensioned" warning message during compile time.

Unless the program was compiled with the /d switch, there are no automatic run-time checks for a "Subscript out of range" error caused by an attempt to read from, or write to, an array element outside the declared subscript range. If executed, such statements will produce unpredictable results.[2] It is the programmer's responsibility to include the proper precautions.

QBASIC helps by providing two constants for each dimension of each array variable. LBOUND(<array>(n)) provides the minimum subscript value for the nth dimension of <array>, and UBOUND(<array>(n)) provides the maximum subscript value. If <array> has only one dimension, the "(n)" can be omitted, as in line 27 of Listing 4-1.

Static and Dynamic Arrays

Static and dynamic arrays differ in the way memory space is allocated for them and in the way the program accesses the memory elements. There are two metacommands, $STATIC and $DYNAMIC, that have secondary control over which type of array variable is declared in DIM statements.

Dimensioning an array in any of the following forms will determine whether the array is static or dynamic, irrespective of which array metacommand is in force at the time:

- Any implicitly declared array will be a static array.
- Any array dimensioned in a DIM statement with a variable subscript value will be a dynamic array.
- Any array initially declared in a COMMON statement and later dimensioned in a DIM statement (with either constant or variable subscripts) will be a dynamic array.

Arrays first declared in DIM statements with constants for the maximum subscript values will be either static or dynamic, depending on which array metacommand is in force at the time. $STATIC is the default case and need not be supplied except to override a previously listed $DYNAMIC metacommand. Thus, line 13 of Listing 4-1 has no effect on the action of SIEVE.BAS as written.

Memory space for static arrays is allocated in the dataspace portion of DGROUP by the compiler and cannot be deallocated during program run time. Declaring an array too large to fit into the maximum-size DGROUP will produce a compile-time severe error.

When a static array is ERASEd, the element values are set to 0 for numeric arrays (to null for string array descriptors), but the space for them still exists. Any attempt to REDIM or DIM a static array after it is first declared produces a severe compile-time error.

When a dynamic array is declared, permanent memory space is allocated during compile time only for an array descriptor. A DIM statement involving dynamic arrays is an executable statement. The allocation of temporary space for the array itself occurs during run time; the location of that space depends on the array type. Thus, discovering there is insufficient space to allocate a dynamic array is a run-time error.

Temporary space for dynamic string arrays (an array of string descriptors) is allocated in the upper portion of DGROUP, the top of string space. Temporary space for dynamic numeric arrays (including dynamic arrays of constant-length strings or of records) is allocated in "far object space." The maximum storage space that can be allocated to a single dynamic numeric array is 64K unless the program was compiled with the /ah switch, subject to the further constraint that no array can contain more than 32,767 elements per dimension.

Space for dynamic numeric arrays is allocated starting at the highest available memory space and allocating down. If all the available far object space outside of DGROUP has been used and more is required, the QBASIC memory space manager moves the boundary between far object space and string space down, reducing the size of string space.

When a dynamic array is ERASEd, the temporary space is deallocated and is available for other use. If the ERASEd array was within DGROUP, the space recovered will be available for strings. REDIMing a dynamic array is permitted; it is equivalent to an ERASE statement followed by a DIM statement. However, using a second DIM declaration for the same dynamic array without an intervening ERASE statement is a compile-time severe error.

The SIEVE Benchmark

The "base case" SIEVE program is shown in Listing 4-1. I have used the symbolic constants SPACE, TRUE, and FALSE in SIEVE (line 16) merely to demonstrate use of the CONST statement. (The executable code would have been the same if I had used the appropriate literals in the source code.) There are several restrictions on the use of symbolic constants, which make them much less convenient than the manuals imply.

The type definition of a symbolic constant is determined by the value of that constant, not by any DEF<typ> statements in effect at the time of constant definition. While symbolic constants can be "typed" with a type-definition suffix, the symbolic <name> (not including the suffix) can be used only once (subject to the scope rules). For example, attempting to define the symbolic constant "a%" after defining "a!" or attempting to define a symbolic constant after having used its <name> as a variable are severe compile-time errors.

Symbolic constants follow an anomalous scope rule. Symbolic constants first defined in the main portion of the program have "global" scope *unless* they are also defined within a procedure. When defined in a procedure, symbolic constants have local scope and may even have a different type than when used in previous definitions. Symbolic constants may be redefined in each separate procedure, but cannot be defined in the main portion of the module if that portion *follows* any procedure definition.

Figure 4-1 is a copy of my display screen after running SIEVE (as shown in Listing 4-1) compiled with the /o switch and linked to the BCOM40 library.

Interpreting the results of running a benchmark program is difficult, even if you wrote the benchmark and think you know what it is measuring. In my versions of SIEVE, I am measuring the elapsed time to execute the kernel, and also the available memory space after each run.[3]

Timing Considerations

It is traditional to time 10 iterations of SIEVE, hitting the stopwatch when the sign-on message "10 iterations" appears (line 22 of Listing 4-1) and again when SIEVE's final message "1899 primes found" is shown (line 44). I have used the built-in TIMER function (lines 23 and 43) instead of

```
10 iterations
 1899 primes found
Elapsed time is  26.5 seconds

 44,990 bytes free in string space
376,286 bytes free in memory
```

Figure 4 - 1
Running SIEVE compiled with /o switch

the stopwatch, displaying the results rounded to one-tenth second (line 45).

TIMER reads the PC's internal clock. It returns the number of seconds that have elapsed since midnight, precise to two decimal places. However, the PC's clock only "ticks" about 18.2 times a second, which means that the time returned by TIMER is accurate to only about 0.05 second. Since "PRINT USING" rounds, the times displayed may vary by a tenth of a second between successive runs with the same configuration. Thus, differences in elapsed run time of 0.1 second are not significant.

Run-time Free Space

For all practical purposes, the available program memory space while running a separately compiled QBASIC program is divided into three regions (plus the run-time module if BRUN40.EXE is required). The first is *code space*, consisting of all the concatenated code segments from the several modules and libraries linked together to make up the program. The only limit on the allowable size of code space is available memory. Once linked, there is no way for the program to change the amount of memory space allocated to code.

Almost all data available to the program (and to its run-time support) are contained in DGROUP, which will use as much space as available after the code is loaded — up to a maximum of 64K. After the BASIC initializer finishes its work, DGROUP includes *data space* for all the permanently allocated data used by the program, and *stack space* consisting of 2K. It is not possible to change the size of data space during run time. It is possible to change the size of stack space with the CLEAR statement.

The rest of DGROUP is *string space*, available for temporary allocations during run time. String space is used for the values of string variables (written from the bottom), and for OPEN file buffers and dynamic string arrays (allocated from the top).

All available memory not being used by code space, data space, allocated string space, or BRUN40.EXE (if used) is *far object space* used for storing dynamic numeric arrays and for running SHELL commands in programs compiled with the /o switch.

If the sum of code space, data space, and stack space specified in the linked executable file exceeds the available memory space, DOS will show you the "Program too big to fit in memory" error message and return its prompt. If the executable file is small enough to fit in available memory but there isn't enough room for a full 64K DGROUP, DGROUP will be shrunk (by the QBASIC initializer) to the maximum available size, eliminating as much string space as necessary; far object space will then be the same as unallocated string space. If the program uses the run-time module and there isn't enough room for BRUN40.EXE (even with no initial string space), the QBASIC initializer will display "Error in loading BRUN40.EXE RTM - Out of memory" and return the DOS prompt.

All of which leads to the interpretation of the amount of free space displayed after a SIEVE run. Since SIEVE doesn't use string variables, dynamic string arrays, or OPEN files, there is no allocation to string space. The available string space shown (lines 47–48) is a direct indication of the amount of data space required by the program (including the BASIC support routines) for each version run.

If you subtract the available memory space shown by a SIEVE run (lines 49–50) from the "available memory" shown by a CHKDSK run on the same system, this would be a fair approximation of the minimum memory size required to run that version of SIEVE, since no dynamic numeric arrays were ERASEd. On a comparative basis, the greater the free memory space shown, the less the minimum memory required to make that run. Since DOS manages memory space in paragraph (16-byte) chunks, these values are accurate to that limit.

While it is not wise to attempt to draw too many conclusions from the results of running a benchmark, there are some observations that appear to be valid. In what follows, I will show the effects of running SIEVE with changes in the way the program was compiled and with modifica-

Array mode	Compile mode	Time	String space	Memory space
Static	BC SIEVE;	26.5	40,654 bytes	327,694 bytes
	BC SIEVE/D;	245.0	40,654 bytes	327,486 bytes
	BC SIEVE/O;	26.5	44,990 bytes	376,286 bytes
	BC SIEVE/O/D;	245.0	44,894 bytes	375,086 bytes
	BC SIEVE/O/E;	26.5	44,990 bytes	376,286 bytes
	BC SIEVE/O/X;	28.5	44,490 bytes	376,126 bytes
	BC SIEVE/O/V;	82.2	44,366 bytes	366,126 bytes
	BC SIEVE/O/W;	26.5	44,366 bytes	366,318 bytes
Dynamic	BC SIEVE;	30.4	57,022 bytes	327,614 bytes
	BC SIEVE/O;	30.4	61,358 bytes	376,206 bytes

Figure 4 - 2
Effect of compile switches on running SIEVE

tions to the program itself. The program modifications are described in detail and are relative to the source code shown in Listing 4-1.

Effects of Compiler Switches

The data obtained from running SIEVE after separately compiling it with various compiler switches are tabulated in Figure 4-2. The elapsed-time penalties of compiling in the default mode, rather than using the /o switch, are not shown. These are due to the necessity of loading BRUN40.EXE before the timing begins and of reloading COM-MAND.COM after the program finishes.

The data are clear that it takes less memory to run a program compiled with the /o switch than the same program compiled without it. In the comparable cases shown, the difference is about 47 kilobytes, somewhat less when the /d switch is used. When an additional compiler switch is used, more code and data may be linked into the stand-alone executable code from the BCOM40 library, duplicating code in the run-time module that was not required without the switch. Only the relative effects of adding the /d switch are shown.

I have cheated a little in my /e, and /x compilations, because SIEVE doesn't contain any BASIC line numbers or any "ON ERROR GOTO" statements. If it did, there would be an increase in required data and code space. There is no penalty shown for using the /e error-trap enabling switch, and the penalty for using /x, which inhibits compiler optimizing across lines, is surprisingly small. Presumably, the compiler treats the IF-block (lines 32–40 of Listing 4-1) as a single logical line.

I have similarly cheated with the /w and /v switches, since there are no "ON <event> GOSUB" statements. Note the large penalty associated with using the /v event-trap enabling switch; /v disables compiler optimization between statements. It apparently has disabled the optimization inside the major IF-block.

The data for "dynamic arrays" were taken after changing line 13 of Listing 4-1 to '$DYNAMIC.

Passing Arrays to Compiled Procedures

When passing an array variable to a compiled procedure, the whole array is passed, either in an argument list or in a COMMON segment. Both methods are illustrated by initializing the FLAGS() array in separately compiled subroutines.

Using an Argument List

The data for static arrays in Figure 4-3 were obtained by compiling and linking the subroutine in FILL_1.BAS (Listing 4-2) to a slightly modified version of SIEVE.BAS. FILL_1.BAS will initialize all elements of any one-dimension integer array passed in an argument list. The passed array in FILL_1's formal parameter list is specified as ARRAY(), not explicitly providing any information as to size and location of the array. The information used in the subroutine (including the values of LBOUND and UBOUND) were obtained from the array descriptor.

SIEVE.BAS was modified by deleting lines 27–29 of Listing 4-1 and inserting the following CALL statement instead:

```
CALL FILLCHAR(FLAGS(),-1)
```

Array mode	Compile mode	Time	String space	Memory space
Static	BC SIEVE;	28.5	40,662 bytes	327,550 bytes
	BC SIEVE/O;	28.5	44,958 bytes	376,014 bytes
Dynamic	BC SIEVE;	31.1	57,006 bytes	327,502 bytes
	BC SIEVE/O;	31.1	61,342 bytes	375,966 bytes

Figure 4 - 3
Array passed to compiled subroutine in argument list

After compiling both SIEVE and FILL_1 with the appropriate switches, they were linked with the command:

```
LINK SIEVE FILL_1;
```

The data for dynamic arrays in Figure 4-3 were obtained by changing line 13 of Listing 4-1 to '$DYNAMIC, again compiling SIEVE; and linking it to the unchanged FILL_1.OBJ.

Using Named COMMON

Although QBASIC permits the use of *blank* COMMON, it is considered good programming practice to use only *named* COMMON segments when passing variables to procedures, with the name of the COMMON being associated with the receiving procedure. The standard form of a COMMON statement in QBASIC is

```
COMMON [SHARED] [/<name>/] <variablelist>
```

where <variablelist> is a list of all the variables contained in <name> COMMON, separated by commas.

The relationship between <variablelist>s in the same named COMMON in different modules is similar to that between the variables in an argument list and its corresponding formal parameter list, with a couple of important differences. The first difference is due to a linker characteristic. The linker overlays same-named COMMON segments in multiple

```
 1:   '*********************************************************************
 2:   '                              FILL_1.BAS                           *
 3:   '    A compiled subroutine using an array passed in an argument list to *
 4:   ' fill the FLAGS() array in SIEVE.BAS.                             *
 5:   '        CALL with:  "CALL FILLCHAR(FLAGS(),<n>)"                   *
 6:   '                    where <n> is the integer to fill the array.    *
 7:   '               Written by M. L. Lesser, 10/27/86                   *
 8:   '       Modified for Microsoft QuickBASIC BC version 4.0, 11/13/87  *
 9:   '*********************************************************************
10:        DEFINT A-Z
11:
12:   SUB FILLCHAR(ARRAY(),N) STATIC
13:        FOR I = LBOUND(ARRAY) TO UBOUND(ARRAY)
14:             LET ARRAY(I) = N
15:        NEXT I
16:   END SUB
```

Listing 4 - 2

linked modules, giving enough space in the resulting executable code to contain the longest that-named COMMON segment in any module. Therefore, the <variablelist>s in same-named COMMONs in different modules may have a different number of variables. Corresponding variables, starting at the left end of all lists, must match in data space required; any missing variables in the shorter lists can be dropped only from the right end. In general, data-space identity is guaranteed if all variables named in corresponding positions are of the same type and if all array variables are of the same mode — with static arrays having the same number of elements.

The other difference from the argument-list format is that *expressions* are not allowed in COMMON <variablelist>s. All items must be actual variables. Thus, there is no way to prevent a procedure sharing any COMMON segment from modifying variables whose normal scope is only the main program.

When a static array is passed to a procedure module in a COMMON segment, the array DIM statement must precede the COMMON statement in both the main module and in the procedure module, so the entire array is available to both modules. Thus, the version of FILL_2.BAS shown in Listing 4-3 will accept only one-dimension static integer arrays having 8191 elements.

Array mode	Compile mode	Time	String space	Memory space
Static	BC SIEVE;	27.1	40,590 bytes	327,534 bytes
	BC SIEVE/O;	27.1	44,926 bytes	375,998 bytes
Dynamic	BC SIEVE;	31.0	56,974 bytes	327,470 bytes
	BC SIEVE/O;	31.0	61,310 bytes	375,974 bytes

Figure 4 - 4
Array passed to compiled subroutine in COMMON

Figure 4-4 shows the effect on SIEVE of passing arrays to a
FILLCHAR subroutine by using FILLIT COMMON. For static arrays,
Listing 4-1 was modified by inserting the statement

```
COMMON /FILLIT/ FLAGS()
```

in line 20 and replacing lines 27–29 with the single line

```
CALL FILLCHAR(-1)
```

FILL_2.BAS was used as written.

The data in Figure 4-4 for dynamic arrays were obtained by making
the following changes in Listing 4-1. The COMMON statement was inserted in line 18, *before* the DIM statement. This forced the FLAGS() array
to be compiled as dynamic, in spite of the unchanged $STATIC metacom-
mand, and the FILLIT segment to contain only the array descriptor. Lines
27–29 were replaced with the same CALL statement as used for the static
case. FILL_2.BAS (Listing 4-3) was modified by deleting lines 11–12, indicating to the module that only the array descriptor is found in the FIL-
LIT segment.

When you compare the data in Figures 4-4 and 4-3, you will note that
the performance gains (as compared to using an argument list) are significant only with the static array.

```
 1:  '*********************************************************************
 2:  '                        FILL_2.BAS                                  *
 3:  '    A compiled subroutine passing a static array in a named COMMON to  *
 4:  ' fill the FLAGS() array in SIEVE.BAS.                               *
 5:  '         CALL with:  "CALL FILLCHAR(<n>)"                           *
 6:  '                  where <n> is the integer to fill the array.       *
 7:  '                  Written by M. L. Lesser, 10/27/86                *
 8:  '                  Modified for Microsoft BC version 4.0, 11/13/87  *
 9:  '*********************************************************************
10:      DEFINT A-Z
11:      CONST SPACE = 8190
12:      DIM ARRAY(SPACE)
13:      COMMON SHARED /FILLIT/ ARRAY()
14:
15:  SUB FILLCHAR(N) STATIC
16:      FOR I = LBOUND(ARRAY) TO UBOUND(ARRAY)
17:          LET ARRAY(I) = N
18:      NEXT I
19:  END SUB
```

Listing 4 - 3

Passing Arrays to Assembled Procedures

Passing an array variable to an assembled procedure differs in concept
from passing that same variable to a compiled procedure. The address of
the first element in the array and the length of the array must be passed
explicitly to the assembled procedure. Passing the address of the first
array element by naming it in the argument list works properly for static
arrays and dynamic string arrays, but a different technique must be used
for dynamic arrays stored in far object space.

Passing Static Arrays

FILL_3.ASM (Listing 4-4) is an example of an assembled subroutine to ful-
fill the FILLCHAR function. This subroutine is called by replacing lines
27–29 of Listing 4-1 with the single statement:

```
CALL FILLCHAR(FLAGS(0),UBOUND(FLAGS)-LBOUND(FLAGS),-1)
```

The three arguments passed are the first element of FLAGS(), an expression indicating its length, and the constant to be used in filling the
array elements.

```
 1:             PAGE    ,105
 2:             TITLE   FILL_3
 3:             .MODEL  MEDIUM
 4:  ;**********************************************************************
 5:  ;                           FILL_3.ASM                              *
 6:  ;   An assembled subroutine to fill the FLAGS() static array in     *
 7:  ; SIEVE.BAS.  Array characteristics passed to the subroutine in an  *
 8:  ; argument list.                                                    *
 9:  ;    Call with:                                                     *
10:  ;        "CALL FILLCHAR(FLAGS(0),UBOUND(FLAGS)-LBOUND(FLAGS),<n>)"  *
11:  ;          where <n> is the integer to fill the array.             *
12:  ;                   Written by M. L. Lesser, 10/28/86              *
13:  ;              Modified for Microsoft MASM 5.0, 11/13/87           *
14:  ;**********************************************************************
15:
16:  ;   Symbol definitions used to get addresses of multiple arguments:
17:  ARG_1     EQU    10                     ;FLAGS(0)
18:  ARG_2     EQU    8                      ;UBOUND(FLAGS)-LBOUND(FLAGS)
19:  ARG_3     EQU    6                      ;<n>
20:
21:  .CODE
22:
23:            PUBLIC  FILLCHAR
24:  FILLCHAR PROC
25:            PUSH    BP
26:            MOV     BP,SP
27:            PUSH    DI                     ;Will use, so must save
28:            MOV     DI,ARG_1[BP]           ;Get address of FLAGS(0)
29:  ;  Put value of UBOUND(FLAGS)-LBOUND(FLAGS) in CX:
30:            MOV     BX,ARG_2[BP]           ;Address of temp variable
31:            MOV     CX,[BX]                ;One less than # elements
32:            INC     CX                     ;Number of elements in array
33:            CMP     CX,0                   ;Check for number >  0
34:            JLE     FINI                   ;If not, exit with no activity
35:            MOV     BX,ARG_3[BP]           ;Temp variable with <n>
36:            MOV     AX,[BX]
37:            CLD                            ;Load it into entire array
38:  REP       STOSW
39:  FINI:     POP     DI                     ;Restore in reverse order
40:            POP     BP                     ;    to pushes
41:
42:            RET     6
43:  FILLCHAR ENDP
44:
45:            END
```

Listing 4 - 4

Because more than one argument is passed to the assembled FILLCHAR, I have inserted a dummy "formal parameter list" in lines 17 –19 of Listing 4-4. The three constants are the offsets from BP, in the stack, of the addresses passed by the CALL statement.

The check for a positive nonzero value in CX (lines 33–34) is a safety feature and should be included in all assembled subroutines that write to

Array mode	Compile mode	Time	String space	Memory space
Static	BC SIEVE;	24.6	40,638 bytes	327,630 bytes
	BC SIEVE/O;	24.6	44,974 bytes	376,222 bytes
Dynamic	BC SIEVE;	27.1	57,022 bytes	327,582 bytes
	BC SIEVE/O;	27.1	61.358 bytes	376,174 bytes

Figure 4 - 5
Array passed to assembled subroutine

memory [CX] times. Otherwise, you are likely to obliterate all or most of DGROUP.

The "static array mode" data in Figure 4-5 were obtained by assembling FILL_3.ASM and linking it to the modified SIEVE.BAS as compiled in the modes shown.

Passing Dynamic Arrays

You cannot use the form of argument list used with a static (or dynamic string) array to pass a dynamic numeric array to an assembled procedure. If you try, the compiler treats the array element argument as an expression, copying its value into a temporary location in data space and passing that address. You need the actual segment:offset address of the array in far object space, obtained by using the two built-in functions, VARPTR and VARSEG.

The VARPTR function returns the address of the first memory byte containing the variable, as an offset from the origin of the segment containing that variable. Data in DGROUP is immediately available to assembled procedures by using the VARPTR offset with the DGROUP segment address already in the DS register.

For array elements in far object space, the VARSEG function returns the corresponding segment address, which must be loaded into a segment register to retrieve the variable. It takes four arguments to pass the necessary information to an assembled procedure to fill a dynamic numeric array. I have used FILLIT COMMON to pass the four arguments to the assembled subroutine.

The following modifications were made to SIEVE.BAS (Listing 4-1) to produce the "dynamic array" data in Figure 4-5. Since FLAGS() was not first declared in FILLIT, the array was declared dynamic by changing the metacommand in line 13 to $DYNAMIC. FILLIT COMMON was declared in line 18 (since the COMMON declaration must precede the now-executable DIM statement) with:

```
COMMON /FILLIT/ FLAGSEG,FLAGOFF,LENGTH,N
```

Expressions are not permitted in COMMON <variablelist>s; the values will be assigned to FLAGSEG, FLAGOFF, LENGTH, and N during run time.

Lines 27–29 were replaced with the following code:

```
LET FLAGSEG = VARSEG(FLAGS(0))
LET FLAGOFF = VARPTR(FLAGS(0))
LET LENGTH = UBOUND(FLAGS) - LBOUND(FLAGS)
LET N = -1
CALL FILLCHAR
```

The corresponding assembled subroutine is FILL_4.ASM (Listing 4-5). Since we are using a COMMON region in DGROUP, it is necessary to define the segment (lines 17–24) and put it into DGROUP (line 26). If blank COMMON were being used, line 17 would read:

```
COMMON SEGMENT WORD COMMON 'BLANK'
```

Line 24 would be "COMMON ENDS" and COMMON would be put into DGROUP (line 26).

Since the array is not in DGROUP, ES is set to the array element segment address (lines 35–36). The remainder of FILL_4.ASM is essentially the same as FILL_3.ASM, allowing for the effects of the "shared" variables in COMMON.

The data in Figures 4-2 through 4-5 show that initializing 8,190 array elements with an assembled subroutine uses about three to four seconds less time (on my system) than does performing the same task with the

```
 1:            PAGE    ,105
 2:            TITLE   FILL_4
 3:            .MODEL  MEDIUM
 4: ;**********************************************************************
 5: ;                              FILL_4.ASM                            *
 6: ;    An assembled subroutine to fill the FLAGS() dynamic array in    *
 7: ; SIEVE.BAS.  Array characteristics passed to the subroutine in a    *
 8: ; named COMMON segment.                                              *
 9: ;      Call with: "CALL FILLCHAR"                                    *
10: ;                 after calling PTR86 to get FLAGSEG and FLAGOFF,    *
11: ;                 and assigning the proper values to LENGTH and N    *
12: ;                                                                    *
13: ;                 Written by M. L. Lesser, 10/28/86                  *
14: ;              Modified for Microsoft MASM 5.0, 11/13/87             *
15: ;**********************************************************************
16:
17: FILLIT  SEGMENT WORD COMMON 'BC_VARS'
18: ;  Common contains the values of the variables noted:
19: FLAGSEG DW      ?                               ;Segment address of FLAGS(0)
20: FLAGOFF DW      ?                               ;Offset address of FLAGS(0)
21: LNGTH   DW      ?                               ;UBOUND(FLAGS) - LBOUND(FLAGS)
22: N       DW      ?                               ;Value to write into elements
23:
24: FILLIT  ENDS
25:
26: DGROUP  GROUP   FILLIT
27:
28: .CODE
29:
30:            PUBLIC  FILLCHAR
31: FILLCHAR PROC
32:            PUSH    BP
33:            PUSH    DI
34: ;  ARRAY(0) segment:offset in ES:DI:
35:            MOV     AX,FLAGSEG
36:            MOV     ES,AX
37:            MOV     DI,FLAGOFF
38: ;  Number of elements in array in CX:
39:            MOV     CX,LNGTH              ;One less than # elements
40:            INC     CX                    ;Number of elements in array
41:            CMP     CX,0                  ;Check for number > 0
42:            JLE     FINI                  ;If not, exit with no activity
43: ;  Value to load into array elements in AX:
44:            MOV     AX,N
45:            CLD
46: REP        STOSW
47: FINI:      POP     DI
48:            POP     BP
49:            RET
50: FILLCHAR ENDP
51:
52:            END
53:
```

Listing 4 - 5

```
defint a-z
option base 1
dim array(3,4)
for i = 1 to 3
    for j = 1 to 4
        let array(i,j) = 10 * i + j
    next j
next i
let where = varptr(array(1,1))
for i = 0 to 11
    print using "####"; peek(where + 2 * i);
next i
print
```

Figure 4-6
ARRAY.BAS, an array storage-order demonstration

best-performing compiled subroutine, and about two to three seconds less time than when performing it in in-line compiled code.[4]

Array Element Storage Sequence

Array element storage sequence is of no importance unless you are writing an assembled procedure that is going to treat some elements of the array differently than others. For one-dimension arrays, the elements are stored contiguously, in order of subscript. For higher-dimension arrays, the elements are stored in *column major* sequence, a sequence determined by varying the subscripts most rapidly from left to right.

Figure 4-6 is a demonstration program to illustrate the memory sequence BASIC uses to store a two-dimension array. Each element of the array is assigned an integer value consisting of the two digits indicating the row and column subscript of that element. The low-order byte of each word containing an array element is then displayed in the sequence the elements are stored in data space. Figure 4-7 shows the output from compiling and linking ARRAY.BAS.

You might check the effect of using the /r switch in the compilation. If you are going to use arrays having more than two dimensions, you might also repeat the little experiment with an array having three or more

```
11  21  31  12  22  32  13  23  33  14  24  34
```

Figure 4 - 7
Running ARRAY.BAS

dimensions, just to make sure you understand what "column major" means when the array has more than "rows" and "columns."

Notes

1. Jim Gilbreath, "A High-Level Language Benchmark," *Byte*, September 1981, pp. 180–191. For examples of how easy it is to bias SIEVE (or any other benchmark) to favor a specific implementation of any programming language, also see Jim Gilbreath and Gary Gilbreath, "Eratosthenes Revisited: Once More through the Sieve," Byte, January 1983, pp. 283–326.

2. *Unpredictable results* is a computerese euphemism meaning "you'll be sorry!" What happens depends on the circumstances, and can vary from a "String space corrupt" nonrecoverable error to a trip to never-never land (an infinite loop).

3. When I compiled the "base case" SIEVE (Listing 4-1) with QBASIC version 3.0 — QB SIEVE/O; — it ran in slightly less than half the time shown for QBASIC 4.0 in Figure 4-1. I assume this "performance degradation" stems from changes in the way arrays are accessed in QBASIC 4.0. Although a pathological case, SIEVE is one of the standard benchmarks used to advertise language processors. So I imagine that improving the performance of QBASIC when running SIEVE is a high-priority project at Microsoft, and would expect to see the effects of the effort in the next release.

4. The differences shown for SIEVE, between using assembled and compiled code to perform the same task, are examples of the typical programming trade-off between performance and

convenience. In general, it pays to use assembled procedures with high-level language programs only when it is difficult to perform the task in the high-level language, or when the assembled procedure is going to be used often enough to pay for the inconvenience. Unfortunately, as with many other easily stated cost-benefit rules, there is no analytic procedure to determine whether the payoff is worth the effort. Programming is an art form; which language to use in a particular circumstance is a matter of style.

Chapter 5

Elements of Program Structure

A program's *structure* is a road map of the flow of control during program execution.[1] Very few useful applications can be programmed with the ideal structure — a straight line from beginning to end.

The "decision-making" power of a computer program stems from the ability of the automatic computing engine to change the path of program execution based on circumstances encountered during run time. The conditional transfer of control is one of the few absolutely required operations in the computer's repertoire and must be available in any programming language that is to be used for nontrivial applications. BASIC offers several conditional-transfer constructs, including built-in error trapping.

This chapter opens with a review of the loop constructs available in BASIC, followed by a discussion of the error-trapping procedures used in the main program and in private-library compiled modules.

An assembled-language function allows keystroke polling (instead of event trapping) to recognize the "extended code" (function or cursor) keys without interfering with normal INPUT statements. Both this declared function and error trapping within a compiled library module are used to enhance the "user friendliness" of the LIST utility.

Control Transfer Fundamentals

The most fundamental and easiest to understand embodiment of the conditional transfer of control is given by a statement of the form:

```
IF <condition> THEN GOTO <label>
```

Although this statement underlies all programmed loops, computer languages include a number of specialized loop constructs, some of which offer genuine convenience and others which merely hide the GOTOs. While QBASIC includes enough of these GOTO substitutes to allow you to write programs with no visible GOTOs, doing so requires giving up much of the clarity and elegance of a well-structured program.

The Much-maligned GOTO

Many neophyte programmers believe there is something unclean about using a visible GOTO, and no "good" programmer would ever do so. Since most of these true believers don't know the origin of their superstition, here is a short bit of computer history.

It all started in 1965 when Professor Dijkstra delivered a paper making a plea for clarity in program source code.[2] Most of what he had to say is long forgotten, but a few statements had a profound effect on computer science as it is taught today. Dijkstra told how "two programming department managers . . . [had] communicated to me, independently . . . that the quality of their programmers was inversely proportional to the density of goto statements in their programs. This [was] an incentive to do away with the goto statement."

So he reprogrammed some problems "in modified versions of ALGOL 60 in which the goto statement was abolished and the for statement — being pompous and over-elaborate — was replaced by a primitive repetition clause . . . In all cases tried . . . the program without the goto statements turned out to be shorter and more lucid."

While not specifically stated, Dijkstra's conjecture was obvious. If he could *always* produce better ("more lucid") programs by using a GOTO substitute (the "primitive repetition clause") instead of the naked GOTO, poor programmers would become better programmers if only the GOTO were abolished from the programming languages. The "goto is harmful" school of computer science was born.

Nobody in this school seems to have noticed all the programs for which the naked GOTO is the *best* programming construct, both in terms of program clarity and in performance. One major class of these consists of programs characterized by being easily described with a state diagram where at least one state has two or more successor states, at least one of which also has two or more successor states. Compiler parsers, although sometimes written in strange languages that do not have a real GOTO, are members of this class.

It should have been obvious to everyone that the "goto is harmful" argument is based on a fallacy. Removing a useful, if sometimes misused, tool from the programmers' toolbox cannot possibly make better programmers out of poor programmers. The result of the nonsense is a generation of programmers not skilled enough to know how to use a GOTO. Instead, this generation believes that any program with no visible GOTO is a sign of a good programmer, and so clutters up its programs with a rash of useless, specialized GOTO substitutes.

Labels

In the fundamental transfer of control statement, <label> is the name of the label on the entry point — the next line to be executed if the control transfer is taken. The compiler will return a severe error message if there is no valid line identified with a label specified in a transfer statement, or if there is more than one line in the module identified with the same label. In QBASIC a label can be either a line number or an alphanumeric line label. It must be the first non-white-space entry on a logical line.

Line numbers identifying entry points can be any valid BASIC numeric value greater than zero. Line numbers between 1 and 65,529, inclusive, can also be used to identify the source line of errors (the ERL function).

It is considered good programming style to use mnemonic alphanumeric line labels rather than line numbers, as a form of self-commenting. Naming conventions for alphanumeric labels are similar to those for variables: labels must consist of alphabetic characters and digits, can include periods as separators, and may contain up to forty symbols. Alphanumeric labels are not case-sensitive and are separated from the rest of the line they identify by a following colon.

No label has scope outside of the module containing it. Labels within the main portion of the module do not have scope within any multiline defined function or compiled procedure, and labels within each such substructure have scope only within that portion. Attempts to transfer control to a label not having scope over the portion of program containing the transfer statement is a compiler severe error.

Relational and Logical Operators

In the generalized transfer of control statement, the transfer will take place if <condition> is any nonzero numeric expression. Conditional transfers of control are usually initiated as the result of testing for the truth or falsity of an assertion about the relationship between two or more entities. Thus, typical statements start with "IF A > B THEN . . . " or "IF C = D THEN . . . " In these examples, the symbols ">" and "=" are *relational* operators.

In Microsoft BASIC, relational operators are evaluated as integer functions having the operands as arguments. Unless the two operands are either both numeric expressions or both string expressions, the compiler will return a "Type mismatch" severe error. Relational operations return the integer -1 if the tested relationship is "true," or the integer 0 if it is "false." As with any BASIC function, this result can be used immediately or can be stored in an integer variable for later use. A variable storing the results of one or more relational tests is sometimes referred to as a *flag*.

When relational operators appear in an expression, the operations are performed in pairs, in strict left-to-right sequence unless parentheses are used, after all arithmetic operations in the expression have been evaluated and before any logical operations are performed. If there are more than two values being compared, the *result* of each pair tested becomes the left-hand operand of the next operator. Just to add a little confusion, BASIC uses the same symbol for both the assignment operator and for the relational "is equal to" operator.

The BASIC formal assignment operator has the form

```
LET <variable> = <expression>
```

where the LET is optional. Since the LET is optional, BASIC recognizes the assignment operator by position. Ignoring labels and LETs, only the

"=" following a variable name that is the first word in a statement, or the first word following THEN or ELSE, is evaluated as an assignment operator. All other "=" symbols in the statement are relational operators. Thus, in the statement

```
LET FLAG = A = B
```

FLAG will be assigned the value -1 if A does equal B, or the value 0 if A does not equal B.

As an example of multiple comparisons, consider:

```
LET FLAG = A = B = C
```

FLAG will have the value -1 if A = B and C = -1, or if A <> B and C = 0. FLAG will have the value 0 for all other combinations of A, B, and C.

The results of two or more relational tests can be combined in a single expression with *logical* operators. For example:

```
IF A > B AND C = D THEN...
```

requires that both A > B and C = D be true for <condition> to be true.

QBASIC logical operators are evaluated as either integer or long integer functions, depending on the magnitude of the operands. These functions return the result of performing the requested Boolean operation on each corresponding bit of two operands (on one operand for the unary operator NOT). If an operand of a logical operator is not an integer, it will be *rounded* to an integer (or long integer, if necessary) before the function is evaluated.

Logical operations in a statement are performed (after all relational operations) in precedence order unless changed by parentheses. The unary operator NOT has the highest precedence. Thus, "NOT A OR B" is evaluated as "(NOT A) OR B." If you really want "NOT (A OR B)," you must supply the parentheses.

Since BASIC has only the bit-wise Boolean logical operators, "true" must be coded as -1 (FFFF in hex) if "NOT true" is to have the same value as "false" (0000) in conditional statements. Initializing constant flags to +1 for "true" works some of the time but not always — another source of hard-to-find bugs.

Top-tested Loops

Under most circumstances, a program is more reliable if loop constructs are tested at the top, on entry, rather than at the bottom, for exit. In this manner, if the controlling variable(s) are outside the programmed loop execution range, the entire active portion of the loop will be skipped. The traditional BASIC top-tested hidden-GOTO loop constructs are FOR...NEXT and WHILE...WEND.

FOR...NEXT

The FOR...NEXT loop was the first hidden-GOTO loop construct and is very convenient when used correctly.[3] The defining statement is

```
FOR <counter> = <start> TO <end> [STEP <increment>]
```

where <counter> must be a variable; <start>, <end>, and the optional <increment> may be either constants or variables. It is conventional to declare FOR...NEXT variables as integers, largely for performance reasons.

If you are using integers, there is one built-in booby trap in the FOR...NEXT loop. If the sum of <end> and <increment> is outside the allowable integer limits (-32,768 through +32,767), the integer overflow will put you into an endless loop. Of course, you can always compile with the /d switch to catch this run-time error, at a great penalty in performance. Good programming practice would be to test variable <end> and <increment> values *before* entering the loop.

The FOR...NEXT construct may be considered to translate into four sequences of machine code. The FOR statement produces both the initializer and the following test. If <end> and/or <increment> are variables, they are initialized to the values they have at entry and used as constants during the remainder of the loop execution. If there is no "STEP <increment>" portion, <increment> will be initialized to +1. The initializer finishes by setting <counter> to the value <start> has on entry, and transfers control to the test code.

The test code (the rest of the FOR statement) evaluates the implied <condition> to determine if the loop has been fully executed. If <increment> is positive and the current value of <counter> is greater than <end>, or if <increment> is negative and the current value of <counter>

is less than <end>, control is transferred to the implicit label on the first statement following the NEXT statement; otherwise, control passes to the implicit label at the start of the third code sequence, the body of the loop. The test is on an inequality; the final value of <counter> will always be outside of <end>. When execution reaches the NEXT statement, <increment> is added to the current value of <counter> and an unconditional GOTO is taken to the start of the test sequence.

FOR...NEXT loops may be nested within other FOR...NEXT loops (having different counter variables) and within WHILE...WEND loops. However, only *static nesting* is permitted by the compiler. Each nested loop must be fully contained in its outer loop in source-code listing sequence. (In BASICA, the requirement is for *dynamic nesting* — loops must be contained in outer loops in execution sequence.)

QBASIC now has the specialized GOTO substitute "EXIT FOR." A conditional "EXIT FOR" forces a jump to the implicit label on the first statement following the current NEXT if <condition> is satisfied.

When it is necessary to leave a loop prematurely, it is always better programming style to use a real conditional GOTO instead of a GOTO substitute. If you really want to go to the first instruction following the NEXT, the explicit label required by the GOTO not only reminds the programmer of where control is going, but also provides useful information for the later reader; the executable code for both constructs will be identical. But if you need to go somewhere else, say directly to the surface from the innermost nested FOR...NEXT loop, using a conditional GOTO will save at least one dummy variable and a sequence of additional <condition> tests; the source code with the GOTO will be "more lucid" and the executable code will be shorter and faster.

Jumping *into* a FOR...NEXT loop is frowned upon as poor programming practice.

WHILE...WEND

The WHILE...WEND loop (under many aliases) is the classic "structured programming" hidden-GOTO loop construct. The body of the loop is surrounded by an opening "WHILE <condition>" statement and a closing "WEND" statement.

The compiler translates the "WHILE <condition>" into a conditional GOTO. If <condition> is true, execution falls through to the body of the loop; if <condition> is false, control is transferred to an implied label on the first line following the WEND. The WEND is shorthand for an unconditional GOTO to the implicit label on the WHILE statement.

In general, the restrictions on using WHILE...WEND loops are similar to those for FOR...NEXT loops. The compiler assigns GOTO-label pairs between each WEND and the most recent unpaired WHILE, in source-code listing order. It cannot catch nesting errors unless there is cross- nesting with another construct or an unequal number of WHILEs and WENDs.

WHILE...WEND loops are very convenient, but they do not include any explicit identifiers. Nested WHILE...WEND loops, especially if carried over more than one page of listing, are very difficult to decipher (by humans) without lots of comments. There are times when using an equivalent GOTO loop with explicit labels produces "more lucid" code.

QBASIC also allows the "DO WHILE/UNTIL...LOOP" construct. "DO WHILE <condition>" is logically identical to "WHILE <condition>," but LOOP must be the closing statement of the loop, rather than WEND. "DO UNTIL <condition>" translates directly into "DO WHILE NOT <condition>." The DO...LOOP construct allows you to use the specialized GOTO substitute "EXIT DO." Using "EXIT DO" is just as poor programming style as is using "EXIT FOR."

Bottom-tested Loops

Usually, it is good programming practice to test loops at the top (before entry) to prevent performing the body of the loop inadvertently if the entry conditions are already outside the looping conditions. However, there are circumstances where the application requires performing the body of the loop at least once, irrespective of the entry conditions. In these circumstances, the bottom-tested conditional GOTO loop is the best construct to use. The first statement of the loop body carries a label, and the closing statement is a conditional GOTO transferring control back to the label unless the exit conditions are satisfied.

There is no rational reason to use a bottom-tested hidden-GOTO loop construct in a language that offers a real GOTO, since all the specialized substitute does is hide useful information from the reader without offering any convenience in exchange. However, you can change the DO-loop construct to a bottom-tested loop by attaching the WHILE/UNTIL clause to the LOOP statement instead of to the DO statement. If your DO...LOOP structure contains neither a WHILE nor an UNTIL, you have written an infinite loop.

Error Trapping

BASIC is one of the few languages offering automatic error trapping. The run-time support intercepts most operational errors. Except for a few non-recoverable errors, the programmer has the choice of allowing the error to terminate the program or of trapping the interruption and making a programmed correction.

You cannot trap errors not checked for by the BASIC support system, although you can supply your own tests for such conditions. You should not trap errors unless you expect them to occur and know what to do to correct the condition. The most common correctable errors are related to "file not found" or "device not ready" conditions.

According to the *Learning and Using Microsoft QuickBASIC* manual, unless the program was compiled with the /d switch, the support system does not check for errors due to arithmetic overflow, array out of bounds, or RETURN without a preceding GOSUB (in execution order). This statement is not entirely true. The support system always checks for floating-point overflow.

Error trapping is initiated by the executable statement

```
ON ERROR GOTO <trap>
```

where <trap> is a label identifying the code segment to be executed if an error occurs. This statement reroutes the "normal" error exit to the section of code identified by <trap>, which must lie within the main portion of the module.

The trap code identifies the source of the error (usually as an IF-block test condition), makes corrections, and then RESUMEs operation at the appropriate point in the program. RESUME is a specialized GOTO that also rearms the error-trapping mechanism (errors occurring within an error trap cannot be trapped). "RESUME <label>" is subject to the usual label scope rules.

If the error was *not* one of those being trapped, an ELSE statement in the IF-block should execute the statement

```
ON ERROR GOTO 0
```

to reroute the error interrupt back to its normal exit.

If error trapping is used in a module, that module must have been compiled with either the /e or the /x switch, depending on the form of the RESUME statement. If only "RESUME <label>" is used, compilation can be done with the /e switch. If either "RESUME" or "RESUME NEXT" is used, compilation must be done with the /x switch, which adds a further space and running-time penalty.

Main-module Traps

One of the more difficult aspects of error trapping is identifying the occurring error — making sure that it is the one expected and that it can be corrected. One way is to trap by error number. ERR will return the number Microsoft assigned to the error causing the interrupt, and can be interrogated as part of the IF-block making up the error trap. Each run-time error number is assigned to a specific error message, as listed in Appendix D of the *BASIC Language Reference* manual distributed with QBASIC. Unfortunately, Microsoft is not too consistent about the way error messages are assigned to what appear to be the same error, so you must do a little experimenting before you write your trap routine.

For example, if you try to run LIST (Listing 3-3) with no <filename> on the command line, LIST will supply only the BAS extension, and you will get the error message shown in Figure 5-1. Reference to the manual shows that "File not found" is ERR code 53. If you try it again with a <filespec> that has more than eight characters in its <filename>, you will get the more reasonable error message, "Bad file name" (ERR code 64). If you happen to try it with a solitary period, you will get the strange message "Path/File access error" (ERR 75). There may be others I haven't tried.

All these messages are followed by the "Hit any key . . ." instruction to return you to the system. This nuisance is a "fix" for the design problem involved in ENDing any program with an error message while in a graphics mode, as discussed in the next chapter.

```
File not found in module LIST       at address 3854:018E

Hit any key to return to system
```

Figure 5 - 1
Error message from LIST due to file name not given

Figure 5-2 is a sample error trap to handle these three situations. It is designed to be tested by inserting it into the version of LIST.BAS shown in Listing 3-3, between lines 108 and 109. Also insert the label "RESTART:" between lines 54 and 55, and the statement

```
ON ERROR GOTO TRAP
```

in line 32.

There is no reason to use the "RESUME NEXT" or "RESUME" form of the error-trap rearming statement when the error being trapped is in the main module, so you don't have to compile with the /x switch. Test this example by copying the header file PQB.BI to the default drive, compiling the edited LIST with the /e switch, and then linking it to PQB.LIB.

Now when you forget to ask LIST for a file, or give it an improper <filespec>, it will give you another chance without requiring you to recall

```
trap:
    if err = 53 or err = 64 or err = 75 then
        print "Cannot find " chr$(34) file chr$(34)
        input "Enter a new  <filespec>:  ", file
        resume restart
    else
        on error goto 0
    end if
```

Figure 5 - 2
Sample error trap for LIST.BAS

it and wait for the program to reload. Instead, it will keep bugging you for a file it can find and list. Of course, you can always get out of the loop by pressing Ctrl-C or Ctrl-Break in response to the INPUT request.

In this example, the expected errors are identified by ERR code number. If you would rather identify them by line number (since there is only one line in which the trapped errors can occur), you could use an appropriate line number on the line containing the OPEN statement, and another line number on the next line. (At least two line numbers are required, since the ERL function returns the last line number it has seen, in listing sequence.) In general, it is safer to trap on ERR than on ERL.

For example, there is a fourth potential error source on that same line. If you specify a drive to the version of LIST using the error trap of Figure 5-2 and that drive has an open door, the terminating error message (after the DOS time-out) will be "Disk not ready" (ERR code 71). But if you had tested on ERL instead of ERR, you would have gotten the same "Cannot find" message for the additional error source.

To trap on an open diskette door, add the appropriate ELSEIF block to the error trap, displaying the appropriate message. You might be a little more friendly than DOS's "Abort, Retry, Ignore?" while you are at it.

A Library-module Trap: FINDFILE.BAS

If you confine all your error trapping to library procedure modules, you can compile all your main modules without using either the /e or the /x switch; the executable code will take up less space and run faster.

You can't use "RESUME <label>" when trapping an error in a compiled procedure because of the label scope rules. Since the error trap must be in the main portion of the module code, it cannot transfer control by label to a recovery point located in the procedure. You must use either "RESUME" or "RESUME NEXT" to rearm the error trap and resume execution after the correction has been made, so the library module must be compiled with the /x switch.

FINDFILE.BAS (Listing 5-1) is such a library subroutine module. When given a file name (which must be the value of a string variable) to look for, FINDFILE first looks in the directory specified in the CALL argument. If it can't find the file, it searches through the directories in the PATH environment string obtained by using the built-in ENVIRON$ function (line 34). If FINDFILE finds the requested file, it "returns" a complete <filespec> in the argument variable, including the drive code and path portions. If it can't find the requested file, it returns a null value as an error signal.

The error line is defined in FINDFILE by switching on the trap mechanism just before the only line in which the error might occur, and switching it off on the line following (lines 37–39). The trap (lines 58–75) will return control to the error line with the RESUME statement after every trap, as long as there are any directories left in the PATH string. If there are no more directories to try, the "RESUME NEXT" statement (line 61) returns control to the line following the error statement, turning off the error trap and returning to the calling program. MAKNAME (lines 44–55) has been written as a separate subroutine, rather than having been included in TRAP, to allow its use by other programs.

In spite of the pedagogical discourse on "Disk not ready" errors in the preceding subsection, FINDFILE does not distinguish between a "Disk not ready" and other "no file" errors. You can correct this omission if you feel it important.

After you have tested FINDFILE thoroughly, add FINDFILE.OBJ to your private library by copying PQB.LIB to the default drive and then using the library-management command:

```
lib pqb+findfile,pqb.idx;
```

When LIB finishes, you will find both PQB.BAK and PQB.LIB along with the new PQB.IDX file. After you check PQB.IDX to make sure the FINDFILE module was indeed added, replace the original PQB.LIB file in your LIB directory with the new version. Also append the declarations for the two subroutines, FINDFILE and MAKNAME, to your PQB.BI file. Store backup copies of the module source-code file, the new PQB.LIB file, and the new PQB.IDX file on your procedure archive diskette. Store the listings of FINDFILE.BAS, the current PQB.BI file, and the current PQB.IDX file in your programmer's notebook.

Keystroke Polling: KBPEEK.ASM

As mentioned in Chapter 2, I have never used event trapping. Since I can't tell you anything about it except what is in the manual, and you can read

```
 1:    '*****************************************************************
 2:    '                        FINDFILE.BAS                           *
 3:    '     FINDFILE is a compiled subroutine to be linked to programs *
 4:    ' written for the Microsoft QuickBASIC compiler.  It locates a file *
 5:    ' stored in the specified directory or in a directory on the PATH *
 6:    ' environment string.                                           *
 7:    '     To use:       CALL FINDFILE(<filename>)                    *
 8:    '           where <filename> is a string variable containing the *
 9:    '           <filespec> to be searched for.                      *
10:    '               On return, <filename> will contain the full <filespec> *
11:    '           to the requested file, including drive and directory path *
12:    '           as required.                                         *
13:    '               If the requested file cannot be found after the PATH *
14:    '           environment string search, <filename> will contain a null *
15:    '           string.                                             *
16:    '               On return, <filename> will not be OPEN.          *
17:    '     MAKNAME.OBJ is a compiled subroutine to remove any drive or path *
18:    ' portion of <filename>.  Call with:  CALL MAKNAME(<filename>)   *
19:    '           where <filename> is a string variable containing a   *
20:    '           <filespec>.                                          *
21:    '               On return, <filename> will contain only the file name *
22:    '           and extension portion of the original value.         *
23:    '               Written by M. L. Lesser, September 27, 1986      *
24:    '               Modified for Microsoft BC version 4.0, 11-17-87  *
25:    '                    Compiled with switch /X                     *
26:    '*****************************************************************
27:    '    Setup:
28:            DEFSTR F,P
29:            DEFINT I-K
30:            DIM I, FPATH
31:            DIM SHARED FILE, PATH
32:
33:    SUB FINDFILE(FILENAME) STATIC
34:            LET PATH = ENVIRON$("PATH")        'Get PATH environment string
35:            LET FILE = FILENAME                'Make <filespec> global variable
36:            LET KEEPER = FREEFILE              'Next unused file number
37:         ON ERROR GOTO TRAP                    'Trap if FILE not found
38:            OPEN FILE FOR INPUT AS KEEPER
39:         ON ERROR GOTO 0                       'Turn off error trapping
40:            CLOSE KEEPER                       'Close file (clearing buffer)
41:            LET FILENAME = FILE                'Return "found" <filespec>
42:    END SUB
43:
44:    SUB MAKNAME(FILENAME) STATIC
45:            LET J = INSTR(FILENAME,"\")        'Separator in <filespec> "path"
46:            LET K = 0                          'Place mark
47:            WHILE J <> 0
48:               LET K = J                                'K will be location of
49:               LET J = INSTR(K+1,FILENAME,"\")          ' last "\" in FILE
50:            WEND
51:            IF K = 0 _                                  'If there is no "path"
52:               THEN LET K = INSTR(FILENAME,":")         '  look for drive code
53:            IF K <> 0 _                                 'If either, strip it off
54:               THEN LET FILENAME = MID$(FILENAME,K+1)
55:    END SUB
56:
```

Listing 5 - 1 (continued)

```
57:   '  Error trap (Executable code in module outside of called subroutine):
58:   TRAP:    LET I = INSTR(PATH,";")        'Separator in PATH string
59:            IF PATH = "" THEN              'If no more directories to try
60:               LET FILE = ""                 'Error signal and forced
61:               RESUME NEXT                   '   return from subroutine
62:            END IF
63:            IF I <> 0 THEN                 'If more than one "path" left
64:               LET FPATH = LEFT$(PATH,I-1)    'Try next one and
65:               LET PATH = MID$(PATH,I+1)      ' strip it off string
66:            ELSE                          'This is last one on string
67:               LET FPATH = PATH              'So use it
68:               LET PATH = ""                 '   and set PATH at null
69:            END IF
70:            IF RIGHT$(FPATH,1) <> "\" THEN 'If not a root directory
71:               LET FPATH = FPATH + "\"     '  add trailing "\"
72:            END IF
73:            CALL MAKNAME(FILE)            'Delete old "path" from FILE
74:            LET FILE = FPATH + FILE       '  and insert new value
75:            RESUME                        'Try next <filespec>
76:   '   End of subroutine module
```

Listing 5 - 1

that for yourself, I don't intend to say much. I consider event polling, if feasible, a better approach.

The objective of keystroke polling is the same as that of keystroke trapping: to identify keystrokes having meaning other than text entry without interfering with normal input. Most certainly, keystroke polling is easier to program, and is probably faster, than keystroke trapping. Keystroke polling, by its nature, "interrupts" the program only at designated points in the running code; it takes extra programming to force keystroke trapping to be this considerate.

BASIC's keystroke trapping works on key scan codes, which are associated directly with each individual key. Duplicate keys having the same function have different scan codes. ROM BIOS converts keystroke scan codes (including those for any of the shift keys — Shift, Alt, and Ctrl — pressed simultaneously) into a code representing the symbol entered, and stores the result in the type-ahead buffer.

If the pressed key/shift combination is not one of the 256 "extended ASCII" symbols,[4] an *extended code* is entered into the buffer. Unlike scan codes, extended codes are associated with the function, not with the key. Thus, the duplicate cursor keys in the new enhanced IBM keyboards produce the same extended code as do the old cursor keys, even though they have different scan codes.

You can read extended code symbols using INKEY$, except for Ctrl-Break (extended code zero). However, INKEY$ always removes the pending symbol from the buffer, and there is no way in BASIC to put it back.

KBPEEK.ASM (Listing 5-2) is an assembled function that determines whether or not there is a pending symbol in the PC's type-ahead buffer. KBPEEK returns an integer argument: if no symbol is pending, -1 is returned; if an ASCII symbol is pending, 256 is returned and the symbol is left in the buffer to be read by normal input commands. If an extended code symbol is pending, KBPEEK returns that value, and the extended code symbol is removed from the buffer.

KBPEEK, as does DOS, discards codes produced by any keys on the new enhanced (101-key) IBM keyboard that do not have an equivalent function on the original PC keyboards (e.g., the F11 and F12 keys). The extended codes returned by KBPEEK are tabulated in Appendix B.

A couple of caveats: I have no idea what KBPEEK will return if you are using one of those "terminate and stay resident" programs that interfere with the keystroke coding. I do know that if you assign a "softkey" value to a function key in BASIC, KBPEEK will return the extended code value of that key; INKEY$ and INPUT$(*n*) will return the softkey string, piecemeal.

Most language extensions can be written either as subroutines or as functions. In some instances, the decision can be based on what is to be done with the "returned" value. If it is most likely that the returned value will be assigned to a named variable, you might as well write the extension as a subroutine and use that variable as one of its arguments. If it is intended to make immediate use of the returned value, it makes sense to write the extension as a declared function.

Since I intend to evaluate the returns from KBPEEK in a "SELECT CASE" block (most of the time), I wrote it as a function. The function value is returned to the QBASIC program as an integer in register AX (lines 30, 35, and 38 of Listing 5-2). But, since KBPEEK is a function that destroys its source data when an extended-code symbol is pending, writing a proper test driver is somewhat easier if you assign the returned value to a variable before examining it. I leave writing the driver for KBPEEK as an exercise for the reader.

EMERGEX.BAS (Listing 5-3) is a small demonstration compiled subroutine to allow emergency exit (at a specified point) from a repetitive program using *either* Ctrl-C or Ctrl-Break. Notice that a single call of EMERGEX will remove (at most) one symbol from the type-ahead buff-

```
 1:          PAGE    ,105
 2:          TITLE   KBPEEK
 3:          .MODEL  MEDIUM
 4: ;*******************************************************************
 5: ;                          KBPEEK.ASM                            *
 6: ;     KBPEEK is a function to be linked to QuickBASIC programs.  It    *
 7: ; looks at the next character in the type-ahead buffer and returns the *
 8: ; following integer values:                                     *
 9: ;                  -1 if no character is pending                *
10: ;                 256 if an ASCII symbol is pending             *
11: ;        Any other value is the extended code symbol, which is purged  *
12: ;           from the type-ahead buffer.                         *
13: ;   Declare with:  DECLARE FUNCTION KBPEEK% ()                  *
14: ;                 Written by M. L. Lesser, May 5, 1986          *
15: ;         Rewritten as function for Microsoft MASM 5.0, 11/17/87    *
16: ;*******************************************************************
17:
18: .CODE
19:
20:          PUBLIC KBPEEK
21: KBPEEK   PROC
22:          PUSH    BP                      ;Safety, no arguments passed
23: ;Check whether character is pending in type-ahead buffer:
24:          MOV     AH,01
25:          INT     16H
26:          JZ      NO_CHR                  ;Zero flag set if buffer empty
27: ;Is pending character "Extended Code" symbol (AL = 0)?
28:          OR      AL,AL
29:          JZ      GETIT                   ;If so, remove from buffer
30:          MOV     AX,256                  ;Else return ASCII char signal
31:          JMP     SHORT DONE
32: ;Remove pending "Extended Code" symbol from buffer:
33: GETIT:   MOV     AH,0
34:          INT     16H
35:          XCHG    AH,AL                   ;Integer value of extended code
36:          JMP     SHORT DONE              ;  in AX
37: ;Signal no character pending:
38: NO_CHR:  MOV     AX,-1
39: DONE:    POP     BP
40:          RET
41:
42: KBPEEK   ENDP
43:
44:          END
```

Listing 5 - 2

er. If you add both KBPEEK and EMERGEX to your private subroutine library (and the proper DECLARE statements to your "include" file), the KBPEEK module will be loaded automatically for any program that calls EMERGEX, irrespective of the order in which the two modules were added to the libraries.

```
 1:  '******************************************************************
 2:  '                         EMERGEX.BAS                            *
 3:  '    EMERGEX is a QuickBASIC compiled called subroutine to allow  *
 4:  ' ending a QuickBASIC program on demand with a pending Ctrl-Break or *
 5:  ' Ctrl-C keystroke.  EMERGEX uses the assembled function KBPEEK.  *
 6:  '    If any keystroke symbols are pending, EMERGEX removes the first *
 7:  ' one.  If that symbol is a "break" symbol, the program ends.    *
 8:  '             Written by M. L. Lesser, November 23, 1986         *
 9:  '             Modified for Microsoft BC version 4.0, 11/17/87    *
10:  '******************************************************************
11:
12:      DECLARE FUNCTION KBPEEK% ()
13:      SUB EMERGEX STATIC
14:          SELECT CASE KBPEEK
15:              CASE 0                              'Ctrl-Break
16:                  END
17:              CASE 256                            'ASCII character pending
18:                  IF INKEY$ = CHR$(3) THEN END   'Ctrl-C
19:              CASE ELSE                           'Required dummy
20:          END SELECT
21:      END SUB
```

Listing 5 - 3

LIST.BAS (Version 1.1)

As you probably noticed if you tried out LIST.BAS as modified by the error trap described earlier, any file name not entered on the DOS command line became case-sensitive. Also, by now you should be somewhat tired of watching the display generated by compiled programs crawl up from the bottom of your screen. (Starting with version 4.0, QBASIC programs do not clear the screen as part of the initialization routine.)

Listing 5-4 is a modified version of LIST.BAS, adding the library modules described in this chapter. Do not retranscribe Listing 5-4. I wrote LIST version 1.1 by editing my original version. Use your text editor to make the same changes to the version you have already customized for your system configuration. If you have an editor that shows the "current" line number the cursor is resting on (as does the QB editor in "document" mode), the replacements are easiest to make if you start from the bottom, as unedited text will have unchanged line numbers. Thus:

- Replace lines 87–88 of Listing 3-3 with the new line 105 of Listing 5-4.

```
1:   '***************************************************************
2:   '                     LIST.BAS (Version 1.1)                   *
3:   '      LIST lists ASCII source-code files having a 72-column maximum  *
4:   ' line length on an IBM Proprinter XL in 12-pitch NLQ mode, listing 55 *
5:   ' lines per page with a header on each page and pseudo line numbers on *
6:   ' each line.  LIST can easily be customized for other printers.  *
7:   '      To customize, set the printer characteristics as follows:  *
8:   '          PAGE.WIDTH is the maximum number of characters per line, as  *
9:   '              limited by pitch and either paper width or printer.  *
10:  '          PAGE.OFFSET is the number of <LF>s necessary to move from the *
11:  '              paper "home" position (perforations at the tear-bar) *
12:  '              to setting the first print line at the top of the next *
13:  '              page.  Use "PAGE.OFFSET = 36" for the IBM Graphics  *
14:  '              printer and equivalents.                           *
15:  '          PROPRINTER is an on/off switch.  Set "PROPRINTER = -1" if an  *
16:  '              IBM Proprinter is installed and you wish to print in  *
17:  '              12-pitch NLQ mode.  Set "PROPRINTER = 0" for all other *
18:  '              configurations.                                    *
19:  '      To omit pseudo line numbers, comment out line 98.  This will  *
20:  ' increase the maximum allowable source text line length to 80    *
21:  ' columns.  If the printer allows, longer line lengths can be listed  *
22:  ' by changing the constants in lines 48, 50, and 79.              *
23:  '      LIST.BAS modified to version 1.1, M. L. Lesser, 11/23/86   *
24:  '          Modified for Microsoft BC version 4.0, 11/17/87        *
25:  '***************************************************************
26:  '   Setup (nonexecutable statements):
27:      DEFINT A-Z
28:      DEFSTR F,H,R,T
29:      DIM COUNT, FILE, FILENAME, LINE.NUM, MARGIN, PAGE.WIDTH, PAGE.OFFSET
30:      DIM PROPRINTER, TEXT, TIME
31:  '      $INCLUDE: 'PQB.BI'
32:
33:  '   Printer characteristics:
34:      PAGE.WIDTH = 102                    '8.5-inch paper at 12 pitch
35:      PAGE.OFFSET = 0                     'No initial paper offset
36:      PROPRINTER = -1                     'Proprinter installed
37:
38:  '   Defined header function:
39:  DEF FNHEADER
40:      STATIC PAGE.NUM                     'Static local variable
41:
42:      LET PAGE.NUM = PAGE.NUM + 1
43:      LET FNHEADER = "Listing page" + STR$(PAGE.NUM)
44:      LET COUNT = 0                       'Reset page line count
45:      LPRINT                              'Top blank line
46:      LPRINT TAB(MARGIN + 1);             'First header line
47:      LPRINT "Listed on " DATE$;
48:      LPRINT TAB(80 + MARGIN - LEN(FILE)) FILE
49:      LPRINT TAB(MARGIN + 8) "at " TIME;  'Second header line
50:      LPRINT TAB(MARGIN + 73) "page" PAGE.NUM
51:      CALL PSKIP(3)                       'Three more blanks
52:  END DEF
53:
54:  '   Main program:
55:      LET FILE = COMMAND$                 '<filespec> from command line
56:  RESTART:                                'Restart point if no file found
```

Listing 5 - 4 (continued)

```
57:         IF LEN(FILE) = 0 THEN                    'If no or incorrect <filespec>
58:             PRINT "Enter <filespec> to be listed:   ";   'prompt for new
59:             INPUT "", FILE                                    'entry, and
60:             LET FILE = UCASE$(FILE)                           'make all caps
61:         END IF
62:         IF INSTR(FILE,".") = 0 _                 'If no <ext> on <filespec>
63:             THEN LET FILE = FILE + ".BAS"        '   add ".BAS"
64:         LET FILENAME = FILE                      'Input <filespec> to find
65:         CALL MAKNAME(FILE)                       '<filename> without path
66:         CALL FINDFILE(FILENAME)                  'Locate directory with FILENAME
67:         CLS                                      'Clean off earlier messages
68:         IF LEN(FILENAME) = 0 THEN                '<filespec> not found
69:             PRINT "I cannot find " CHR$(34) FILE CHR$(34);
70:             PRINT " - Please try again."
71:             LET FILE = ""                        'Clean off to try again
72:             GOTO RESTART
73:         ELSE
74:             OPEN FILENAME FOR INPUT AS #1
75:         END IF
76:   '   Customize for printer and list first page header:
77:         LET TIME = TIMESTAMP
78:         WIDTH LPRINT 255                         'Bug killer
79:         LET MARGIN = (PAGE.WIDTH - 80)/2
80:         IF PROPRINTER THEN CALL PROPRIN          'Set Proprinter for 12-pitch NLQ
81:         IF PAGE.OFFSET THEN                      'If using IBM Graphics printer
82:             CALL PSKIP(PAGE.OFFSET)              '   set print line at top of page
83:             CALL PAGELEN(66)                     '   and reset form-feed point
84:         END IF
85:         PRINT "Listing the file: " FILE
86:         PRINT CHR$(9) FNHEADER                   'First page header
87:   '   Read and list file:
88:         WHILE NOT EOF(1)                         'As long as there is any text left
89:             LINE INPUT #1, TEXT                  'Read a line of text
90:             LET LINE.NUM = LINE.NUM + 1          'Update line number
91:             LET COUNT = COUNT + 1                'Update page line count
92:             IF LEFT$(TEXT,1) = CHR$(12) THEN          'If first byte is <FF>
93:                 CALL PFORM                            '   eject page
94:                 PRINT CHR$(9) FNHEADER                '   list new header
95:                 LET TEXT = MID$(TEXT,2)               '   delete <FF>
96:             END IF
97:             LPRINT TAB(MARGIN + 1);
98:             LPRINT USING "#####:   "; LINE.NUM;
99:             CALL TABBER                          'Detab text line
100:            LPRINT TEXT                          '   and list it
101:            IF COUNT = 55 AND NOT EOF(1) THEN    'If 55 lines on page
102:                CALL PFORM                            '   Skip to top of next page
103:                PRINT CHR$(9) FNHEADER                '   and list new header
104:            END IF
105:            CALL EMERGEX                         'Exit on Ctrl-C or Ctrl-Break
106:        WEND                                     'Continue until file listed
107:        CALL PFORM                               'Eject remainder of last page
108:        IF PAGE.OFFSET THEN                      'If graphics printer
109:            CALL PSKIP(66 - PAGE.OFFSET)         '   skip to tearbar
110:            CALL PAGELEN(66)                     '   and reset top of form
111:        END IF
112: END                       'End of main program
```

Listing 5 - 4   (continued)

```
113:
114:    '  Compiled subroutine to expand <HT>s to every eighth column:
115:  SUB TABBER STATIC
116:      SHARED TEXT
117:
118:      LET I = INSTR(TEXT,CHR$(9))          'Find first <HT>
119:      WHILE I <> 0                        'As long there are any <HT>s
120:          LET REST = MID$(TEXT,I+1)        'Unexpanded portion of TEXT
121:          LET TEXT = LEFT$(TEXT,I-1)       'Expanded portion of TEXT
122:          LET N = 8 - (I-1) MOD 8          'No. of <SP>s to insert for <HT>
123:          LET TEXT = TEXT + SPACE$(N) + REST
124:          LET I = INSTR(TEXT,CHR$(9))       'Any more to deal with?
125:      WEND                                'Continue until done
126:  END SUB
127:    '  End of source code
```

Listing 5 - 4

- Replace lines 56–58 of Listing 3-3 with the new lines 56–75. Note the use of UCASE$ (line 60) to force the input <filespec> to upper-case, and the addition of the CLS (line 67) to perform the screen-cleaning task.
- Add FILENAME to the variable "declaration" list in line 29, and change the prologue date notices (lines 23–24).
- Recompile, relink to the private library, and test version 1.1 of LIST.

Enhancements still to be provided: means to allow the program to customize itself for the user's display/printer configuration, and to adjust the margins for the maximum length of line to be listed.

Notes

1. Do not confuse *program structure* with "structured programming." The latter is a rigid set of rules for programming style, favored by people who believe that programming is a science, not an art form.
2. E. Dijkstra, "Programming Considered as a Human Activity," originally in *Proceedings of the 1965 IFIP Congress*, reprinted in Edward Nash Yourdon, ed., *Classics in Software Engineering*, Yourdon Press, New York, 1979, pp. 3–9.

3. BASIC's FOR...NEXT is a direct descendent of FORTRAN's DO loop. When John Backus and colleagues invented FORTRAN (in the mid-1950s), expediency made DO a bottom-tested loop construct. Programmers soon found the built-in booby trap; the loop would always be taken at least once, even when it shouldn't have been taken at all. By the early 1960s, good programmers had learned to put in their own top test (with a GOTO) before entering a DO loop having variable limits. FOR...NEXT loops in early BASICs were also bottom-tested. The 1978 ANSI standard for BASIC established FOR...NEXT as a top-tested loop. Microsoft's first implementation of this change was released in 1979.

4. ASCII is an acronym for "American Standard Code for Information Interchange," although the standard describing the code is named "USA Standard Code for Information Interchange." Standard ASCII has only 128 symbols. "Extended ASCII" defines the entire IBM PC set of 256 symbols, including the foreign letters, mathematical symbols, and block graphics used by all IBM PC display adapters (in text mode) and "character set 2" of most IBM PC printers, as shown in Appendix A of the *BASIC Language Reference* manual.

Chapter 6
Advanced Display Control

There are many display adapters that can be installed in PC systems. Until recently, the three most common were: the mono display adapter (MDA), the color/graphics display adapter (CGA), and the enhanced graphics adapter (EGA). The newer IBM machines use either the multicolor graphics adapter (MCGA) or the video graphics adapter (VGA). In addition to supporting all of these, QBASIC 4.0 also supports a Hercules Graphics Card driving a mono display.[1]

IBM has gone to great lengths in the design of ROM BIOS to keep all its display adapters fairly compatible in text mode, but they have highly different capabilities in the graphics modes. Since there is no such thing as *device independence* when the devices have different capabilities, DOS supports only the most basic text-mode functions.[2]

QBASIC supports the IBM-compatible adapters by writing text directly to display memory and by making direct calls on ROM BIOS for the graphics modes, rather than by going through DOS. Thus, it offers considerably better-than-DOS support for text mode, and excellent support for available graphics modes.

Assembled language extensions presented in this chapter allow a program to determine whether an IBM-compatible graphics adapter is installed, and (to some extent) the type of display attached. The only graphics program presented lets the user determine the effective aspect ratio of an installed graphics display.

Much of the chapter is devoted to extending the display-control support by providing "window" facilities for text mode. The final extension is a declared function for adding "pop-up" menus to text-mode programs. These extensions are "device independent" in that they work with any of the adapters and any appropriate display.

One of the benefits of an extendible language is the ability to design the extensions to fit individual preferences. The display extensions shown in this chapter are based on my design decisions, both in the way the functions are performed and in their interfaces to the rest of the program. I would remind you that these are only examples; there are many other approaches to providing the same capabilities.

Display Characteristics

When the IBM PC was first introduced, either of two display adapters (and corresponding display devices) could be installed. The mono display and printer adapter (to give it its formal name) drives a special high-resolution, long-persistence green-phosphor display, providing excellent text resolution but no graphics. For a long period, this adapter/display combination was the best available for working with text applications.

The color/graphics adapter driving the IBM PC color display was the alternate choice. This combination offers medium-resolution graphics (called high resolution in BASIC) in two colors, low-resolution graphics in four colors, and text in sixteen colors against an eight-color background. Unfortunately, its text-display characteristics are miserable. The characters have a low-quality, dot-matrix appearance, and the display blinks every time it scrolls a line. The poor text quality makes the combination unsuitable for extended business or professional use.

The characteristics of the CGA result from the adapter having been designed for compatibility with the U.S. color television standard, a design decision that permits producing a cheap display by driving a black-and-white television monitor from the "composite" signal output. This composite mono display (found in the IBM Portable and in many low-cost clones) is the worst of both worlds: a combination of the CGA's miserable text mode (without color enhancement) and two-color graphics.

The later-announced enhanced graphics adapter and enhanced color display (ECD) are much more satisfactory than their predecessors. The text mode has MDA-resolution characters, with choice of color and in a slightly larger size, while the graphics capability is a reasonable 640 by 350 pixels in sixteen colors. Although this is not adequate for some design work, it is sufficient for most presentation graphics. The EGA will not drive a composite display device, but it will drive either the IBM mono display or the PC color display. The mono display produces the same text as does the MDA, with the addition of 640 x 350-pixel mono graphics. There is no advantage in using an EGA to drive the color display except for the availability of sixteen-color low- and medium-resolution graphics.

IBM has introduced two new display adapters and new displays with the Personal System/2 machines. The video graphics array (VGA), standard on the PS/2 models 50, 60, and 80, can emulate a 256K EGA as well as provide very high resolution (640-by-480-pixel) graphics. The multicolor graphics array (MCGA), standard on models 25 and 30, emulates a no-blink CGA having EGA quality text and can also produce high-resolution graphics — but only in two-attribute (SCREEN 11) mode. The MCGA drives the new IBM mono display as a composite mono display, providing shades of gray instead of the colors.

Identifying the Display Adapter

The QBASIC graphics support is device dependent. The allowable SCREEN modes depend on the type of graphics adapter installed.

The only built-in QBASIC test for determining the available graphics modes is to try an appropriate SCREEN statement and trap on an error interruption.[3] I have provided two assembled modules of display adapter "recognizer" routines, ISCOLOR.ASM and ISEGA.ASM, to supplement this primitive test procedure. ISCOLOR (Listing 6-1) returns "true" (-1) if any display adapter capable of operating in a color-graphics SCREEN mode is attached and active; these include the CGA or MCGA driving any display (even a composite mono), and the EGA or VGA when driving a color display. ISCOLOR returns "false" (0) if a mono display adapter is active, or if an active EGA or VGA is driving a mono display.

I wrote the ISEGA function (Listing 6-2, lines 16–52) to recognize the presence of an active EGA driving either an ECD or mono display — one

```
 1:              PAGE    ,105
 2:              TITLE   ISCOLOR
 3:              .MODEL  MEDIUM
 4: ;*******************************************************************
 5: ;                          ISCOLOR.ASM                            *
 6: ; ISCOLOR is an assembled integer function for QBASIC to determine *
 7: ;    whether color-graphics capabilities are active.              *
 8: ;             Declare with:  DECLARE FUNCTION ISCOLOR% ()          *
 9: ;    ISCOLOR returns:  -1 if display memory origin is at segment B800 *
10: ;                      (CGA/MCGA with any monitor, or EGA/VGA with *
11: ;                       color monitor)                            *
12: ;                       0 if display memory origin is at segment B000 *
13: ;                      (mono adapter or EGA/VGA with mono display) *
14: ;             Written by M. L. Lesser, August 29, 1986            *
15: ;         Modified for Microsoft BC 4.0 and MASM 5.0, 10/27/87     *
16: ;*******************************************************************
17:
18: .CODE
19:              PUBLIC  ISCOLOR
20: ISCOLOR PROC
21:              PUSH    BP
22:              MOV     BP,SP
23:              INT     11H                      ;Get equipment flag in AX
24:              AND     AX,30H                   ;Isolate display bits
25:              SUB     AL,30H                   ;Test for mono adapter
26:              JZ      RETURN                   ;Zero in AX if mono
27:              MOV     AX,-1                    ;Color return
28: RETURN: POP      BP
29:              RET
30: ISCOLOR ENDP
31:              END
```

Listing 6 - 1

capable of operating in 43-line mode. It also recognizes a VGA driving any of the Personal System/2 displays. ISEGA returns "true" only for one of these configurations and returns "false" for all other active display configurations — including an EGA driving an ECD while set to "compatible" mode (imitating the color display). I consider the latter a useless EGA mode, but you might wish to add the proper recognizer code to the subroutine.[4]

EGAMEM (Listing 6-2, lines 54–72) was written primarily to determine the amount of EGA memory installed, as this information is required when using BASIC's graphics GET and PUT commands while in SCREEN 9 mode. Any return other than 16 shows an EGA is installed in the system, even if it is inactive. EGAMEM will indicate a 256K EGA memory if the VGA is installed.

Combinations of these routines resolve many situations. For example, if the return from ISEGA is "true" and that from ISCOLOR is

```
 1:          PAGE    ,105
 2:          TITLE   ISEGA
 3:          .MODEL  MEDIUM
 4: ;****************************************************************
 5: ;                        ISEGA.ASM                            *
 6: ;    A pair of assembled integer functions for QBASIC to determine   *
 7: ; whether an EGA or VGA (emulating an EGA) display adapter is    *
 8: ; installed.                                                  *
 9: ;            Written by M. L. Lesser, August 29, 1986         *
10: ;       Modified for Microsoft BC 4.0 and MASM 5.0, 10/27/87  *
11: ;****************************************************************
12:
13: .CODE
14:
15: ;  Local subroutine:
16: GET_INFO:                        ;Uses ROM BIOS "get EGA info" call
17:          MOV     BH,0FFH         ;   inserting invalid "output" register
18:          MOV     CL,0FFH         ;   information, which will remain
19:          MOV     AH,12H          ;   unchanged if EGA is not installed
20:          MOV     BL,10H
21:          INT     10H
22:          RET
23: ;   End of local subroutine
24:
25:          PUBLIC  ISEGA
26: ISEGA    PROC    FAR
27: ;****************************************************************
28: ;     ISEGA tests for an active EGA or VGA driving a display capable of *
29: ; high-resolution (350-line or greater) displays.             *
30: ;                 Declare with:  DECLARE FUNCTION ISEGA% ()   *
31: ;     Returns:  -1 if EGA driving a mono display or ECD, or a VGA   *
32: ;                   any PS/2 display.                         *
33: ;                0 if either EGA driving color display or no EGA/VGA  *
34: ;                   active.                                   *
35: ;****************************************************************
36:          PUSH    BP
37:          CALL    GET_INFO             ;Check for EGA presence
38:          MOV     AX,40H               ;Set up for EGA-active test
39:          MOV     ES,AX
40:          TEST    BYTE PTR ES:[87H],8  ;Bit on - EGA installed/inactive
41:          MOV     AX,-1                ;Set return value for EGA active
42:          JNZ     NO_EGA               ;Jump if EGA inactive
43:          CMP     BH,01                ;Else test for mono display
44:          JZ      RETURN               ;EGA active with mono display
45:          CMP     CL,09                ;Else test for ECD in high-res
46:          JZ      RETURN               ;  mode - EGA primary adapter
47:          CMP     CL,03                ;Else test for ECD in high-res
48:          JZ      RETURN               ;  mode - EGA secondary adapter
49: NO_EGA:  XOR     AX,AX                ;Return value for no active EGA
50: RETURN:  POP     BP
51:          RET
52: ISEGA    ENDP
53:
```

Listing 6 - 2 (continued)

```
54:            PUBLIC  EGAMEM
55: EGAMEM  PROC FAR
56: ;**************************************************************************
57: ;     EGAMEM returns code indicating the amount of EGA/VGA graphics    *
58: ; memory installed.                                                     *
59: ;             Declare with:  DECLARE FUNCTION EGAMEM% ()                *
60: ;     Returns code>:  0 if 64K EGA memory                              *
61: ;                     1 if 128K                                         *
62: ;                     2 if 192K                                         *
63: ;                     3 if 256K                                         *
64: ;                    16 if no EGA installed.                            *
65: ;**************************************************************************
66:            PUSH    BP
67:            CALL    GET_INFO
68:            XOR     AH,AH                    ;Clear AH and
69:            MOV     AL,BL                    ; move memory return to AL
70:            JMP     RETURN
71: EGAMEM  ENDP
72:            END
```

Listing 6 - 2

"false," the active display is a mono display driven by an EGA or VGA. If ISEGA returns "false," ISCOLOR returns "true," and EGAMEM shows no EGA memory, you have a CGA or an MCGA. Unfortunately, you cannot tell if it is driving a color display or a mono display. You will have to ask the user to tell you, in cases where it matters. (See the section on "System Profiles" in the next chapter.)

However, there is one ambiguous case. If the ISEGA return is "false," ISCOLOR returns "true," but EGAMEM shows the presence of an EGA, one of two possibilities exists. You may have an EGA driving a standard color display (the only possibility in a one-display system). Or you may have a two-display system with the CGA as the active display and an EGA driving a mono display as the inactive adapter. You can resolve this ambiguity by trying a SCREEN 7 statement; you will get an "Illegal function call" error interrupt if a CGA is installed.

QBASIC Display Idiosyncrasies

QBASIC (as of version 4.0) uses ROM BIOS routines to determine the type of display adapter installed, as part of its initialization routine. It then executes PRINT statements by writing text strings directly to the display memory, starting each string at the cursor location stored by ROM BIOS. This technique produces almost instantaneous text display. After writing the string, QBASIC moves ROM BIOS's cursor position to the nominal beginning of the next PRINT statement. PRINT statements expand the <HT> symbol by writing the appropriate number of space symbols, but do not expand the <BS> symbol — both printable symbols in the IBM extended ASCII set.

QBASIC text-mode programs normally use only the first 24 rows of the display screen, and scroll after writing to row 24 unless that PRINT statement is terminated with a semicolon. You can write to row 25 of the screen with an appropriate LOCATE statement. However, unless the following PRINT statement ends with a semicolon, writing to row 25 will scroll the rest of the screen up one line from row 24, leaving row 24 blank and the text unchanged in row 25.

You can cause QBASIC to expand its text "window" to the full 25 rows with a "VIEW PRINT 1 TO 25" statement. QBASIC will locate the cursor at the beginning of the top row specified, and the next PRINT statement will start writing from there. However, since "VIEW PRINT" does not automatically clear its window, PRINT statements will overwrite any material that was in the window region before the statement was executed. You must use a CLS or CLS 2 statement to clear the window screen before writing to it. In full-screen text mode, a PRINT statement to row 25 (if not terminated with a semicolon) causes a scroll from row 25 immediately after the line is printed, leaving row 25 blank.

When a separately compiled QBASIC program ENDs in text mode, a row of 80 spaces (using "COLOR 7,0" attribute) is written to row 25 before the program terminates. If the program terminates in a graphics mode, the END routine resets the screen to text mode (thereby clearing the display) to prevent the display system from being left in a graphics mode. If you want to stare at your graphics masterpiece before it is lost, you have to prevent automatic termination at the end of the program by inserting a "Press any key" wait loop. QBASIC error and Ctrl-Break terminations always include the wait loop, irrespective of whether the system is in a graphics mode at the time.

Display Aspect Ratio

A proper treatment of display graphics is beyond the scope of this book, so I will limit discussion of graphics to one small demonstration program. ARTEST.BAS (Listing 6-3) allows you to determine the effective aspect ratio of your screen for use with graphics statements.

```
  1:  '****************************************************************************
  2:  '                              ARTEST.BAS                                   *
  3:  '     ARTEST allows the user to determine the effective display screen *
  4:  ' aspect ratio for PCs having a display adapter capable of operating   *
  5:  ' in BASIC's SCREEN 2 mode (CGA or MCGA with any display; EGA or VGA   *
  6:  ' with a color display).                                               *
  7:  '            Written by M. L. Lesser, December 29, 1986                *
  8:  '            Modified for Microsoft BC version 4.0, 11-23-87           *
  9:  '****************************************************************************
 10:
 11:      DEFINT I
 12:      DIM AR, DELTA, I            'AR is tested <aspect>
 13:  '   $INCLUDE: 'PQB.BI'
 14:
 15:      LET AR = 5/12              'BASIC default value for SCREEN 2
 16:      LET DELTA = .10            'Initial AR adjustment increment
 17:      CLS
 18:      LOCATE 3,1                 'Start sign-on message here
 19:      PRINT TAB(36) "ARTEST": PRINT
 20:      PRINT TAB(10) _                        '(continued on next line)
 21:          "A program to determine the effective display aspect ratio"
 22:      PRINT:PRINT
 23:      IF NOT ISCOLOR THEN
 24:        PRINT TAB(16) "  This program requires a CGA, an MCGA or"
 25:        PRINT TAB(16) "either an EGA or VGA driving a color monitor"
 26:        PRINT
 27:        PRINT TAB(16) "        -- Terminating program --"
 28:        END
 29:      ELSE
 30:        PRINT TAB(15) "If concentric ellipses are displayed, adjust them"
 31:        PRINT TAB(17) "toward circles by pressing:"
 32:        PRINT TAB(20) CHR$(26);
 33:        PRINT       " [Cursor Right] to make the ellipses wider"
 34:        PRINT TAB(20) CHR$(27);
 35:        PRINT       " [Cursor Left] to make the ellipses narrower"
 36:        PRINT TAB(15) "Either key will display an adjusted pattern."
 37:        PRINT
 38:        PRINT TAB(15) "Press ENTER when satisfactory circles are shown."
 39:        PRINT TAB(15) "This will display the values of <aspect> to use"
 40:        PRINT TAB(17) "with CIRCLE statements for each SCREEN mode."
 41:        PRINT
 42:        PRINT TAB(15) "NOTE:  The <aspect> adjustment increment is cut in"
 43:        PRINT TAB(15) "       half each time the adjustment direction is"
 44:        PRINT TAB(15) "       reversed, permitting fine-tuning."
 45:        PRINT: PRINT
 46:        PRINT TAB(27) "Press ENTER to continue"
 47:      END IF
 48:      WHILE INKEY$ <> CHR$(13): WEND              'Wait for <CR>
 49:      SCREEN 2
 50:  ' Iterative test cycle starts here:
 51:  START:                                    'Start of infinite loop
 52:      CLS
 53:      FOR I = 0 TO 205 STEP 5                    'Draw target ellipses
 54:        IF I MOD 30 <> 0 THEN
 55:            CIRCLE (320,100),I,,,,AR
 56:        END IF
```

Listing 6 - 3 (continued)

```
57:      NEXT I
58:      PRINT "<aspect> = " USING "#.###"; AR
59:  ' Examine pending keystroke before adjusting for next test display
60:  '      cutting DELTA in half with a direction change:
61:  CHANGE:
62:      SELECT CASE KBPEEK
63:          CASE 75                                  'Cursor left
64:              IF DELTA < 0 THEN LET DELTA = -DELTA/2
65:          CASE 77                                  'Cursor right
66:              IF DELTA > 0 THEN LET DELTA = -DELTA/2
67:          CASE 256                            'ASCII key pending
68:              IF INKEY$ = CHR$(13) THEN        'ENTER key
69:                  GOTO NORMAL
70:              ELSE                           'Ignore other ASCII
71:                  GOTO CHANGE                '    keys
72:              END IF
73:          CASE ELSE
74:              GOTO CHANGE                    'Ignore all other keys
75:  END SELECT
76:      IF ABS(DELTA) < .001 THEN GOTO UNDER        'Minimum effective value
77:          LET AR = AR + DELTA
78:      IF AR < 0 THEN GOTO WRONG                 'Minimum allowable value
79:      GOTO START                        'Infinite loop until stopped
80:
81:  WRONG:                       'AR reduced to below zero
82:      SCREEN 0
83:      LOCATE 5,1
84:      PRINT TAB(10) "Aspect ratio out of valid range.  Rerun program."
85:  END                          'Abnormal end
86:
87:  UNDER:                       'DELTA below significant level
88:      SCREEN 0
89:      LOCATE 5,1
90:      PRINT TAB(10) "Cannot adjust any finer than this"
91:  NORMAL:                      'Normal end to test procedure
92:      SCREEN 0
93:      LOCATE 8,1
94:      PRINT TAB(20) "Last aspect ratio shown was"; USING " #.###"; AR
95:      PRINT
96:      PRINT TAB(10) "Use <aspect> = ";
97:      PRINT USING "#.###"; 2 * AR;
98:      PRINT " for SCREEN 1 and SCREEN 7 graphics."
99:      PRINT TAB(10) "Use <aspect> = ";
100:     PRINT USING "#.###"; AR;
101:     PRINT " for SCREEN 2 and SCREEN 8 graphics."
102:     PRINT TAB(10) "Use <aspect> = ";
103:     PRINT USING "#.###"; 1.75 * AR;
104:     PRINT " for SCREEN 9 graphics."
105: END                          'Normal end
106: '       End of source code
```

Listing 6 - 3

The *aspect ratio* of an image is the width of the image divided by its height. Somehow, the idea has gotten around that the "standard" display screen aspect ratio is 4/3, although none of the screen images I have measured had that value. This 4/3 assumption is the source of the default values of <aspect> used by BASIC in executing CIRCLE statements.

The value of <aspect> that would produce perfect circles on a linear display device is the ratio of the number of vertical pixels per inch to the number of horizontal pixels per inch for the device and graphics mode being used. You could calculate this <aspect> value by measuring the actual aspect ratio of your screen, and then multiplying that aspect ratio by the ratio of vertical to horizontal pixels for the graphics mode. If you assume the aspect ratio of the screen to be 4/3, you will get BASIC's default <aspect> of 5/12 (0.417) for SCREEN 2 mode (200 vertical, 640 horizontal pixels).

However, direct measurement may not produce the best results, since few display devices are linear over the entire screen. The better way is to draw a lot of circles, look at them, and then adjust <aspect> until the results are most pleasing. This is exactly what the demonstration program ARTEST.BAS does. Display devices I tested with ARTEST had most pleasing centered circles at values of <aspect> ranging from about 0.43 to 0.46.

The circle drawing is terminated either by the user with an Enter keystroke, or by the program if the value of either <aspect> or the change in <aspect> (DELTA) is out of range.

I set up ARTEST to work in SCREEN 2 mode, since this is common to most graphics display systems supported by QBASIC. The working part of the program is an unconditional-GOTO infinite loop (lines 51–79) that draws the circle pattern and then polls for an adjusting keystroke. The keystroke poll uses the KBPEEK function in a SELECT CASE block (lines 62–75) containing a nested IF-block (lines 68–72), all of which keeps looping until it finds a pending keystroke that it recognizes. All others are thrown away.

ARTEST does not check for display linearity. You might write another test program that draws lots of squares on the screen using repeated LINE statements in a pair of FOR...NEXT loops. If the STEP <increment> for drawing the horizontal lines is DELTA.Y, the <increment> for drawing the vertical lines should be DELTA.Y/<aspect>. The more linear the display device, the more square the "squares" around the edges will be.

```
let ar = .455
PRINT TAB(20) "Last aspect ratio shown was "; USING " #.###"; AR
PRINT
PRINT TAB(10) "Use aspect = "; USING "#.###"; 2 * AR;
PRINT " for SCREEN 1 and SCREEN 7 graphics."
```

Figure 6 - 1

PRINTEST.BAS a QB/BC bug demonstration

The Vanishing Bug

While modifying ARTEST for QBASIC 4.0, I found an interesting bug in the compiler that is not caught by running the same program under the development environment. The small piece of demonstration code shown in Figure 6-1 shows the original structure of lines 94 –98 of Listing 6-3, and will reproduce the error found. When run under the development environment, the code in Figure 6-1 runs as expected. But when the same source code is compiled with BC 4.0 and linked, running it produces a "Type mismatch" error interrupt immediately following the "Use <aspect> = 0.910" display produced by the fourth line shown. Why the error only in the separately compiled version?

The only obvious difference between the structure of the second and fourth lines in Figure 6-1 is the closing semicolon on the fourth line. The second, third, and fourth lines executed correctly; the run-time error interrupt was actually for the fifth line, which has no "Type mismatch" error in its code.

After carefully reading the listing while considering the symptoms, I decided that the compiler was associating the string constant in the fifth line with the USING numerical format string in the fourth line. Hence the "Type mismatch." The problem is in BC's optimizer, an error that would not be caught by the development environment (nor by any source-code debugger I know of). It would appear that BC 4.0 did too good an optimization job when it spotted the successive PRINT statements separated by a semicolon; it removed the second call to its PRINT library routine, not noticing a USING in between the two.

The solution to living with a compiler bug is to code a "workaround" that should not be required by the language, but prevents the bug from appearing. I tried splitting the fourth-line compound statement (into lines 96–97 of Listing 6-3) to put the USING into its own PRINT statement. This workaround produced executable code that runs correctly.

I imagine this will be one of the first bugs to be killed in the next release of QuickBASIC, so it may not exist by the time you read this book. But it serves to demonstrate that you can't count on the development environment to show you how to "fix" a bug that isn't really in your program. No automatic debugging tool can show you how to work around the inevitable compiler bugs. The only debugging tool that works every time is a neatly organized source-code listing, carefully read by a programmer who uses common sense and an understanding of the language architecture to correlate the observed symptoms with the written code.

Text-Mode Windows

The hardest part of writing ARTEST.BAS was centering the messages on the display screen. When using bare PRINT statements, the programmer has to count line lengths and add TAB functions or put spaces into the text strings. This is a dumb task better left to computing engines than to programmers.

My solution to the problem was a mixed bag of assembled and compiled language extensions allowing "windows" to be set up in text mode. Once the boundaries of the window have been defined, text lines can be written to any row in that window, with the options of starting at the left edge of the window, being centered within the window, or starting at any arbitrary column within the window. Windows can include the entire screen or can be as small as one character.

The display-control language extensions shown are true "bottom-up" programming. The hardware-control assembled subroutines were written first, implementing the minimal capabilities I thought necessary. The compiled subroutines that write to the windows were written next, calling on the hardware-control routines. The two modules establish the interface rules for using the text-mode window facility I have added to the language. These interface rules must be followed by any program using the window facilities, just as any program must follow the syntax rules of the language. Bottom-up programming is very effective when implementing a family of application programs in any language permitting procedures to be stored in private searchable libraries.

WINDOW.ASM

The underlying window facility is provided by WINDOW.ASM (Listing 6-4), which allows blanking an entire defined window (CLEARIT, lines 36–69) or scrolling up one row within the window, blanking only the bottom row (SCROLLIT, lines 72–94, 59–68).

The major decisions were how to pass the window coordinates to the subroutines and how to establish the display attribute (as defined by a COLOR statement) for the blanked rows. The minimum information to pass a window definition from a BASIC program is four integers: the top row number, the left column number, the bottom row number, and the right column number. I passed these in a COMMON named CURSOR (lines 24–30). MASM 5.0 does not automatically define COMMON segments to be in DGROUP, possibly because the form of COMMON segment used by QBASIC is unique to that language. So I told MASM that CURSOR is in DGROUP (line 32).

You cannot use periods as spacers in variable names in assembly-language programs. The usual convention is to use the underscore character for local names. The corresponding BASIC variables use periods, instead. The location numbers are passed in BASIC notation (top left position is 1,1) and converted to ROM BIOS notation (top left position is 0,0) when used within the subroutine.

There are no tests in WINDOW.ASM to insure that any of the cursor-location integers passed are valid display-screen locations. Such checking should be done by the calling program. The window can be of any size as long as it is contained within the display-screen coordinates: the valid ROW integers are between 1 and 25, inclusive, and the valid COL integers are between 1 and 80, inclusive. ROW.T and COL.T must be less than or equal to ROW.B and COL.B, respectively.

I adopted the conventions for the source of the blanking attribute from the Microsoft Business BASIC compiler and the ROM BIOS "write tty" routine. CLEARIT blanks the entire window to the attribute of the character in its upper left corner (lines 52–65); SCROLLIT blanks the bottom row to the attribute originally in the first column of that row (lines

```
 1:           PAGE    ,105
 2:           TITLE   WINDOW
 3:           .MODEL  MEDIUM
 4: ;**************************************************************************
 5: ;                              WINDOW.ASM                                 *
 6: ;    WINDOW is a module of two text-mode display-control assembled        *
 7: ; subroutines for linking to QBASIC programs.  Both subroutines           *
 8: ; operate in a "window" defined by the top left and bottom right          *
 9: ; display locations passed by the calling program in COMMON /CURSOR/.     *
10: ;    Row and column positions in CURSOR are integers in the BASIC         *
11: ; display coordinate system (top left of screen is location 1,1).         *
12: ;    CLEARIT clears the window, setting the display attribute to the      *
13: ; value contained in the upper left window location before the call.      *
14: ;    SCROLLIT scrolls the text in the window up one line, setting the     *
15: ; blanked-out bottom line to the attribute in the left most window        *
16: ; column of that line before the call.                                    *
17: ;    WARNING:  After return from either subroutine, the cursor should     *
18: ; be reset with a LOCATE statement before further PRINT statements are    *
19: ; executed.                                                               *
20: ;             Written by M. L. Lesser, December 30, 1986                  *
21: ;             Modified for Microsoft MASM 5.0, 10-22-87                   *
22: ;**************************************************************************
23:
24: CURSOR  SEGMENT WORD COMMON 'BC_VARS'
25: ;  Contains window boundaries passed from calling program
26: ROW_T   DW      ?                       ;Upper left row position
27: COL_T   DW      ?                       ;Upper left column position
28: ROW_B   DW      ?                       ;Lower right row position
29: COL_B   DW      ?                       ;Lower right column position
30: CURSOR  ENDS
31:
32: DGROUP  GROUP CURSOR
33:
34: .CODE
35:
36:           PUBLIC  CLEARIT
37: CLEARIT PROC
38: ;**************************************************************************
39: ;    CLEARIT uses the ROM BIOS "scroll up" routine with AL set to 0 to    *
40: ; clear entire window.  The entire window is set to the attribute of      *
41: ; the former upper left corner location.                                  *
42: ;**************************************************************************
43:           PUSH    BP
44:           MOV     AH,0FH                  ;Get display mode to put active
45:           INT     10H                     ;  page number in BH
46:           MOV     DH,BYTE PTR ROW_T       ;Put top left window location
47:           MOV     DL,BYTE PTR COL_T       ;  into DX
48:           DEC     DL                      ;Convert from BASIC cursor
49:           DEC     DH                      ;  coordinates to ROM BIOS
50:           MOV     AH,2                    ;Put cursor in top left
51:           INT     10H                     ;  window location,
52:           MOV     CX,DX                   ;Move top left to CX,
53:           MOV     DH,BYTE PTR ROW_B       ;  bottom right to DX,
54:           MOV     DL,BYTE PTR COL_B
55:           DEC     DH
56:           DEC     DL
```

Listing 6 - 4 (continued)

```
57:           MOV     AL,0                    ;  and set AL for scroll
58: ; Get display atttribute at cursor location, scroll window:
59: DOIT:     PUSH    AX                      ;Save contents of AL
60:           MOV     AH,8                    ;Read attribute/character
61:           INT     10H
62:           MOV     BH,AH                   ;Attribute for blanked lines
63:           POP     AX                      ;Recover scroll control in AL
64:           MOV     AH,6                    ;  and scroll window up to clear
65:           INT     10H
66: ;  Return to BASIC
67:           POP     BP
68:           RET
69: CLEARIT ENDP
70:
71:           PUBLIC  SCROLLIT
72: SCROLLIT PROC FAR
73: ;**********************************************************************
74: ;    SCROLLIT scrolls the window up one row, with AL set to 1 to clear  *
75: ; only the bottom row.  The blanked row is set to the attribute of the *
76: ; former lower left corner location.                                   *
77: ;**********************************************************************
78:           PUSH    BP
79:           MOV     AH,0FH                  ;Get display mode to put active
80:           INT     10H                     ;  page number in BH
81:           MOV     DH,BYTE PTR ROW_B       ;Put bottom left window location
82:           MOV     DL,BYTE PTR COL_T       ;  into DX
83:           DEC     DL                      ;Convert from BASIC cursor
84:           DEC     DH                      ;  coordinates to ROM BIOS
85:           MOV     AH,2                    ;Put cursor in bottom left
86:           INT     10H                     ;  window location,
87:           MOV     CH,BYTE PTR ROW_T       ;Move top left of window to CX,
88:           DEC     CH
89:           MOV     CL,DL
90:           MOV     DL,BYTE PTR COL_B       ;  bottom right to DX,
91:           DEC     DL
92:           MOV     AL,1                    ;  and set AL for scroll
93:           JMP     DOIT
94: SCROLLIT ENDP
95:
96:           END
```

Listing 6 - 4

87–93, 59–65). QBASIC programs can write the attribute to the appropriate location with a COLOR statement, followed by a LOCATE statement, followed by PRINTing a space character.

DWINDOW.BAS

Writing to the window is controlled by calls to the compiled subroutines in DWINDOW.BAS (Listing 6-5). The variables used are set up in the same COMMON /CURSOR/ region used by WINDOW.ASM (and by any program calling the subroutines) and marked SHARED to be global over

```
 1:  '************************************************************************
 2:  '                          DWINDOW.BAS                                 *
 3:  '    DWINDOW is a module of compiled subroutines to display lines of   *
 4:  ' text at a row and column position within a window area defined by     *
 5:  ' the integer variables in COMMON /CURSOR/.                            *
 6:  '    The window is defined by the screen locations corresponding to the *
 7:  ' top left corner (ROW.T, COL.T) and the bottom right corner (ROW.B,   *
 8:  ' COL.B), where ROW.B can equal 25.                                    *
 9:  '    PWINDOW(TEXT) prints the string TEXT starting at the location     *
10:  ' ROW, COL.T, providing TEXT will fit inside one line of the window    *
11:  ' and ROW lies within the window.                                      *
12:  '    CWINDOW(TEXT) prints the string TEXT at ROW, COL, where COL is    *
13:  ' calculated by the subroutine to center the string horizontally in    *
14:  ' the window.                                                          *
15:  '    When either of these subroutines exit, COL contains the values set *
16:  ' for the start of the displayed line, and control is passed to:       *
17:  '     DWINDOW(TEXT) displays the string TEXT starting at column COL and *
18:  ' row ROW.  If ROW is above window, TEXT will be displayed in ROW.T.   *
19:  ' If ROW is below window, the text in the window will be scrolled up    *
20:  ' one line and TEXT will be displayed in ROW.B.  After TEXT is         *
21:  ' displayed, ROW will be incremented to one higher than used for the   *
22:  ' display, COL will be left unchanged, and the cursor will be left at  *
23:  ' one column past the end-of-TEXT position.                            *
24:  '    NOTE:  If TEXT will not fit in the window, the program will be     *
25:  ' terminated with an "Unprintable error in module DWINDOW."           *
26:  '          Written by M. L. Lesser, December 31, 1986                  *
27:  '          Recompiled with Microsoft BC version 4.0, 11-24-87          *
28:  '************************************************************************
29:      DEFINT C,R
30:      DEFSTR T
31:      COMMON SHARED /CURSOR/ ROW.T, COL.T, ROW.B, COL.B, ROW, COL
32:
33:  SUB PWINDOW(TEXT) STATIC          'Displays TEXT in window
34:      LET COL = COL.T
35:      CALL DWINDOW(TEXT)
36:  END SUB
37:
38:  SUB CWINDOW(TEXT) STATIC          'Displays TEXT centered horizontally
39:      LET COL = COL.T + (COL.B - COL.T + 1 - LEN(TEXT))/2
40:      CALL DWINDOW(TEXT)
41:  END SUB
42:
43:  SUB DWINDOW(TEXT) STATIC
44:  ' Test if TEXT will fit inside window, starting at COL:
45:      IF (COL < COL.T) OR (LEN(TEXT) > (COL.B - COL + 1)) THEN ERROR 255
46:  ' Test ROW to see if it is inside window, scroll if necessary:
47:      IF (ROW < ROW.T) THEN LET ROW = ROW.T      'Out of window at top
48:      IF (ROW > ROW.B) THEN                       'Out of window at bottom
49:          CALL SCROLLIT
50:          LET ROW = ROW.B                         'PRINT in ROW.B
51:      END IF
52:      LOCATE ROW,COL
53:      PRINT TEXT;                                 'No automatic <CR><LF>
54:      LET ROW = ROW + 1                           'Increment to next row
55:  END SUB
```

Listing 6 - 5

the entire module (line 31). The variables ROW and COL did not appear in the same-named COMMON in WINDOW.ASM, but are used for marking the origin of the string to be displayed by the DWINDOW subroutine. Since the added integer variables are at the right-hand end of the COMMON statement, the two differently defined COMMON segments will be properly overlayed at link time.

PWINDOW(<text>) (lines 33–36) writes the string passed in <text> starting at the leftmost column of the window. CWINDOW(<text>) (lines 38–41) writes <text> centered horizontally in the window. DWINDOW(<text>) (lines 43–55) does all the work. It is called by both PWINDOW() and CWINDOW(), or can be called directly from other QBASIC modules.

DWINDOW() tests to insure that <text> can be written (horizontally) within the window as specified. If it cannot, an error 255 is forced (line 45), which terminates the program with an "Unprintable error in module DWINDOW" interrupt. This is *very* unfriendly programming and is used only because the size of the window and the lengths of the strings are assumed to have been established explicitly by the program; error 255 should occur only during program implementation. If you are contemplating a program that writes console input directly to a window and do not otherwise control the length of the input string, you might wish to add recovery from error 255 to this module.

DWINDOW() attempts to write <text> in the row having the value of ROW. If this row number is less than ROW.T, <text> is written into the top row of the window. If ROW is greater than ROW.B, the window is scrolled and <text> is written into the bottom row. This lets scrolling occur first, with text written into the bottom row of the window afterward. I believe it produces more pleasing displays than the usual BASIC and DOS conventions, as it doesn't leave a blank line at the bottom of the window.

When DWINDOW finishes, ROW has a value one greater than the row number written in, COL is left unchanged, and the stored cursor position is left wherever it was at the end of the write to screen. Note that DWINDOW follows its PRINT statement with a semicolon to prevent undesired scrolling by BASIC's default display controls.

MOVESCRN.ASM

If you are going to overwrite portions of the display with temporary messages, it would be nice to copy the original contents of the display screen somewhere else first, so they can be restored afterward. If you are in text mode with a CGA, EGA, MCGA, or VGA, you can use the BASIC PCOPY statement to copy the contents of the "normal" display page (page zero) to one of the other available pages. However, if you have an MDA installed, PCOPY won't work.

MOVESCRN.ASM (Listing 6-6) is the "device-independent" solution to the problem. GETIT (lines 38–58) copies the contents of page zero of the active display adapter into a buffer located in the *code segment* of the module. PUTIT (lines 61–73, 50–58) copies the bytes in the buffer back to page zero of the active display. Although MOVESCRN is quite fast, it will show momentary "snow" on displays driven by a CGA.[5]

Both subroutines use the local procedure ADAPTER (lines 27–35) to find the segment address of the display memory segment. ADAPTER calls the private-library function ISCOLOR to determine which display segment to use. Even though ISCOLOR is programmed as an assembled function, it is actually reached (in machine language) as a FAR CALL. The EXTRN pseudo-op telling MASM to let the linker find ISCOLOR should be outside all defined segments (line 19). As with all integer functions, IS-COLOR returns its value in register AX (line 30). If ISCOLOR returns "true," ADAPTER will leave the segment address of the color display in register BX (lines 31 –32); otherwise, ADAPTER leaves the address of the mono display in BX.

The major design consideration was where to put the buffer. The three obvious choices were in far object space (a 4,000-byte dynamic numeric array), in data space, or in code space. My choice of code space was based on memory-space economics:

- Using far object space requires declaring a dynamic numeric array in the calling module before MOVESCRN is called. The assembled subroutine would not be self-contained, and the complexity of both the calling program and MOVESCRN would be increased. More code space would be required for instructions and more data space for the array descriptor, in addition to the 4,000 bytes of buffer space. Therefore, storing the MOVESCRN buffer in far objet space would increase the size of memory required to run a program using it.
- If 4,000 bytes of data space were used for the buffer, the program would run in the same minimum space as if the buffer were in code space. However, using data space decreases the amount of string

```
 1:              PAGE     ,105
 2:              TITLE    MOVESCRN
 3:              .MODEL   MEDIUM
 4:   ;*******************************************************************
 5:   ;                           MOVESCRN.ASM                         *
 6:   ;     MOVESCRN is a module of two assembled subroutines for linking to  *
 7:   ; programs compiled with Microsoft QuickBASIC.  The routines copy, and *
 8:   ; later restore, the display adapter buffer corresponding to text mode *
 9:   ; page 0.  The routines in this module can be used with any PC display *
10:   ; adapter in text mode.                                          *
11:   ;     GETIT copies text mode page 0 of the active display buffer to a   *
12:   ; buffer hidden in the MOVESCRN_TEXT Code Segment.               *
13:   ;     PUTIT copies the contents of the hidden buffer to page 0.  *
14:   ;     Both routines use the assembled function ISCOLOR           *
15:   ;               Written by M. L. Lesser, January 1, 1987         *
16:   ;          Modified for Microsoft BC 4.0 and MASM 5.0, 10-22-87  *
17:   ;*******************************************************************
18:
19:   EXTRN    ISCOLOR:FAR
20:
21:   .CODE
22:
23:   ;  Local data storage in Code Segment for contents of display buffer:
24:   BUFF     DB       4000 DUP(?)
25:
26:   ;  Local subroutine:
27:   ADAPTER PROC NEAR                    ;Puts segment address of display adapter
28:                                        ;  in BX
29:              CALL     ISCOLOR
30:              OR       AX,AX            ;Is color adapter active?
31:              MOV      BX,0B800H        ;Setup for color adapter
32:              JNZ      DONE             ;Use color adapter segment
33:              MOV      BX,0B000H        ;Setup for mono adapter
34:   DONE:      RET
35:   ADAPTER ENDP
36:
37:              PUBLIC   GETIT
38:   GETIT      PROC FAR                  ;Get current display image in buffer
39:              PUSH     BP
40:              PUSH     DS
41:              PUSH     SI
42:              PUSH     DI
43:              CALL     ADAPTER          ;Get display buffer segment
44:              MOV      DS,BX            ;DS points to display buffer
45:              MOV      AX,CS            ;Establish ES addressability
46:              MOV      ES,AX            ;  to Code Segment
47:              LEA      DI,CS:BUFF       ;Offset of move destination
48:              XOR      SI,SI            ;Offset of display page 0
49:   ;  Move 4,000 bytes between display buffer and BUFF
50:   DOIT:      CLD
51:              MOV      CX,4000          ;Will move 4,000 bytes
52:   REP        MOVSB                     ;Move them all
53:              POP      DI
54:              POP      SI
55:              POP      DS
56:              POP      BP
```

Listing 6 - 6 (continued)

```
57:                RET
58:    GETIT       ENDP
59:
60:                PUBLIC   PUTIT              ;Put buffered display image in display
61:    PUTIT       PROC     FAR
62:                PUSH     BP
63:                PUSH     DS
64:                PUSH     SI
65:                PUSH     DI
66:                CALL     ADAPTER            ;Get display buffer segment
67:                MOV      ES,BX              ;ES points to display buffer
68:                MOV      AX,CS              ;Establish DS addressability
69:                MOV      DS,AX              ;   to Code Segment
70:                LEA      SI,CS:BUFF         ;Offset of move source
71:                XOR      DI,DI              ;Offset of display page 0
72:                JMP      DOIT               ;Transfer bytes and return
73:    PUTIT       ENDP
74:
75:                END
```

Listing 6 - 6

space available to the program if there is enough memory space for more than a minimum DGROUP.

MENU.BAS

The interface conventions for the window routines are demonstrated with the declared function MENU.BAS (Listing 6-7). MENU() allows any text-mode program to pop up a menu from the lower right corner of the display screen. The menu can contain up to twenty-four entries, with each entry having a maximum length of thirty-five characters. MENU() writes the menu in reverse video (COLOR 0,7), with the selected entry in normal video (COLOR 7,0). (Only these attributes are used, since other COLOR combinations tend to be unreadable on systems with a composite mono display.) The DECLARE conventions for MENU() are described in the listing prologue.

MENU() assigns an alphabetic index letter — starting with A — to each entry. Selection can be by cursor key — moving the marker identifying the "selected" entry up or down the menu — and making final selection by pressing the Enter key. Or, as I prefer, immediate selection can be made by pressing the single alpha key corresponding to the index letter. After selection, the original display text is restored.

Purely for demonstration, I have split the variable declaration statements. The DIM statements in the main portion of the module are declared

```
 1:  '***********************************************************************
 2:  '                          MENU.BAS                                   *
 3:  '     MENU is an integer function for including pop-up menus, with up  *
 4:  ' to 24 entries, in QBASIC programs running in text mode.  Menu        *
 5:  ' returns the entry number, n, of the selected entry.                 *
 6:  '     Declare with:  DECLARE MENU% (A$())                             *
 7:  '          A$() is a one-dimension string array as follows:           *
 8:  '                A$(0) contains MKI$(n)                               *
 9:  '                    (where n is the number of menu entries)          *
10:  '                A$(1) contains the name of the menu                  *
11:  '                A$(2) to A$(n+1) contain the entry texts             *
12:  '     Each menu entry will be assigned an alphabetic index starting at *
13:  ' "A".  All menu entries, except the "selected" one, are shown in     *
14:  ' reverse video.  Initially, the first entry is marked as selected.   *
15:  '     Menu selection can be performed in either of two ways:          *
16:  '        Select by cursor control (Up, Down, Home, End):  After each  *
17:  '            cursor keystroke, the new selected entry will be shown.   *
18:  '            Return the selected item number (in <item>) to the calling *
19:  '            program by pressing Enter.                               *
20:  '        Direct selection:  Press the alpha key (either upper- or lower-*
21:  '            case) corresponding to the desired entry index letter.  The *
22:  '            selected item number is returned immediately.            *
23:  '     After selection, the screen is restored to the form it had before *
24:  ' the call to MENU.                                                    *
25:  '     If less than one entry or more than 24 entries are indicated in  *
26:  ' A$(0), MENU() returns a zero.  Menu names or entries longer than 35 *
27:  ' characters will be truncated to that length.                        *
28:  '               Written by M. L. Lesser, January 5, 1987             *
29:  '               Modified for Microsoft BC version 4.0, 11-24-87       *
30:  '***********************************************************************
31:      DEFINT A-Z
32:      DEFSTR P,T
33:      DIM SHARED ITEM, LENGTH, LONGEST, MARK, MAX           'Integers
34:      DIM SHARED PASS, TEXT                                 'Strings
35:      COMMON SHARED /CURSOR/ ROW.T, COL.T, ROW.B, COL.B, ROW, COL
36:  '    $INCLUDE: 'PQB.BI'
37:
38:  FUNCTION MENU%(TEXT()) STATIC
39:  ' Declare local variables:
40:      DIM ROW.CURS, COL.CURS, OLD.ROW.T, OLD.COL.T, OLD.ROW.B, OLD.COL.B
41:      DIM OLD.ROW, OLD.COL, ATTRIB, CFG, CBG
42:  ' Check for allowable number of items in menu array:
43:      LET MAX = CVI(TEXT(0))                     'Number of entries
44:      IF MAX < 1 OR MAX > 24 THEN                'If number out of bounds
45:          LET MENU = 0                           '    return error code
46:          EXIT FUNCTION                          'Abnormal end to function
47:      END IF
48:  ' Check for longest entry (truncate if exceeds 35):
49:      LET LONGEST = 0                            'Initialize for reuse
50:      FOR I = 1 TO MAX + 1                       'Menu name + entries
51:          LET LENGTH = LEN(TEXT(I))
52:          IF LENGTH > 35 THEN                    'If too long for menu array
53:              LET TEXT(I) = LEFT$(TEXT(I),35)
54:              LET LONGEST = 35
55:          ELSE
56:              IF LENGTH > LONGEST THEN LET LONGEST = LENGTH
```

Listing 6 - 7 (continued)

```
57:          END IF
58:       NEXT I
59: ' Build pop-up menu display from right bottom in reverse video:
60:       GOSUB GETSTAT                        'Save original screen status
61:       COLOR 0,7                            'Menu in reverse video
62: ' Define menu window:
63:       LET ROW.T = 25 - MAX: COL.T = 76 - LONGEST  'Window is 5 cols wider
64:       LET ROW.B = 25: COL.B = 80           '    than longest entry
65: ' Write name of menu in row 25, to be scrolled up:
66:       LET ROW = 25
67:       CALL PWINDOW(STRING$(LONGEST + 5,"-"))          'Row of hyphens
68:       LET ROW = 25
69:       CALL CWINDOW(TEXT(1))                'Overlay centered title
70: ' Pop up menu items on screen, writing in row 25 after scroll:
71:       LET COL = COL.T + 1                  'Menu entries start one over
72:       FOR ITEM = 1 TO MAX
73:          GOSUB PLACE                       'Put entry in standard form
74:          CALL DWINDOW(TEXT)
75:       NEXT ITEM
76: ' Mark initial menu entry:
77:       LET ITEM = 1
78:       GOSUB SHOW                           'Writes entry in normal video
79: ' Select entry to be returned:
80: PICK:                           'Start of infinite selection loop:
81:       SELECT CASE KBPEEK
82:          CASE -1                           'Nothing pending
83:             GOTO PICK
84:          CASE 71                           'Home - select first entry
85:             LET ITEM = 1
86:          CASE 72                           'Cursor up - previous entry
87:             IF ITEM > 1 THEN LET ITEM = ITEM - 1
88:          CASE 79                           'End - select last entry
89:             LET ITEM = MAX
90:          CASE 80                           'Cursor down - following
91:             IF ITEM < MAX THEN LET ITEM = ITEM + 1      'entry
92:          CASE 256                          'ASCII symbol pending
93:             LET PASS = INKEY$              'Read pending keystroke
94:             LET PASS = UCASE$(PASS)        'Force alpha uppercase
95:             LET MARK = ASC(PASS) - 64      'Convert to ITEM format
96:             IF PASS = CHR$(13) THEN        'If Enter key pending
97:                GOTO WIN                    '   Return selected entry
98:             ELSEIF PASS = CHR$(32) THEN    '<SP> equivalent to Cursor
99:                IF ITEM < MAX THEN LET ITEM = ITEM + 1          'down
100:            ELSEIF MARK > 0 AND MARK <= MAX THEN          'If valid item
101:               LET ITEM = MARK             'Return selected entry
102:               GOTO WIN
103:            END IF
104:         CASE ELSE                         'All the rest do nothing
105:      END SELECT
106:      LET ROW = ROW - 1                    'Restore previous selection to
107:      CALL DWINDOW(TEXT)                   '   reverse video
108:      GOSUB SHOW                           'Highlight current selection
109:      GOTO PICK                   'Go around infinite loop again
110:
111: WIN:                           'Return selected item to calling program
112:      LET MENU = ITEM
```

Listing 6 - 7 (continued)

```
113:        GOSUB PUTSTAT                        'Restore original screen status
114:    EXIT FUNCTION                    'Normal function end
115:
116:    '  GOSUB subroutines used by MENU in alphabetical order:
117:
118:    GETSTAT:          ' Saves screen entry status, including image
119:        LET ROW.CURS = CSRLIN                    'Cursor position
120:        LET COL.CURS = POS(0)
121:        LET ATTRIB = SCREEN(ROW.CURS,COL.CURS,1)    'Display attribute
122:        LET CFG = (ATTRIB AND &H0F) + (ATTRIB AND &H80)\8  'Foreground color
123:        LET CBG = (ATTRIB AND &H70)\16              'Background color
124:        LET OLD.ROW.T = ROW.T                    'Previous values in
125:        LET OLD.COL.T = COL.T                    ' COMMON /CURSOR/
126:        LET OLD.ROW.B = ROW.B
127:        LET OLD.COL.B = COL.B
128:        LET OLD.ROW = ROW
129:        LET OLD.COL = COL
130:        CALL GETIT                         'Load screen image in buffer
131:    RETURN
132:
133:    PLACE:                  'Put ITEM entry in standard form
134:        LET TEXT = TEXT(ITEM+1) + SPACE$(35)      'Pad with 35 <SP> symbols
135:        LET TEXT = LEFT$(TEXT,LONGEST)              'Truncate to longest
136:    ' Prefix menu entry with associated alpha character:
137:        LET TEXT = CHR$(64 + ITEM) + ". " + TEXT     'Add alpha index
138:    RETURN
139:
140:    PUTSTAT:          ' Restores previous screen status
141:        CALL PUTIT                         'Restore previous screen image
142:        LOCATE ROW.CURS,COL.CURS
143:        COLOR CFG,CBG
144:        ROW.T = OLD.ROW.T
145:        COL.T = OLD.COL.T
146:        ROW.B = OLD.ROW.B
147:        COL.B = OLD.COL.B
148:        ROW = OLD.ROW
149:        COL = OLD.COL
150:    RETURN
151:
152:    SHOW:                  'Display selected entry in normal video
153:        GOSUB PLACE                         'Put ITEM entry in standard form
154:        LET ROW = 25 - (MAX - ITEM)         'Set up to write in entry ROW
155:        COLOR 7,0                         'Reverse the reverse video
156:        CALL DWINDOW(TEXT)
157:        COLOR 0,7
158:    RETURN
159:
160:    END FUNCTION              'End of function definition
```

Listing 6 - 7

SHARED, making those variables global, available to the function (lines 33–34). The remaining (except for the COMMON variables which must be in the main portion) are declared as local variables within the function definition (lines 40–41). These *cannot* be declared SHARED, as they are not declared anywhere outside the function definition.

Entry selection is done by keystroke, using a SELECT CASE block inside of an infinite selection loop (lines 80–109). If no keystroke is pending, the program loops between lines 80 and 83, doing nothing. If an ASCII keystroke is pending, it is examined in the doubly nested IF-block structure (lines 96–103).[6] Any invalid keystroke flashes the selected entry (lines 108–109), very rapidly.

Four GOSUB subroutines (lines 116–158) are used to avoid giving the linker unnecessary public names. As required by the label scope rules, the GOSUB subroutines are inside the declared function definition. Although the definition ends with the "END FUNCTION" statement in line 160, the normal return from MENU() is at the "EXIT FUNCTION" in line 114.

GETSTAT (lines 118–131) "saves" the display status belonging to the calling program; PUTSTAT restores it before the function exits. In addition to moving the display memory image, these save and restore a "window" definition the calling program may have established, along with the cursor position and color attribute that existed before the MENU() call. While BASIC provides the SCREEN function to determine the display attribute at any screen coordinate (line 121), it does not provide any automatic way to make the reverse translation to a COLOR statement. A programmed translation is made in lines 122– 123. The cursor type (visible/invisible) is left unchanged from the calling program. If you used a "LOCATE „1" statement before calling MENU(), the cursor will travel up and down the pop-up menu with the selection marker.

Bringing Up MENU.BAS

MENU.BAS was implemented and tested in sequential phases, using the test driver MENDRIVE.BAS (Listing 6-8). MENDRIVE.BAS also serves to illustrate the interface rules for using the MENU() library function.

MENDRIVE.BAS must be implemented and tested before it can be used as a test driver. (If you are using a composite mono display, MENDRIVE's output may be more readable if you change the COLOR statement in line 11 to COLOR 7,0.) Insert a dummy MENU declared function definition after line 43, consisting of the debugging code shown in Figure 6-2. This causes an instantaneous return from MENU, indicating only that the function did receive the passed array. Once you get

```
1:   '************************************************************************
2:   '                         MENDRIVE.BAS                              *
3:   '        A test driver for the compiled pop-up menu function MENU.BAS  *
4:   '                 Written by M. L. Lesser, January 5, 1987          *
5:   '            Modified for Microsoft BC version 4.0, 11-24-87        *
6:   '************************************************************************
7:
8:        DEFINT A-Z
9:        DEFSTR T
10:       DECLARE FUNCTION MENU% (A$())
11:       COLOR 7,1
12:       CLS                                'Set background color to blue
13:
14:  ' Set up line number display at right side of screen:
15:       FOR I = 1 TO 25
16:            LOCATE I,78
17:            PRINT USING "##"; I;
18:       NEXT I
19:       LOCATE 1,1
20:  START:
21:       PRINT
22:       INPUT "Enter number of entries:  ", I
23:  ' Set up MENU input interface in string array TEXT():
24:       DIM TEXT(I+1)                      'Dynamic string array for driver
25:       LET TEXT(0) = MKI$(I)              'Nunber of entries in TEXT(0)
26:       LET TEXT(1) = "MENU TEST"          'Menu title in TEXT(1)
27:       FOR ITEM = 1 TO I                  'Menu entries in rest of array
28:            LET TEXT(ITEM+1) = "This is entry" + STR$(ITEM)
29:       NEXT ITEM
30:       ITEM = MENU(TEXT())
31:       SELECT CASE ITEM
32:            CASE 0
33:                 PRINT TAB(10) "Number of menu entries out of range"
34:            CASE ELSE
35:                 PRINT TAB(10) TEXT(ITEM+1)
36:       END SELECT
37:       PRINT
38:       PRINT "Do you wish to try again (y/n)? ";
39:       LET T = INPUT$(1)
40:       IF T = "Y" OR T = "y" OR T = " " THEN
41:            ERASE TEXT                    'Must clear before dimensioning
42:            GOTO START                    '  on next pass
43:       END IF
```

Listing 6 - 8

MENDRIVE to separately compile, you can test it by responding to its
input query with an appropriate positive integer.

Since there is nothing to MENDRIVE that isn't displayed, you don't
have to use a debugger to test it. If MENDRIVE is working properly, it
will display twenty-five row numbers at the right edge of your display
screen and ask you for the number of entries the menu should have. For
this debugging version, the response should be an entry number message
corresponding to the input value, as left by the FOR...NEXT loop in lines

```
function menu%(a$()) static
    let menu = cvi(a$(0))
end function
```

Figure 6 - 2
Debugging code for MENDRIVE.BAS

27–29. If it isn't working properly, read the listing of *your* source code and correct the errors you find. Once you have MENDRIVE tested, delete the dummy MENU subroutine and recompile it for use while implementing the real MENU.BAS.

Whenever one brings up a complex program, there will be many cycles of edit, compile, link, and run. MENU.BAS was implemented in three phases, requiring at least three such cycles — even if everything worked correctly the first time. One way to mechanize the dog work is to use a batch file and let DOS's fingers do the walking. Figure 6-3, AGAIN.BAT, shows a suitable file. The second line removes the object file produced by BC if there were any compile-time errors. The fourth line deletes any previous version of MENDRIVE.EXE when the linker cannot find the deleted object file.

The initial version of MENU.BAS only read in the input array and determined that the out-of-bounds check and the GETSTAT, PUTSTAT subroutines worked as they should. It consisted of lines 1–61, followed by the bit of debugging code shown in Figure 6-4, followed by lines 111–131, 140–150, and 160.

After the compile, load, and go session produced by calling AGAIN, I tried several input numbers to test the error return. If this version is working properly, the MENU call in MENDRIVE should produce a cleared screen in reverse video with a cursor blinking in the upper left-hand corner. The return will occur when you press any key. The restored MENDRIVE screen will show the highest entry number (as before), but the "try again" request will show the visible cursor turned on by the LOCATE statement in the MENU.BAS debugging code.

The next phase added the ability to pop up the menu and select the first entry (lines 62–78, 133–138 and 152–158). The first three lines of the debugging code were deleted, leaving only the wait-loop last line in its

```
bc menu;
if errorlevel 1 del menu.obj
link mendrive menu,,,pqb
if errorlevel 1 del mendrive.exe
mendrive
```

Figure 6 - 3
AGAIN.BAT file for MENU.BAS

previous location just before line 111. Testing this version should produce
the pop-up menu with the first entry marked as selected by being in normal video. The return should show entry 1 as long as a valid number of
entries is specified.

The final implementation phase added the ability to select a particular entry. I removed the debugging code and added the PICK routine
(lines 79–109). After running AGAIN again, I tested this version until I
was satisfied with its operation.

Possible Extensions to MENU.BAS

There are several variations possible on the basic structure shown in
MENU.BAS. I limited the width of the pop-up menu to forty columns because I thought I might eventually write nested menus that were displayed side by side. However, I later decided that one menu at a time was

```
cls
locate ,,1
let item = max
while inkey$ = "": wend
```

Figure 6 - 4
Debugging code for first version of MENU.BAS

probably more than enough. You may wish to allow for menu entries up to seventy-five symbols wide.

The selection segment could be modified to react to computer rodents or light-pen response, although this would remove the "device independent" nature of the subroutine. Or you could shorten up the whole affair by eliminating the cursor-key selection entirely, since the letter-key method is both faster and more convenient.

Menu design is an aspect of "user friendly" programming. However, what is "friendly" to one user may be a nuisance to another.

Notes

1. See the README.DOC file distributed with QBASIC for details on the Hercules Graphics Card support.
2. DOS can provide a slightly higher level of text-mode support if you include the relatively clumsy ANSI.SYS device driver in your CONFIG.SYS file. While the ANSI.SYS driver probably is not as dangerous to system integrity as are many proprietary keyboard- interception "terminate and stay resident" programs, its functions are better performed by including direct calls on ROM BIOS only in those programs requiring the additional function. Many applications programs are written under the assumption that they have direct control over the system resources; any interference with that assumption may wreak havoc when such a program is executed.
3. Unlike BASICA and earlier versions of QBASIC, version 4.0 returns an immediate "Illegal function call" error interrupt on an "illegal" SCREEN statement.
4. Useful assembly-language programmers' references for the EGA and VGA are: the IBM Options and Adapters *Technical Reference* manual update for the EGA, and the IBM *Personal System/2 and Personal Computer BIOS Interface Technical Reference*. The latter contains an outline of a display adapter recognition scheme that will identify any of the IBM adapters.
5. If the momentary "snow" while executing the MOVESCRN subroutines with an active CGA bothers you, you can program around the idiosyncrasy. Test for the presence of any color

adapter with ISCOLOR. If one is present, use "PCOPY 0,1" and "PCOPY 1,0" instead of GETIT and PUTIT, respectively.

6. There is no BASICA equivalent to IFs without ELSEs nested in an IF...THEN...ELSEIF structure (Listing 6-7, line 99).

Chapter 7

Advanced Printer Control

Very few printers attached to PCs have only a single "plain vanilla" print mode. Most PC printers can change type styles and line spacing under program control. However, your program cannot use any additional capability the printer may have unless it "knows" the capability is available and, if it is, how to tell the printer to use it.

In most cases, you cannot identify the attached printer from within a program. The only general solution is to ask the computer user. The result of asking the user should be a system profile, suitable for describing the system characteristics to a family of applications programs.

But a program can't use a profile giving printer characteristics unless the program can supply the necessary printer-control sequences. Expanding PRINT.ASM (Listing 3-2) to cover all possible contingencies is not a reasonable proposition. This chapter opens with two library subroutines, one assembled and one compiled, to convert a string expression to a printer-control sequence.

The simple system profile program SYSPRO.BAS produces a SYSTEM.PRO file describing pertinent display and printer characteristics. As an example of SYSTEM.PRO usage, version 2.0 of LIST.BAS customizes itself for the attached display and printer, and chooses between normal and condensed type styles to prevent the longest line in the source text from overflowing the printer (or paper) maximum line width.

Printer-Control Strings

PCONTR.ASM (Listing 7-1) sends the low-order 8 bits of an integer variable or expression to the printer. If the printer recognizes those bits as an ASCII symbol in its repertoire, the printer reacts accordingly. Thus, "CALL PCONTR(<int>)" performs similarly to "LPRINT CHR$(<int>)" but with two advantages. The minor advantage is that PCONTR is slightly faster; the major advantage is that control sequences sent by PCONTR do not clutter up BASIC's printer output buffer, so do not adversely affect the response of BASIC's LPOS(0) function.

The compiled subroutine PCONTROL.BAS (Listing 7-2) accepts a printer- control sequence encoded in a string expression consisting of the decimal ASCII values of the control symbols separated by commas. PCONTROL(<string>) converts each value in the string to its corresponding integer and calls PCONTR to send that integer to the printer.

PCONTROL(<string>) is relatively fail-safe. If <string> is null, PCONTROL sends nothing. If <string> has a leading comma, PCONTROL starts its transmission with a <NUL>, which does nothing (except when within a printer-recognized escape sequence). It ignores blanks between the digit strings and surrounding commas, as well as any erroneous trailing comma.

The argument string is destructively parsed in a WHILE...WEND loop (lines 19–28) that deletes the leading value from the string on each pass, continuing until there is nothing left to parse. Obviously, we cannot parse a formal parameter pointing to an actual "global" variable in this fashion or we would null the argument variable in the process — leading to a subtle bug if there was another call to PCONTROL with the same argument later in the program. There are two ways to prevent this problem.

One way would be to require the programmer using PCONTROL to surround the argument variable name with parentheses of its own in the CALL statement. The compiler would copy the value of the resulting expression into a temporary storage location before shipping the address of

```
 1:            PAGE     ,105
 2:            TITLE    PCONTR
 3:            .MODEL   MEDIUM
 4: ;********************************************************************
 5: ;                          PCONTR.ASM                             *
 6: ;     PCONTR(<int>) accepts the integer expression <int> and sends the *
 7: ; low eight bits to the printer.  It is equivalent to the statement: *
 8: ; LPRINT CHR$(<int>), but ignores the high eight bits of <int> and is *
 9: ; not checked.  Use with the compiled subroutine PCONTROL(<string>) to *
10: ; send arbitrary control strings to the printer.                  *
11: ;            Written by M. L. Lesser, January 14, 1987            *
12: ;            Modified for Microsoft MASM 5.0, 11/30/87            *
13: ;********************************************************************
14:
15: .CODE
16:
17:            PUBLIC   PCONTR
18: PCONTR  PROC
19:            PUSH     BP
20:            MOV      BP,SP
21:            MOV      BX,6[BP]
22:            MOV      AL,[BX]            ;Decimal ASCII value to print
23:            XOR      AH,AH             ; using ROM BIOS print character
24:            XOR      DX,DX             ; on LPT1
25:            INT      17H
26:            POP      BP
27:            RET      2
28: PCONTR  ENDP
29:
30:            END
```

Listing 7 - 1

the temporary to the subroutine, and only the temporary string would be eliminated.

A better approach is to isolate the applications programmer from the problem by containing the solution within the subroutine itself. PCONTROL makes a temporary copy of the argument string by assigning the value of the formal parameter variable to a local variable (line 18) and parses its temporary, instead.

I tested PCONTR and PCONTROL together with a test driver (not shown) that alternated LPRINT strings with control strings to reset my Qume's left margin to differing locations. The same technique can be used with a Proprinter XL.[1] If you cannot set the left margin on your printer, you might print alternate lines in differing type styles, instead. Be sure to test multisymbol escape sequences.

```
1:    ' ***********************************************************************
2:    '                        PCONTROL.BAS                                  *
3:    '        PCONTROL is a compiled subroutine that calls the assembled    *
4:    ' printer-control subroutine PCONTR, to send an arbitrary control      *
5:    ' sequence to the printer.                                             *
6:    '        Call with:  CALL PCONTROL(<text>), where <text> is a string   *
7:    ' expression or variable having the form "<n1>[,<n2>][,<n3>[,...]".    *
8:    ' The n's are string representations of the decimal ASCII values of    *
9:    ' the successive control symbols to be sent to the printer.            *
10:   '              Written by M. L. Lesser, January 15, 1987               *
11:   '              Recompiled with Microsoft BC version 4.0                *
12:   ' ***********************************************************************
13:
14:          DEFINT I
15:          DEFSTR T
16:
17:   SUB PCONTROL(TEXT.IN) STATIC
18:        LET TEXT = TEXT.IN                    'Copy to dissect
19:        WHILE LEN(TEXT)                       'As long as <text> not null
20:             LET ITEM = VAL(TEXT)
21:             CALL PCONTR(ITEM)                '     Ship off leading symbol
22:             LET I = INSTR(TEXT,",")          '     Find next comma
23:             IF I THEN                        '        and strip to next symbol
24:                  LET TEXT = MID$(TEXT,I+1)
25:             ELSE                             '     If there is one
26:                  LET TEXT = ""
27:             END IF
28:        WEND                                  'Repeat loop until done
29:   END SUB
```

Listing 7 - 2

Replacing a Library Module

The PCONTROL-PCONTR pair of subroutines can send any control sequence to any printer receiving signals routed through LPT1. While the printer-control subroutines in PRINT.ASM are now redundant, they are still convenient. I continue to use all of them except PROPRIN, and even PROPRIN remains in my library to provide compatibility when recompiling and relinking old programs.

Although PCONTR.ASM is shown as a separate listing, it is not a separate module in my library. I inserted the PCONTR subroutine into the source- code text of PRINT.ASM with my text editor, inserting the following lines from Listing 7-1 between lines 109 and 110 of Listing 3-2: lines 17–18, 4, 6–10, 13, 19–29. This created PRINT.ASM version 2.0 (not shown). I used the LIB utility in its "replace" mode to delete the old print module from the PQB library, replacing it with the new one.

```
pcontrol        Offset: 00002bb0H Code and data size: eaH
  PCONTROL
print           Offset: 00003000H Code and data size: 7cH
  PAGELEN       PCONTR        PFORM              PROPRIN
  PSKIP
```

Figure 7 - 1
Excerpt from PQD.IDX

You can load the compiled PCONTROL.OBJ and the revised and reassembled PRINT.OBJ modules into the library with a single command:

```
lib pqb+pcontrol-+print,pqb.idx;
```

Note that the "minus" must precede the "plus" or you will get a LIB syntax error message. The library manager will first remove the old print module, then add the PCONTROL module at the end of the remaining library, and finally add the new print module.

Figure 7-1 is an excerpt from my PQB.IDX file, showing the new location, size, and contents of the print module. (Compare with Figure 3-4.)

If you wish, you can produce a neater library index by rearranging your library so the modules are in alphabetic order, using LIB in a manner analogous to a bubble sort. Extract modules and then replace them at the end of the library. The form is

```
lib pqb-*<modname>+<modname>,pqb.idx;
```

where <modname> is the name of the module to be moved. The "-*" sequence deletes the module but writes a <modname>.OBJ file to the default directory. The "+" reloads that object file at the end of the library. Each <modname> to be moved must be entered on the LIB command line twice, as shown.

A System Profile

Only a minimal system profile program is shown here. The file it builds consists of a single record containing terms in a format analogous to the PC-DOS command-line "switches."

The information provided consists of the desired foreground and background text-display colors, any printer initialization string, the printer initial page offset, the maximum number of characters per line in "normal" type style, the control string to produce normal type, the number of characters in a line in "condensed" type style (zero if condensed type not available), and the control string to produce condensed type.

This profile is sufficient for the programs shown in the remainder of this book to customize themselves for the hardware they are running on. However, there are applications (such as a word processor) that would require considerably more elaborate system profiles to be effective.

SYSPRO.BAS

SYSPRO.BAS (Listing 7-3) is an interactive program that uses the MENU.BAS subroutine to interrogate the user and then writes a single-record SYSTEM.PRO file containing the profile thus obtained. All printer-control sequences are written in the form required by PCONTROL. SYSPRO.BAS demonstrates further use of the "window" subroutines, since both the main program and the menu declared function maintain their individual window structures.

The following remarks on language usage expand the comments in the listing. The program uses five menus. The menu entries are contained in the four DATA sequences in lines 20–32 (COLORS is used twice). Each menu is initialized by an individual code sequence (e.g., lines 51–54) followed by a call to the GOSUB subroutine DO.MENU. The user prompt string for the menu is stored in the simple string variable TEXT (line 51), and the menu entry data is stored in the eighteen-element string array TEXT() (lines 53, 105–108), demonstrating BASIC's ability to separate simple and array variables having the same name. DO.MENU (lines 103–112) builds the menu array, calls on the MENU() function, and displays the selected entry name following the prompt.

The first menu response (type of display) is analyzed by a single IF-block (lines 56–58) since only entry 3 has any effect on the outcome. The

```
1:     '******************************************************************
2:     '                          SYSPRO.BAS                             *
3:     '     SYSPRO interrogates the user (by menu) to obtain a system profile *
4:     ' describing the display and printer characteristics not available *
5:     ' from internal tests.  On request, this profile is written to a  *
6:     ' SYSTEM.PRO file in the default directory.  SYSTEM.PRO can be read by *
7:     ' other programs to configure themselves for the system.  See     *
8:     ' LIST.BAS, version 2.0, for details.                             *
9:     '     SYSPRO.BAS calls the library subroutines in the modules MENU.BAS, *
10:    ' WINDOW.ASM, and DWINDOW.BAS, requiring use of COMMON /CURSOR/.  *
11:    '           Written by M. L. Lesser, January 18, 1987             *
12:    '         Modified for Microsoft BC version 4.0, 11/30/87         *
13:    '******************************************************************
14:        DEFINT C,E,I,R
15:        DEFSTR P,T
16:        DIM CBG, CBTEMP, CFG, CFTEMP, ENTRIES, ENTRY, I, PASS
17:        DIM TEXT, TEXT(17), TEXT.OUT
18:        COMMON /CURSOR/ ROW.T, COL.T, ROW.B, COL.B, ROW, COL
19:    '    $INCLUDE: 'PQB.BI'
20:    ' Menu entries:
21:    DISPLAYS:
22:        DATA "Mono", "Composite Mono", "Color"
23:    COLORS:
24:        DATA "Black", "Blue", "Green", "Cyan", "Red", "Magenta", "Brown"
25:        DATA "White", "Gray", "Light Blue", "Light Green", "Light Cyan"
26:        DATA "Light Red", "Light Magenta", "Yellow", "High-intensity White"
27:    PRINTERS:
28:        DATA "IBM Graphics Printer", "Proprinter", "Proprinter XL"
29:        DATA "Printer not listed"
30:    CHOICES:
31:        DATA "Terminate Program", "Repeat Selection Process"
32:        DATA "Write SYSTEM.PRO file"
33:
34:    ' Main program loop:
35:    RESTART:
36:        LET CFG = 7: CBG = 0                    'Default values
37:        COLOR CFG,CBG                           'Clear screen to normal video
38:        CLS
39:        LET ROW.T = 1: COL.T = 1: ROW.B = 25: COL.B = 80    'Full screen
40:        LET ROW = 2                             'Start display on Row 2
41:        CALL CWINDOW("Building a System Profile File")
42:        CALL DWINDOW("")                        'Skip a row
43:        LET TEXT = "Make menu selection with Cursor keys " + _
44:                   "followed by pressing ENTER key"
45:        CALL CWINDOW(TEXT)
46:        CALL CWINDOW("or")
47:        LET TEXT = "Make direct selection by pressing index letter key"
48:        CALL CWINDOW(TEXT)
49:    ' Select display colors:
50:        CALL DWINDOW("")                        'Skip a row
51:        LET TEXT = "Select display type:  "     'Menu sign-on message
52:        LET ENTRIES = 3                         'Number of entries in menu
53:        LET TEXT(1) = "Display Types"           'Menu title
54:        RESTORE DISPLAYS                        'Menu entries for display choice
55:        GOSUB DO.MENU                           'Make menu selection
56:        IF ENTRY = 3 THEN                       'Color display
```

Listing 7 - 3   (continued)

```
 57:        GOSUB SETCOLOR                     '  so specify colors
 58:     END IF                              '(All others are default colors)
 59: ' Write display color choice in output string:
 60:     LET TEXT.OUT = "/CFG=" + STR$(CFG) + "/CBG=" + STR$(CBG)
 61: ' Select printer type:
 62:     LET TEXT = "Select printer type:   "
 63:     RESTORE PRINTERS                     'Printer menu entries
 64:     LET ENTRIES = 4
 65:     LET TEXT(1) = "Available Printers"
 66:     GOSUB DO.MENU
 67: ' If listed printer, prepare text of output file:
 68:     SELECT CASE ENTRY
 69:         CASE 1                            'IBM Graphics Printer
 70:            LET TEXT.OUT = TEXT.OUT + "/POFF=36" + _
 71:                           "/WID.N=80/WID.C=132" + _
 72:                           "/NORM=18/COND=15"
 73:         CASE 2                        'Proprinter
 74:            LET TEXT.OUT = TEXT.OUT + "/WID.N=96/WID.C=137" + _
 75:                           "/INIT=27,73,2" +  _      'NLQ standard font
 76:                           "/NORM=27,58/COND=18,15"
 77:         CASE 3                        'Proprinter XL
 78:            LET TEXT.OUT = TEXT.OUT + "/WID.N=102/WID.C=145" + _
 79:                           "/INIT=27,73,2,27,88,1,255" + _   'Sets margins
 80:                           "/NORM=27,58/COND=18,15"          '  at ends
 81:         CASE ELSE            'If printer not listed
 82:            GOSUB SETPRINT           'Set up printer characteristics
 83:     END SELECT
 84: ' Final disposition:
 85:     LET ENTRIES = 3
 86:     LET TEXT(1) = "Program Output"
 87:     LET TEXT = "Select disposition of profile:   "
 88:     RESTORE CHOICES                   'Menu for final choice
 89:     GOSUB DO.MENU
 90:     SELECT CASE ENTRY
 91:        CASE 1                          'Terminate program
 92:            END
 93:        CASE 2                          'Try whole loop over
 94:            GOTO RESTART
 95:        CASE ELSE                       'OK to file
 96:            OPEN "SYSTEM.PRO" FOR OUTPUT AS #1
 97:            WRITE #1, TEXT.OUT
 98:            CLOSE #1
 99:     END SELECT
100: END             'End of main program
101:
102: ' GOSUB subroutines, in order first called:
103: DO.MENU: 'Set up for MENU call
104:     LET COL = 10
105:     LET TEXT(0) = MKI$(ENTRIES)        'Number of entries in menu
106:     FOR I = 1 TO ENTRIES              'Menu entries
107:        READ TEXT(I+1)
108:     NEXT I
109:     CALL DWINDOW(TEXT)                'Selection sign-on
110:     LET ENTRY = MENU(TEXT())
111:     PRINT TEXT(ENTRY+1);                  'Print response
112: RETURN           'End of DO.MENU
```

Listing 7 - 3 (continued)

```
113:
114: SETCOLOR:  ' Color selection for Color Displays:
115:      LET CFG = 7: CBG = 0
116:      GOSUB CLEAR.WIN                       'Clear window starting row 4
117:      LET TEXT = "Select foreground color:  "
118:      RESTORE COLORS                        'Foreground color menu entries
119:      LET ENTRIES = 16
120:      LET TEXT(1) = "Foreground Colors"
121:      GOSUB DO.MENU
122:      LET CFTEMP = ENTRY - 1      'Temporary foreground color
123:      LET TEXT = "Select background color:  "
124:      LET TEXT(1) = "Background colors"
125:      RESTORE COLORS                        'Background same as foreground
126:      LET ENTRIES = 8                       '  except fewer entries
127:      GOSUB DO.MENU
128:      LET CBTEMP = ENTRY - 1      'Temporary background color
129:      CALL DWINDOW("")
130:      IF CFTEMP = CBTEMP THEN               'If both the same
131:           COLOR 0,7                        '  tell user and
132:           CALL DWINDOW("Illegal choice: foreground same as background")
133:           CALL DWINDOW("Press any key to reselect colors")
134:           WHILE INKEY$ = "": WEND
135:           GOTO SETCOLOR                    '  force color reselect
136:      ELSE                                  'Try temporary colors
137:           LET CFG = CFTEMP: CBG = CBTEMP
138:           GOSUB CLEAR.WIN
139:           LET TEXT = "Are these colors satisfactory (press 'y' or 'n')?  "
140:           CALL DWINDOW(TEXT)
141:           LET PASS = INPUT$(1)
142:           IF PASS = "Y" OR PASS = "y" OR PASS = " " THEN          'OK
143:                PRINT "Yes";
144:                CALL DWINDOW("")
145:           ELSE                             'Any other keypress is "No"
146:                GOTO SETCOLOR               '  Frustration but no harm!
147:           END IF
148:      END IF
149: RETURN             'End of SETCOLOR
150:
151: CLEAR.WIN: 'Clear inner window starting at row 4:
152:      COLOR CFG,CBG
153:      LET ROW.T = 4: ROW = 4               'Will start display in row 4
154:      LOCATE ROW.T,COL.T                   'Clear subwindow
155:      PRINT " ";                           'Blanking attribute
156:      CALL CLEARIT
157: RETURN             'End of CLEAR.WIN
158:
159: SETPRINT:  'Set up characteristics of unlisted printer:
160:      GOSUB CLEAR.WIN
161:      CALL CWINDOW("Enter unlisted printer characteristics")
162:      LET TEXT = "Enter control sequences as decimal ASCII values."
163:      CALL DWINDOW("")
164:      CALL CWINDOW(TEXT)
165:      LET TEXT = "If there is more than one value in string, " + _
166:                     "separate them by commas."
167:      CALL CWINDOW(TEXT)
168:      CALL CWINDOW("For example:  Enter '<ESC> A' as '27,65'")
```

Listing 7 - 3 (continued)

```
169:        LET COL = 10: CALL DWINDOW("")
170:        LET TEXT = "Does printer have an initialization sequence " + _
171:                    "(press y/n)?   "
172:        CALL DWINDOW(TEXT)
173:        LET PASS = INPUT$(1)
174:        IF PASS = "Y" OR PASS = "y" OR PASS = " " THEN
175:            PRINT "Yes";
176:            CALL DWINDOW("Enter initialization string:   ")
177:            LINE INPUT; PASS
178:            LET TEXT.OUT = TEXT.OUT + "/INIT=" + PASS
179:        ELSE
180:            PRINT "No";
181:        END IF
182:        CALL DWINDOW("")
183:        CALL CWINDOW("PageOffset is number of <LF>s to move paper from")
184:        CALL CWINDOW("perforations at tear bar to print at top of page")
185:        LET COL = 10: CALL DWINDOW("")
186:        CALL DWINDOW("Enter value of PageOffset (may be zero):   ")
187:        LINE INPUT; PASS
188:        LET TEXT.OUT = TEXT.OUT + "/POFF=" + PASS
189:        LET TEXT = "Enter number of characters in normal print line:   "
190:        CALL DWINDOW(TEXT)
191:        LINE INPUT; PASS
192:        LET TEXT.OUT = TEXT.OUT + "/WID.N=" + PASS
193:        CALL DWINDOW("Can printer print in condensed type (y/n)?:   ")
194:        LET PASS = INPUT$(1)
195:        IF PASS = "Y" OR PASS = "y" OR PASS = " " THEN
196:            PRINT "Yes";
197:            LET TEXT = "Enter number of characters in condensed " + _
198:                        "print line:   "
199:            CALL DWINDOW(TEXT)
200:            LINE INPUT; PASS
201:            LET TEXT.OUT = TEXT.OUT + "/WID.C=" + PASS
202:            CALL DWINDOW("Enter control string for normal type:   ")
203:            LINE INPUT; PASS
204:            LET TEXT.OUT = TEXT.OUT + "/NORM=" + PASS
205:            CALL DWINDOW("Enter control string for condensed type:   ")
206:            LINE INPUT; PASS
207:            LET TEXT.OUT = TEXT.OUT + "/COND=" + PASS
208:        ELSE
209:            PRINT "No";
210:            LET TEXT.OUT = TEXT.OUT + "/WID.C=0"
211:        END IF
212:        CALL DWINDOW("")
213: RETURN            'End of SETPRINT
214: '                         'End of source code
```

Listing 7-3

remaining MENU() responses are analyzed by SELECT CASE blocks (e.g., lines 68–99). Since the possible responses for each SELECT CASE block are known, there is no error-prevention requirement for a CASE ELSE statement within the block. However, the executable code is shorter (and hence faster) if CASE ELSE is used for the final CASE statement in each block, rather than an explicit constant (e.g., line 95).

SYSPRO is structured as closely to a straight line as seems reasonable. Only GOSUB subroutines are used, to take advantage of the global variables. Two are multiuse; the other two are called on from only one place in the program, but are separated from the in-line code for readability.

SETCOLOR (lines 114–149) consists of a nested pair of bottom-tested loops. The single label in line 114 serves to identify the start of the GOSUB subroutine and also the start of each loop. SETCOLOR will be repeated automatically if the color choice is the same for foreground and background colors (lines 130–135) or on demand if the color choice is not pleasing to the user (lines 136–147). While the whole substructure *could* have replaced the "GOSUB SETCOLOR" in line 57 (deleting *only* the RETURN in line 149), I felt the resulting code would be too difficult for a reader to follow without a road map.

SETPRINT (lines 159–213) is a single-use subroutine to obtain the characteristics of a printer not listed in the printer menu.

The entire program operates within text "windows" defined for the DWINDOW subroutines, requiring certain precautions to prevent the BASIC support routines from inadvertently scrolling the display.

All PRINT statements are terminated by a semicolon (line 111). Blank rows can be produced either by calling DWINDOW with a null string argument (line 42) or by increasing the value of ROW by one (not shown). The former method will always ensure a blank row; the latter will not if the original value of ROW was beyond the last row in the window.

No INPUT statements are used. Entries requiring the Enter key (even those asking for a single integer) use "LINE INPUT" (with a semicolon) to a string variable, to prevent BASIC's <CR><LF> line-end pair and any possibility of its "?Redo from start" error message. The corresponding prompt message is displayed with a DWINDOW call (e.g., lines 191–193).

Single-character yes/no responses are read with the INPUT$(1) statement and interpreted with an IF-block (e.g., lines 141–148). You may wish to change my yes/no conventions to suit your own idiosyncrasies. I accept y, Y, or a <SP> as "yes"; any other keystroke is "no."

The final output of SYSPRO is the SYSTEM.PRO file written to the default directory. The WRITE# statement is used (lines 96–98) to surround the entire file record with quotation marks, so it can be read by a single INPUT# command, irrespective of the number of pseudo switches it contains.

```
                 Building a System Profile File

            Enter unlisted printer characteristics

           Enter control sequences as decimal ASCII values.
  If there is more than one value in string, separate them by commas.
              For example: Enter '<ESC> A' as '27,65'
    Does printer have an initialization sequence (press y/n)? Yes
    Enter initialization string:  27,9,1,27,57

          PageOffset is number of <LF>s to move paper from
          perforations at tear bar to print at top of page

   Enter value of PageOffset (may be zero): 0
   Enter number of characters in normal print line: 102
   Can printer print in condensed type (y/n)?: No

   Select disposition of profile: Write SYSTEM.PRO file
```

Figure 7 - 2
Writing SYSTEM.PRO file for Qume printer

Bringing Up SYSPRO.BAS

SYSPRO is truly a "what you see is what there is" program, so trace debuggers are of no help. I wrote and tested it in sequential stages, one menu at a time. If the display after each addition was not as expected, I searched the source-code listing until I found the cause of the error, made the correction, and retried the new code.

If you are testing on a system with a mono or composite mono display, you can select "Color" and enter reverse video (black on white) to test the SETCOLOR and CLEAR.WIN subroutines. Even if you have one of the listed printers, you can test the SETPRINT routine for appearance and results by describing a dummy printer. Figure 7-2 is a copy of my display screen after entering the characteristics of my Qume printer. The initializing string shown moves the print head to the left end of the carriage and sets the left margin at that point.

The final proof of the pudding is to write several different SYSTEM.PRO files to the default drive, reading each one with DOS's TYPE

```
"/CFG= 7/CBG= 1/INIT=27,9,1,27,57/POFF=0/WID.N=102/WID.C=0"
```

Figure 7 - 3
SYSTEM.PRO file for Qume printer at 12 pitch

command. Figure 7-3 is a copy of SYSTEM.PRO for my PC-XT with the EGA/ECD and Qume printer.

Once you have SYSPRO implemented, construct a SYSTEM.PRO file for your working system. Put a permanent copy in a directory in the PATH environment string where FINDFILE can find it.

Potential Enhancements

The most obvious enhancement to SYSPRO would be to add printers to its list. If you have access to printers not presently on the menu list, it isn't difficult to add them. Insert the new printer name(s) in the PRINTER entry DATA list (lines 27–29) between the last listed printer name shown and "Printer not listed," adjusting the value of ENTRIES in line 64 accordingly. If the total number of printer entries exceeds fifteen, adjust the DIM statement for TEXT() (line 17). Insert the new printer CASEs into the printer select SELECT CASE block between lines 80 and 81, leaving the CASE ELSE to handle unlisted printers.

You might wish to make SYSPRO a little more "bulletproof" by guarding against inadvertent choices due to extraneous symbols in the type-ahead buffer. You can flush the buffer with a

```
WHILE INKEY$ <> "": WEND
```

before every line requesting keyboard input. If you wish to be doubly safe, you could insert similar safeguards in MENU.BAS (Listing 6-7). However, think carefully before you insert these bits of "user friendly" coding. While beginners might appreciate being saved from their own foolishness, experienced users prefer the ability to preenter information — even menu choices — once they are familiar with the program.

LIST.BAS (Version 2.0)

The first program I wrote using the SYSTEM.PRO file was version 2.0 of LIST.BAS (Listing 7-4). If you compare this listing with the previous version (Listing 5-5), you will see that the rewrite was primarily by addition — the great majority of the previous code remains unchanged.

This self-customizing version of LIST allows listing without headers (the /H switch) and/or without pseudo line numbers (the /N switch). The longest text line is centered in the available printing width. The body of the listing is printed in condensed type (if available) when the longest line is over eighty characters. Listing is suppressed if the longest line is longer than the printer (or paper width) can accommodate.

In what follows, I will discuss the additions in the order I made them. All line-number references are to Listing 7-4.

Parsing SYSTEM.PRO

Delete the "Printer characteristics" constants in the old version and substitute the default display and printer constants (lines 24–35). These values, describing a "plain vanilla" eighty-character-per-line printer, will be used if the SYSTEM.PRO file cannot be found and there are no equivalent command-line switch entries.

The "startup" code, after RESTART, has been modified. The prompt now indicates that switches are acceptable, and the former "INPUT" is now a "LINE INPUT" since keyed switches may contain commas (lines 83–84). The <filespec> is separated from any appended switches, and any white space between the actual <filespec> and the first switch is deleted (lines 87–98). The trailing <SP> or <HT> removal loop (lines 96–98) could have been replaced by a single RTRIM$ statement, but RTRIM$ deletes only <SP> symbols, starting from the rightmost end of the string, and will quit if it finds an <HT>. The last insert in the main program, for this phase, is the "GOSUB PARSER" in line 115.

PARSER (lines 173–223) is an example of *defensive programming* against many common input errors. PARSER is not upset by blank spaces

```
 1: '****************************************************************************
 2: '                     LIST.BAS (Version 2.0)                              *
 3: '      LIST lists ASCII source-code files using display and printer       *
 4: ' characteristics obtained from the SYSTEM.PRO file as written by         *
 5: ' SYSPRO.BAS.  LIST prints 55 lines per page, supplying page headers      *
 6: ' and pseudo line numbers.                                                *
 7: '        Call with:  LIST <filespec>[/N][/H]                              *
 8: ' where /N causes the pseudo line numbers to be omitted, and /H          *
 9: ' eliminates page headers, printing 60 lines per page.                    *
10: '             Written by M. L. Lesser, October 1, 1986                    *
11: '             Modified to version 1.1, November 23, 1986                  *
12: '             Modified to version 2.0, January 23, 1987                   *
13: '             Modified for Microsoft BC version 4.0, 12/1/87              *
14: '****************************************************************************
15: '    Setup (nonexecutable statements):
16:     DEFINT A-Z
17:     DEFSTR D,F,H,R,S,T
18:     DIM COMP, COUNT, FILE, FILENAME, LINE.NUM, L.NUM, LINE.ONE, LONGEST
19:     DIM MARGIN, P.HEAD, PAGE.NUM, PAGE.WIDTH.C, PAGE.WIDTH.N
20:     DIM PAGE.OFFSET, SWITCH, SWITCHES, S.COND, S.INIT, S.NORM, TEST
21:     DIM TEXT, TIME, TOKEN
22: '    $INCLUDE: 'PQB.BI'
23:
24: '   Default system characteristics:
25:     CFG = 7: CBG = 0                    'Standard video display
26:     PAGE.WIDTH.N = 80                   '8.0-inch line at 10 cpi
27:     PAGE.WIDTH.C = 0                    'No condensed print size
28:     PAGE.OFFSET = 0                     'No initial paper offset
29:     S.INIT = ""                         'No initialization sequence
30:     S.NORM = ""                         'No "normal print" sequence
31:     S.COND = ""                         'No "condensed print" sequence
32: '   Default listing style:
33:     COMP = 0                            'Not printing in condensed type
34:     P.HEAD = -1                         'Printing with page headers
35:     L.NUM = -1                          'Printing line numbers
36:
37: '   Defined header function:
38: DEF FNHEADER                    'Normal header
39:     STATIC PAGE.NUM                         'Static local variable
40:     LET PAGE.NUM = PAGE.NUM + 1
41:     LET FNHEADER = "Listing page" + STR$(PAGE.NUM)
42:     CALL PCONTROL(S.NORM)               'Set for normal type size
43:     LPRINT                              'One blank line at top
44:     LET LINE.ONE = -1                   'Set "first line" flag
45:     IF P.HEAD THEN                      'If printing page headers
46:         LET MARGIN = (PAGE.WIDTH.N - 80)/2     'Margin for headers
47:         LET COUNT = 0
48: ' Print the header
49:         LPRINT TAB(MARGIN + 1);                 'First header line
50:         LPRINT "Listed on " DATE$;
51:         LPRINT TAB(80 + MARGIN - LEN(FILE)) FILE
52:         LPRINT TAB(MARGIN + 8) "at " TIME;      'Second header line
53:         LPRINT TAB(MARGIN + 73) "page" PAGE.NUM
54:         CALL PSKIP(3)                           'Three more blanks
55:     ELSE                                'No headers
56:         LET COUNT = -5                  'Will produce 60-line page
```

Listing 7 - 4 (continued)

```
57:         END IF
58: ' Reset line width for body:
59:     IF COMP THEN                          'If printing in condensed type
60:         CALL PCONTROL(S.COND)             'Set condensed typeface
61:         LET MARGIN = (PAGE.WIDTH.C - LONGEST)/2
62:     ELSE
63:         LET MARGIN = (PAGE.WIDTH.N - LONGEST)/2
64:     END IF
65: END DEF
66:
67: DEF FNDUMHEAD                        'Dummy header for analysis
68:     STATIC PAGE.NUM                       'Static local variable
69:     LET PAGE.NUM = PAGE.NUM + 1
70:     LET FNDUMHEAD = "Analyzing page" + STR$(PAGE.NUM)
71:     LET LINE.ONE = -1                     'Set "first line" flag
72:     IF P.HEAD THEN                        'If printing page headers
73:         LET COUNT = 0
74:     ELSE                                  'No headers
75:         LET COUNT = -5                    'Will produce 60-line page
76:     END IF
77: END DEF
78:
79: '  Main program:
80:     LET FILE = COMMAND$                   '<filespec> from command line
81: RESTART:                                  'Restart point if no file found
82:     IF LEN(FILE) = 0 THEN                 'If no or incorrect <filespec>
83:         PRINT "Enter '<filespec>[/N][/H]' for listing:  ";
84:         LINE INPUT FILE                   'Enter <filespec> and switches
85:         LET FILE = UCASE$(FILE)           ' and make all caps
86:     END IF
87: ' Separate any appended switches:
88:     LET I = INSTR(FILE,"/")
89:     IF I THEN
90:         LET SWITCHES = MID$(FILE,I)       'SWITCHES has leading "/"
91:         LET FILE = LEFT$(FILE,I-1)
92:     ELSE
93:         LET SWITCHES = ""                 'To delete any earlier entry
94:     END IF
95: ' Delete any <SP> or <HT> on end of FILE:
96:     WHILE RIGHT$(FILE,1) = " " OR RIGHT$(FILE,1) = CHR$(9)
97:         LET FILE = LEFT$(FILE,LEN(FILE)-1)
98:     WEND
99: ' Add .BAS if no <ext> on FILE
100:     IF INSTR(FILE,".") = 0 _              'If no <ext> on <filespec>
101:         THEN LET FILE = FILE + ".BAS"     '  add ".BAS"
102:     LET FILENAME = FILE                   'Input <filespec> to find
103:     CALL MAKNAME(FILE)                    '<filename> without path
104:     CALL FINDFILE(FILENAME)               'Locate directory with FILENAME
105:     CLS                                   'Clean off earlier messages
106:     IF LEN(FILENAME) = 0 THEN             '<filespec> not found
107:         PRINT "I cannot find " CHR$(34) FILE CHR$(34);
108:         PRINT " - Please try again."
109:         LET FILE = ""                     'Clean off to try again
110:         GOTO RESTART
111:     ELSE
112:         OPEN FILENAME FOR INPUT AS #1
```

Listing 7 - 4 (continued)

```
113:        END IF
114:  '  Customize for printer and list first page header:
115:        GOSUB PARSER
116:        GOSUB ANALYZE                        'Set print style
117:        LET TIME = TIMESTAMP
118:        WIDTH LPRINT 255                     'Bug killer
119:        CALL PCONTROL(S.INIT)
120:        IF PAGE.OFFSET THEN                  'If using IBM Graphics printer
121:            CALL PSKIP(PAGE.OFFSET)          '   set print line at top of page
122:            CALL PAGELEN(66)                 '   and reset form-feed point
123:        END IF
124:        PRINT "Listing the file: " FILE
125:        PRINT CHR$(9) FNHEADER                'First page header
126:  '  Read and list file:
127:        WHILE NOT EOF(1)                     'As long as there is any text left
128:            LINE INPUT #1, TEXT              'Read a line of text
129:            LET LINE.NUM = LINE.NUM + 1      'Update line number
130:            LET COUNT = COUNT + 1            'Update page line count
131:            IF LEFT$(TEXT,1) = CHR$(12) THEN     'If first byte is <FF>
132:                LET TEXT = MID$(TEXT,2)      '   delete <FF>
133:                IF NOT LINE.ONE THEN         'If not first line
134:                    CALL PFORM               '   eject page
135:                    PRINT CHR$(9) FNHEADER   '   list new header
136:                END IF
137:            END IF
138:            LPRINT TAB(MARGIN + 1);
139:            IF L.NUM THEN                        'Line number switch on
140:                LPRINT USING "#####:  "; LINE.NUM;
141:            END IF
142:            CALL TABBER                      'Detab text line
143:            LPRINT TEXT                      '   and list it
144:            IF COUNT = 55 AND NOT EOF(1) THEN    'If 55 lines on page
145:                CALL PFORM                   '   Skip to top of next page
146:                PRINT CHR$(9) FNHEADER       '   and list new header
147:            END IF
148:            CALL EMERGEX                     'Exit on Ctrl-C or Ctrl-Break
149:            LET LINE.ONE = 0                 'Turn off flag after one line
150:        WEND                                 'Continue until file listed
151:        CALL PFORM                           'Eject remainder of last page
152:        IF PAGE.OFFSET THEN                  'If graphics printer
153:            CALL PSKIP(66 - PAGE.OFFSET)     '   skip to tearbar
154:            CALL PAGELEN(66)                 '   and reset top of form
155:        END IF
156:  END                    'End of main program
157:
158:  '  Compiled subroutine to expand <HT>s to every eighth column:
159:  SUB TABBER STATIC
160:        SHARED TEXT
161:
162:        LET I = INSTR(TEXT,CHR$(9))          'Find first <HT>
163:        WHILE I <> 0                         'As long there are any <HT>s
164:            LET REST = MID$(TEXT,I+1)        'Unexpanded portion of TEXT
165:            LET TEXT = LEFT$(TEXT,I-1)       'Expanded portion of TEXT
166:            LET N = 8 - (I-1) MOD 8          'No. of <SP>s to insert for <HT>
167:            LET TEXT = TEXT + SPACE$(N) + REST
168:            LET I = INSTR(TEXT,CHR$(9))      'Any more to deal with?
```

Listing 7 - 4 (continued)

```
169:        WEND                                    'Continue until done
170:  END SUB
171:
172:  ' GOSUB subroutines in order of first call:
173:  PARSER: 'Customize program for system and switches:
174:        LET FILENAME = "SYSTEM.PRO"
175:        CALL FINDFILE(FILENAME)
176:        IF LEN(FILENAME) THEN                    'If SYSTEM.PRO exists
177:            OPEN FILENAME FOR INPUT AS #2
178:            INPUT #2, TEXT
179:            CLOSE #2
180:            LET SWITCHES = TEXT + SWITCHES  'Command-line switches last
181:        END IF
182:  ' Parse SWITCHES, setting all system characteristics accordingly:
183:        WHILE LEN(SWITCHES)                    'As long as any left:
184:            LET I = INSTR(2,SWITCHES,"/")   'Check for more switches
185:            IF I THEN                                'If more
186:                LET SWITCH = LEFT$(SWITCHES,I-1)    ' separate off first
187:                LET SWITCHES = MID$(SWITCHES,I)
188:            ELSE
189:                LET SWITCH = SWITCHES
190:                LET SWITCHES = ""
191:            END IF
192:            LET J = INSTR(SWITCH,"=")          'Not all switches have "="
193:            IF J THEN
194:                LET TEMP = MID$(SWITCH,J+1)            'Possible control string
195:                LET I = VAL(TEMP)                      'Possible switch value
196:            END IF
197:            LET TEST = LEFT$(SWITCH,6)
198:  '   Check in order of default system characteristics:
199:            IF LEFT$(TEST,4) = "/CFG" THEN          'Set foreground flag
200:                LET CFG = I
201:            ELSEIF LEFT$(TEST,4) = "/CBG" THEN      'Set background flag
202:                LET CBG = I
203:            ELSEIF TEST = "/WID.N" THEN             'Normal print line
204:                LET PAGE.WIDTH.N = I
205:            ELSEIF TEST = "/WID.C" THEN             'Condensed print line
206:                LET PAGE.WIDTH.C = I
207:            ELSEIF TEST = "/POFF=" THEN             'Initial page offset
208:                LET PAGE.OFFSET = I
209:            ELSEIF TEST = "/INIT=" THEN             'Control string for
210:                LET S.INIT = TEMP                   '    initialization
211:            ELSEIF TEST = "/NORM=" THEN             'Control string for
212:                LET S.NORM = TEMP                   '    normal print
213:            ELSEIF TEST = "/COND=" THEN             'Control string for
214:                LET S.COND = TEMP                   '    condensed print
215:            ELSEIF LEFT$(TEST,2) = "/H" THEN        'No page headers
216:                LET P.HEAD = 0
217:            ELSEIF LEFT$(TEST,2) = "/N" THEN        'No line numbers
218:                LET L.NUM = 0
219:            END IF
220:        WEND
221:        COLOR CFG,CBG
222:        CLS
223:  RETURN              'End of parser GOSUB subroutine
224:
```

Listing 7 - 4   (continued)

```
225:   ANALYZE:          'Find longest line, set typeface flag:
226:       PRINT "Analyzing " FILE " for listing with ";
227:       IF NOT P.HEAD THEN PRINT "no ";
228:       PRINT "page headers"
229:       PRINT TAB(25) "and ";
230:       IF NOT L.NUM THEN PRINT "no ";
231:       PRINT "pseudo line numbers."
232:       LET PAGE.NUM = 0
233:       PRINT CHR$(9) FNDUMHEAD                'Dummy header
234:       WHILE NOT EOF(1)                       'As long as there is any text left
235:           LINE INPUT #1, TEXT               'Read a line of text
236:           LET LINE.NUM = LINE.NUM + 1       'Update line number
237:           LET COUNT = COUNT + 1             'Update page line count
238:           IF LEFT$(TEXT,1) = CHR$(12) THEN          'If first byte is <FF>
239:               LET TEXT = MID$(TEXT,2)       '  delete <FF>
240:               IF NOT LINE.ONE THEN          'If not first line
241:                   PRINT CHR$(9) FNDUMHEAD   '  count another page
242:               END IF
243:           END IF
244:           CALL TABBER                       'Detab text line
245:           LET I = LEN(TEXT)
246:           IF L.NUM THEN LET I = I + 8
247:           IF I > LONGEST THEN LET LONGEST = I
248:           IF COUNT = 55 AND NOT EOF(1) THEN    'If 55 lines on page,
249:               PRINT CHR$(9) FNDUMHEAD       '  start new page
250:           END IF
251:           CALL EMERGEX                      'Exit on Ctrl-C or Ctrl-Break
252:           LET LINE.ONE = 0                  'Turn off flag after one line
253:       WEND                                  'Continue until file analyzed
254:       SEEK #1, 1                            '"Rewind" file for next use
255: ' Establish typeface for body of listing:
256:       IF LONGEST > 80 AND LONGEST <= PAGE.WIDTH.C THEN
257:           LET COMP = -1                     'Print in compressed type
258:       END IF
259:       PRINT
260:       IF (NOT COMP) AND (LONGEST > PAGE.WIDTH.N) THEN
261:           PRINT "Cannot list " FILE " because longest line has";
262:           PRINT LONGEST "symbols."
263:           PRINT "Terminating program."
264:           END
265:       ELSE
266:           PRINT FILE " will be listed in ";
267:           IF COMP THEN
268:               PRINT "condensed type."
269:           ELSE
270:               PRINT "normal type."
271:           END IF
272:           PRINT "There are" LINE.NUM "lines.";
273:           PRINT "  The longest line has" LONGEST "symbols."
274:           PRINT "Is this OK (y/n)? ";
275:           LET TOKEN = INPUT$(1)
276:           IF TOKEN = "y" OR TOKEN = "Y" OR TOKEN = " " THEN
277:               PRINT "Yes"
278:           ELSE
279:               PRINT "No"
280:               PRINT "Terminating program."
```

Listing 7 - 4 (continued)

```
281:              END
282:           END IF
283:        END IF
284:        LET LINE.NUM = 0                    'Initialize for listing
285:        PRINT
286: RETURN                      'End of analyze GOSUB subroutine
287: '  End of source code
```

Listing 7 - 4

between switches, nor by switches it cannot recognize. If PARSER recognizes the same switch more than once, it "remembers" only the last value entered.

If PARSER finds a SYSTEM.PRO file, it places that file in the SWITCHES string *in front of* any switches entered with <filespec>. Thus, any switch in SYSTEM.PRO can be overridden by the user from the keyboard. I use this facility to get "fast" debugging listings on my Proprinter XL by entering a new "/INIT=" string that doesn't turn on NLQ (near-letter-quality) printing.

PARSER peels off and checks one switch at a time in a WHILE...WEND loop (lines 183–220). It uses an IF-block (lines 199–219) to implement the switches and ignores any it can't recognize. You may wish to add an ELSE "safety" code block to signal unrecognizable switches and send the program back to RESTART. If so, don't forget to CLOSE the open files and reset FILE to a null string as part of the ELSE code.

I tested this phase of the program by inserting a block of temporary debugging code between lines 223 and 224 (not shown). My debugging code displayed the final values of the "system characteristics" constants, followed by an END statement. PARSER was tested by using SYSPRO to "invent" printer characteristics, and also by entering command-line switches.

Line Number and Header Switches

The final proof of the parser is to make sure the default print characteristics are altered. I edited the FNHEADER defined function as shown in lines 38–65, to print the headers in normal type style even if the body of the listing is in condensed type (not tested in this phase), and to list files without headers if the /H switch is used. The no-header switch was added for listing MASM <filename>.LST files, which include their own page headers as part of the file. The no-header maximum line count per page is increased to sixty by initializing COUNT to -5.[2] The LINE.ONE flag prevents blank pages when the first line on a new page contains a <FF> symbol.

I modified the segment of code "customizing" the printer by substituting the "CALL PCONTROL(S.INIT)" for the IF-block that previously checked for a Proprinter (line 119), and by inserting the temporary statement "let longest = 80" where the final "GOSUB ANALYZE" would appear (line 116).

The modifications to the "read and list file" segment enable the /N switch to delete pseudo line numbers (lines 139–140) and the LINE.ONE flag to prevent blank pages (lines 133–136, 149).

This version of LIST can list itself as it exists to this point. Try it with and without headers and/or pseudo line numbers. You can minimize the wasted paper by using the emergency exit as soon as the display shows page 2 has been started.

Self-Analysis

The final portion of added code inserts the ANALYZE subroutine (lines 225–286) and its corresponding FNDUMHEAD dummy header function (lines 67–77). The "GOSUB ANALYZE" statement replaces the dummy "longest" assignment in line 116.

Use your text editor to copy the body of FNHEADER (lines 38– 65) to become the body of FNDUMHEAD. Then edit the function code to that shown in lines 67–77. In a similar fashion, lines 234– 253 of the ANALYZE subroutine are based on an edited copy of lines 127–150. The remainder of ANALYZE displays information to the user and requests permission to list the file. After ANALYZE has read the entire source-code file, that file is "rewound" with a SEEK statement (line 254) to be read again for the actual listing operation.

Again, use SYSPRO as a driver to set up various printer capabilities to test ANALYZE. The printer is not exercised if you answer ANALYZE's final question with "no." Figure 7-4 is a copy of my display screen after analyzing the assembler listing file PRINT.LST (version 2.0) for a Proprinter XL. PRINT.LST is obtained by assembling PRINT.ASM with the command:

```
Analyzing PRINT.LST for listing with no page headers
                        and no pseudo line numbers.
          Analyzing page 1
          Analyzing page 2
          Analyzing page 3
          Analyzing page 4
          Analyzing page 5

PRINT.LST will be listed in condensed type.
There are 222 lines.  The longest line has 105 symbols.
Is this OK (y/n)?  No
Terminating program.
```

Figure 7 - 4
Testing the ANALYZE subroutine

```
                MASM PRINT,,;
```

Replace the original prologue of LIST.BAS, and test this final version by listing itself. Test the automatic centering facility by listing PQB.IDX with the /N switch. If you have a printer that can print in condensed type, test the dual-mode print capability by listing an assembler listing file.

A Useful Enhancement

It is very frustrating to be listing a long file and have the paper jam on the next to the last page. It is even more frustrating if your only LIST utility always has to start over at the beginning of the file. I leave it as an exercise for the reader to modify version 2.0 of LIST.BAS by adding an optional "/P=n" switch causing LIST to start printing at page n instead of at page 1.

Notes

---

1. The Proprinter XL does not include moving the print head to the new left margin as a portion of changing that margin setting. You must add a <CR> [,13] to the margin-setting control string.
2. The default listing-file PAGE length for Microsoft MASM is fifty-nine lines.

Chapter 8

The SHELL Game

There are three ways to execute a second program from a compiled QBASIC program: SHELL, RUN, and CHAIN. SHELL transfers control temporarily from the parent program to any executable file (COM, EXE, or BAT), returning control to the parent after the child finishes executing. Although RUN executes only EXE files, it requires considerably less memory than does SHELL, so is the preferred construct where it can be used. CHAIN serves no useful purpose in a compiled environment.

SHELL is particularly well suited for stacked job utilities too complex for normal "batch" operation. The example in this chapter is DOLIB.BAS, an automatic library update utility. SHELL is also useful for running a single second program if RUN is not feasible. DOBACK.BAS provides automatic backup for files changed by a proprietary file- maintenance program, calling an assembled subroutine to read the volume label on the backup diskette before SHELLing XCOPY.

As furnished with BASIC, RUN does not allow any information to be passed to the child program except by writing and reading a file. An assembled extension permits the parent program to pass the equivalent of command-line input to all compiled QBASIC programs and to many proprietary EXE programs. COMPILE.BAS reads a QBASIC source-code

```
cls
print "total free space is" fre(-1) "bytes"
print
shell "chkdsk"
```

Figure 8 - 1
SHELTEST.BAS, a SHELL demonstration

file, looking for both a $INCLUDE statement and an error trap, copies
PQB.BI to the default directory and/or supplies the /e switch (if necessary), and then RUNs BC.EXE to compile the program.

SHELL

While very flexible and highly useful when no other construct will serve,
SHELL suffers from two severe drawbacks: it is expensive in terms of
memory space required, and it does not allow for direct communication
from the child to the parent process.

SHELL operates by loading a second copy of the command processor (COMMAND.COM) into the available memory space and then turning control over to it to run the "command line" given as the SHELL
argument. If there is no command line in the SHELL statement, the second
command processor remains in control until you return to your original
program by entering "exit" on the second processor's command line.

SHELL requires at least enough available memory space to load the
entire command processor — both the resident and transient portions. If
there isn't enough space to load the command processor, an attempt to
execute SHELL will return an "Out of memory" error interrupt. If your
program uses SHELL, it should clean up memory space to the extent possible before executing the SHELL statement. ERASE all dynamic arrays
no longer needed and CLOSE all unneeded files.

You can get an idea of the upper limit of the space you have in your
system for running SHELLed programs by compiling and linking the lit-

tle demonstration program shown in Figure 8-1. You cannot SHELL any child program requiring more available memory than shown by the CHKDSK display. In fact, most real programs take up much more space than does SHELTEST, so most child programs must be much smaller than indicated.

Before running SHELTEST, run CHKDSK directly to get the "base case" statistics for your system as it is configured. The difference in CHKDSK's "available memory" between your base case and the SHEL-TEST display is the "lost" memory space — memory being used by the parent program and by the resident portion of the second command processor.

If you run SHELTEST under the development environment (QB.EXE), you will find you have "lost" about 229K of available memory. Running SHELTEST after compiling with BC.EXE for stand-alone (with the /o switch) shows a loss of about 37K. But running SHELTEST when compiled in the default mode shows only about 15K has been lost; the amount of "available memory" shown by the SHELLed CHKDSK is greater than the total amount of free memory space shown in the first line of SHELTEST's display!

Programs using the SHELL statement are the only programs that run in less total memory space when compiled for the run-time module than when compiled to run alone. However, the decrease in required memory space to run the program is paid for by a performance loss. The QBASIC support code allows the run-time module to be overwritten by the SHELLed command processor and child program, and then reloads BRUN40.EXE from its disk on return to the parent program.

Once the second command processor is in control, the parent program cannot receive any direct messages from that processor or from the child program. For example, if the second command processor doesn't have enough memory to load the child program, the "Program too big to fit in memory" message will be displayed and control will return immediately to the parent program. If you need to be sure that the SHELLed program operated successfully, you have to find a way around this impasse.

The displayed output from a SHELLed program will remain on the screen when the parent program finishes unless it scrolls off the screen or either it or the parent uses a graphics mode.[1] The only problem in keeping normal text messages from disappearing on program end is BASIC's idiosyncrasy of scrolling at display row 24, while DOS (and programs written in most other languages) scroll at display row 25. Thus, the first "PRINT <message>" statement after a return from a SHELL statement might be in row 25, and will be blanked out when the program ENDs. The antidote for this occasional problem is to execute a no-message PRINT before any meaningful display, after a return from SHELL.

COLORIT.BAS

Since none of the three programs described in this chapter use the printer, it seems unreasonable to have to write a parser subroutine for each merely to read SYSTEM.PRO (if it exists) to find the user-preferred display attribute. Instead, I wrote a compiled subroutine that can be used in all such programs.

COLORIT.BAS (Listing 8-1) hunts for a SYSTEM.PRO file. If it can't find one, it resets the foreground and background colors to BASIC's default color scheme (lines 23–24). If COLORIT does find SYSTEM.PRO, it parses the record, looking only for the foreground and background colors. Note the COMMON declaration in line 18. The two integers are returned only if the calling program also declares COMMON /COLORS/.

Stacked Job Utilities

A *stacked job utility* is a program that runs a sequence of (usually) related programs to accomplish a particular task without having to reenter the command line for each program. Some people use stacked job utilities to let the system run a series of tasks while they go out for a cup of coffee. I use stacked job utilities to avoid having to enter redundant data, thus avoiding intermittent problems associated with typographical and other input errors.

The easiest stacked job utility to use is the one built into the command processor. It "runs" the jobs described by the sequence of command lines contained in a BAT file. The AGAIN.BAT file shown in Figure 6-3 is typical. The batch functions allow some decision making based on the

```
 1:  '****************************************************************
 2:  '                        COLORIT.BAS                           *
 3:  '     COLORIT is a compiled subroutine to be linked to QBASIC programs  *
 4:  ' that do not use a printer, so need only the display characteristics  *
 5:  ' data in the SYSTEM.PRO file.                                 *
 6:  '     Call with:  CALL COLORIT.  If the SYSTEM.PRO file is found, the   *
 7:  ' screen will be cleared to the stored attribute.  If no SYSTEM.PRO     *
 8:  ' file is found, the screen will be cleared to the default BASIC        *
 9:  ' attribute.  The color values used are available to the calling        *
10:  ' program in COMMON /COLORS/.                                  *
11:  '           Written by M. L. Lesser, February 1, 1987          *
12:  '           Modified for Microsoft BC version 4.0, 12-4-87     *
13:  '****************************************************************
14:
15:      DEFINT C,I
16:      DEFSTR F,S,T
17:  ' Color values will be returned if calling program also declares common:
18:      COMMON SHARED /COLORS/ CBG, CFG
19:
20:  SUB COLORIT STATIC
21:      LET FILE = "SYSTEM.PRO"
22:      CALL FINDFILE(FILE)
23:      IF LEN(FILE) = 0 THEN              'If no SYSTEM.PRO file, use
24:          LET CFG =7: CBG = 0           '  BASIC's default display mode
25:      ELSE
26:          ITEM = FREEFILE
27:          OPEN FILE FOR INPUT AS #ITEM
28:          INPUT #ITEM, TEXT
29:          CLOSE #ITEM
30:  ' Parse TEXT for display color values:
31:          WHILE LEN(TEXT)                   'As long as any left:
32:              LET I = INSTR(2,TEXT,"/")     'Check for more switches
33:              IF I THEN                         'If more
34:                  LET SWITCH = LEFT$(TEXT,I-1)   ' separate off first
35:                  LET TEXT = MID$(TEXT,I)
36:              ELSE
37:                  LET SWITCH = TEXT
38:                  LET TEXT = ""
39:              END IF
40:              IF LEFT$(SWITCH,4) = "/CFG" THEN     'Set foreground flag
41:                  LET CFG = VAL(MID$(SWITCH,6))
42:              ELSEIF LEFT$(SWITCH,4) = "/CBG" THEN     'Set background flag
43:                  LET CBG = VAL(MID$(SWITCH,6))
44:              END IF
45:          WEND
46:      END IF
47:      COLOR CFG,CBG
48:      CLS                                        'Reset entire display
49:  END SUB
```

Listing 8 - 1

presence or absence of named files, whether or not a previous job "returned" an error code, etc.

The various MAKE programs are more powerful stacked job utilities. In addition to interpreting the set of batchlike commands in a special MAK file, MAKE can expand user-written macros and make decisions on the basis of the date of file creation. MAKE utilities are used extensively by software producers who are juggling a large number of component modules to build several different products and wish to be sure that all "dependent" object and executable files are based on the latest version of their component source modules.

The power of a do-it-yourself stacked job utility is limited only by your imagination. I write them when I wish to make execution decisions based on the *content* of an ASCII file. When DOLIB is adding a compiled module to my private library, it reads the source code looking for an error trap and compiles with the /x switch if necessary.

DOLIB.BAS

DOLIB.BAS (Listing 8-2) automatically updates the private library, PQB.LIB, by adding (or replacing) a named module. The instructions for using DOLIB are given in the listing prologue.

The primary assumption in writing DOLIB was that the procedure module has been thoroughly tested, so there will be no error messages from either the assembler or the compiler. Once DOLIB finds the source file, the only further check is whether an object file is produced each time the assembler or compiler is SHELLed. If there is no object file, DOLIB assumes there is not enough memory space, and the program is terminated with an appropriate error message.

DOLIB has almost a straight sequential structure except for the two GOSUB subroutines to either assemble or compile the module, and the excursions into error traps if the necessary files are not found where they are expected. When I implemented DOLIB, I did so incrementally, carefully testing each phase before I went to the next.

After the sign-on is displayed, DOLIB checks the command line for input, displaying a prompt that asks for the proper input if the command line is empty (lines 33–37). The input source command is checked for the presence of any switch. A switch (nominally /r) tells DOLIB to replace the module in the library rather than to add it (lines 38–45). The module name is put into lowercase with the built-in LCASE$ function and any <path> entered with the module name is deleted with the private library subroutine MAKNAME (lines 46–47). (My first implementation version

The SHELL Game

```
1:  '********************************************************************
2:  '                          DOLIB.BAS                               *
3:  '       DOLIB is an automatic update program for adding (or replacing) *
4:  ' named modules to the private searchable library PQB.LIB.         *
5:  '      The command-line call is "DOLIB [<path>]<modname>[/R]"      *
6:  '       where <modname> is the name of the module to be added.     *
7:  '              /R is a switch to replace an existing <modname>.     *
8:  '              <path> is required if the source-code file for       *
9:  '                     <modname> is not in a directory in the PATH   *
10: '                     environment string.                          *
11: '      If the source file for <modname> is <modname>.ASM, DOLIB will be *
12: ' assembled before adding it to the library.  If the source is     *
13: ' <modname>.BAS, the file will be compiled.  If a BAS file contains a *
14: ' '$INCLUDE statement, the PQB.BI file will be copied to the default *
15: ' directory.  If the source file contains error trapping, the      *
16: ' compilation will be made with the /X switch.                     *
17: '      The original version of PQB.LIB is left unchanged.  It is copied *
18: ' to the default directory, and the copy is updated.               *
19: '              Written by M. L. Lesser, February 11, 1987          *
20: '              Modified for Microsoft BC version 4.0, 12-4-87       *
21: '                  Compiled with the /O/E switches                 *
22: '********************************************************************
23:
24:      DEFINT A-Z
25:      DEFSTR D,F,M,T
26:
27:      DIM DIRECTORY, FILE, I, INCLUDE.FLAG, MODOP, MODNAME, TEXT
28:
29:      CALL COLORIT                               'Set display attributes
30:      PRINT TAB(22) "Private Library Update Program"
31:      PRINT STRING$(80,"-")
32:      LET TEXT = COMMAND$
33: ' Make sure there is a <modname> to add:
34:      WHILE LEN(TEXT) = 0                        'While no source file
35:          LINE INPUT "Enter '[<path>]<modname>[/R]' for update: ", TEXT
36:          LET TEXT = UCASE$(TEXT)
37:      WEND
38: ' Set up library module instruction:
39:      LET I = INSTR(TEXT,"/")
40:      IF I THEN                                  'Any command-line switch
41:          LET TEXT = LEFT$(TEXT,I-1)      '    will be interpreted as
42:          LET MODOP = "-+"                '-   requesting replacement
43:      ELSE
44:          LET MODOP = "+"
45:      END IF
46:      LET MODNAME = LCASE$(TEXT)                 '<modname> is always lowercase
47:      CALL MAKNAME(MODNAME)                      'Remove any <path> string
48: ' Delete any existing <modname>.OBJ file in default directory:
49:      ON ERROR GOTO TRAP.OBJ
50:          KILL MODNAME + ".OBJ"                  'Error if doesn't exist
51:      ON ERROR GOTO 0
52: ' See if module is assembly language or BASIC:
53: OK: LET FILE = TEXT + ".ASM"                    'Try assembled first
54:      CALL FINDFILE(FILE)
55:      IF LEN(FILE) THEN                          'Found it
56:          GOSUB ASSEMBLE                         ' so assemble it
```

Listing 8 - 2 (continued)

```
57:        ELSE
58:            LET FILE = TEXT + ".BAS"           'Maybe its BASIC
59:            CALL FINDFILE(FILE)
60:            IF LEN(FILE) THEN                  'Found BASIC source file
61:                GOSUB COMPILE                  '  so compile it
62:            ELSE                               'No source file found
63:                PRINT TAB(10) "Cannot find source code for ";
64:                PRINT CHR$(34) TEXT CHR$(34)
65:                GOTO ERREND                    ' so terminate program
66:            END IF
67:        END IF
68: ' Check if enough memory space to compile/assemble <modname>:
69:     ON ERROR GOTO TRAP.FULL
70:        OPEN MODNAME + ".OBJ" FOR INPUT AS #1       'Trap if no object file
71:     ON ERROR GOTO 0
72:     CLOSE #1
73: ' Check for presence of PQB.LIB in default directory:
74:     ON ERROR GOTO TRAP.LIB:              'Trap if PQB.LIB not in
75:        OPEN "PQB.LIB" FOR INPUT AS #1    '  default directory
76:     ON ERROR GOTO 0
77:        CLOSE #1
78: LIB:          'Add module to library:
79:     PRINT: PRINT TAB(10);
80:     IF MODOP = "+"  THEN PRINT "ADDING "; MODNAME " To PQB.LIB" _
81:                     ELSE PRINT "REPLACING "; MODNAME " In PQB.LIB"
82:        SHELL "LIB PQB" + MODOP + MODNAME + ",PQB.IDX;"
83: END
84:
85: ERREND: 'Error abnormal end
86:     PRINT: PRINT TAB(24) "--TERMINATING PROGRAM--"
87: END
88:
89: ' GOSUB subroutines in alphabetical order:
90: ASSEMBLE:          'Assembling source file:
91:     PRINT TAB(10) "ASSEMBLING "; FILE
92:     SHELL "MASM " + FILE + ";"
93: RETURN
94:
95: COMPILE:          'Compiling Source File
96:     PRINT TAB(10) "READING "; FILE
97:     OPEN FILE FOR INPUT AS #1
98:     WHILE NOT EOF(1)                      'Read entire file if necessary
99:         LINE INPUT #1, TEXT
100:        LET TEXT = UCASE$(TEXT)
101:        IF LEFT$(TEXT,1) = "'" THEN            'If a remark
102:            IF INSTR(TEXT,"$INCLUDE") THEN     ' and needs include
103:                LET INCLUDE.FLAG = -1          ' file, set flag.
104:            END IF
105:        ELSE               'Assumption:  $INCLUDE before "ON ERROR GOTO"
106:            IF INSTR(TEXT,"ON ERROR GOTO") THEN     'Add error trap
107:                LET FILE = FILE + "/X"               ' switch,
108:                GOTO DONE                            ' and exit loop
109:            END IF
110:        END IF
111:     WEND
112: DONE:   CLOSE #1
```

Listing 8 - 2   (continued)

```
113:   ' Copy PQB.BI to default directory, if necessary:
114:       IF INCLUDE.FLAG THEN              'If PQB.BI required
115:          ON ERROR GOTO TRAP.BI          '  and not in default
116:             OPEN "PQB.BI" FOR INPUT AS #1    '  directory, trap and
117:          ON ERROR GOTO 0                '  move it
118:             CLOSE #1
119:       END IF
120:   BI:              'Compile the module:
121:       PRINT: PRINT TAB(10) "COMPILING "; FILE
122:       SHELL "BC " + FILE + ";"
123:   RETURN
124:
125:   ' Error traps in alphabetical order:
126:   TRAP.BI:           'PQB.BI not in default directory:
127:       PRINT: PRINT TAB(10) "COPYING PQB.BI To Default Directory."
128:       LET DIRECTORY = ENVIRON$("INCLUDE")
129:       LET I = INSTR(DIRECTORY,";")         'Only checks one
130:       IF I THEN LET DIRECTORY = MID$(DIRECTORY,I-1)    ' include entry
131:       IF RIGHT$(DIRECTORY,1) <> "\" THEN
132:           LET DIRECTORY = DIRECTORY + "\"
133:       END IF
134:       SHELL "COPY " + DIRECTORY + "PQB.BI"
135:   RESUME BI
136:
137:   TRAP.FULL:         'Insufficient memory to compile <modname>:
138:       PRINT: PRINT TAB(10) "Insufficient memory to compile/assemble ";
139:       PRINT FILE
140:   GOTO ERREND
141:
142:   TRAP.LIB:          'PQB.LIB not in default directory:
143:       PRINT: PRINT TAB(10) "COPYING PQB.LIB To Default Directory."
144:       LET DIRECTORY = ENVIRON$("LIB")
145:       LET I = INSTR(DIRECTORY,";")         'Only checks one
146:       IF I THEN LET DIRECTORY = MID$(DIRECTORY,I-1)    ' LIB entry
147:       IF RIGHT$(DIRECTORY,1) <> "\" THEN
148:           LET DIRECTORY = DIRECTORY + "\"
149:       END IF
150:       SHELL "COPY " + DIRECTORY + "PQB.LIB"
151:   RESUME LIB
152:
153:   TRAP.OBJ:          'No <modname>.OBJ to KILL:
154:   RESUME OK
155:   ' End of DOLIB.BAS
```

Listing 8 - 2

of DOLIB consisted of the code through line 47, followed by a line of debugging code that displayed MODOP and MODNAME.)

After storing the LIB operation data, DOLIB destroys any existing copy of <modname>.OBJ in the default directory with a KILL statement (lines 48–51). Since attempting to KILL a nonexistent file is a BASIC error, the error is trapped (lines 153–154), with a RESUME to the OK label (line 53). DOLIB then checks the source module to see if it is to be assembled or compiled, and the appropriate GOSUB subroutine is called. This test uses nested IF-blocks (lines 52– 67) to force either GOSUB subroutine to effectively return to line 69. If DOLIB is unable to find the source-code file, the program is terminated (lines 63–65, 85–87).

If the module is to be compiled, it is first read, looking for a $IN-CLUDE in a remark line and an "ON ERROR GOTO" in an executable line (lines 97–112). Certain of my programming-style conventions are assumed in this section of code. All my remark lines start with an apostrophe in the first column; the only $INCLUDE statements I use are for the header file, PQB.BI, and will appear in my source code *before* any executable statements. If your conventions differ, you must modify this portion of the code.[2] If a required PQB.BI file is not already in the default directory, it will be copied from the first directory shown in the INCLUDE environment string (lines 113–119, 126–135).

After either assembling or compiling the module, the existence of the <modname>.OBJ file is checked to make sure there was enough memory to perform the translation (lines 68–72, 137–140). Note that TRAP.FULL does not end with a RESUME statement, since there is no possibility of further error interruptions in this program.

DOLIB works on a copy of the library in the default directory. If PQB.LIB is not already in the default directory, it will be copied from the first directory shown in the LIB environment string (lines 73–77, 126–135). Thus, if you are DOLIBing a series of modules (say, with a batch file), they will all modify the same copy of PQB.LIB. The original version of the library is left unscathed in case of trouble.

The final action of DOLIB is to SHELL the LIB utility to either add <modname> to the copy of PQB.LIB or replace a previous version in that library. If you give DOLIB the name of a module that already exists in the library without adding the "replace" switch, the LIB error will not be caught; the new PQB.LIB file will be the same as its ancestor, PQB.BAK. It wouldn't help to run the LIB program under a BAT file instead of directly, because LIB does not return an error code when it ignores a command. You can check the display for LIB's warning message, which will be the last one left before the DOS prompt returns.

Potential Enhancements for DOLIB

DOLIB, as written, is useful only when run on systems containing a hard disk or on diskette-only systems with at least 720K capacity per diskette (so MASM and the other utilities can reside on the same diskette as BC.EXE and LIB.EXE), having enough memory for a virtual disk. If you are using DOLIB on a diskette-only system with 360K diskettes, you probably should add code to check whether or not the next utility to be SHELLed is on the diskette in the A drive, and (if not) tell the operator to insert the proper diskette and reply to the system with the Enter key.

If you wish to make the procedures in PQB.LIB available to QB's development environment, you can produce an equivalent "Quick" library by adding the statement

```
SHELL "LINK PQB.LIB/Q,,,BQLB40"
```

between lines 82 and 83 of DOLIB. (See the section on "Quick" libraries in Chapter 11 for further details.)

Child-Parent Communication

In DOLIB, the indication of a child program failure was communicated to the parent program by checking for the existence of the file written by the compiler or assembler. It works only because of the assumption that there would be no translation errors other than due to "out of memory."

In the more general case, the only indirect communication means is to run the child program under a BAT file written by the parent. The BAT file not only runs the child, but can also create an error-message file if the child process fails. This scheme will work only if the child program issues an errorlevel code after unsuccessful execution. Both BC and MASM issue such codes.

A Matter of Space

DOLIB requires more available memory to run when compiling a procedure module than it took to compile DOLIB in the first place. The memory space required depends on the size of the module being compiled.

I used the technique described in Chapter 11 to measure the memory space required for DOLIB to replace the MENU subroutine in PQB.LIB. The test DOS configuration was minimal: the only entry in the CONFIG.SYS file was "BUFFERS=4." The size of resident DOS 3.3 thus created, on my PC-XT, was a little less than 44K.

It took a minimum total memory of 198K to compile DOLIB.BAS with BC.EXE version 4.0. Using DOLIB compiled for stand-alone, it required at least 307K of total memory to replace the MENU function in PQB.LIB. When DOLIB was compiled and linked for the run-time module (as would probably be the case in an all-diskette system), this minimum memory requirement decreased to 216K, but the elapsed time became intolerably long—BRUN40.EXE was reloaded from the diskette after every SHELL statement. Just for the exercise, I ran DOLIB under the development environment (with a "Quick" library containing all the library procedures shown to this point). The resulting minimum memory size was 448K.

Backing Up Files

Although a general discussion of the needs and methods for backing up files is beyond the scope of this book, here are a few observations:

- It probably is more important to back up files kept on diskettes than it is to back up files kept on a reliable hard disk. By its nature, a double-sided diskette drive is relatively hard on the diskette. I have lost only one file on my hard disk in the three years I have used my PC-XT, but periodically find unreadable files on damaged diskettes and have to reconstruct them.
- The purpose of a backup file is to let you run an important application if one or more of the needed data files have been lost or damaged. To be useful, application data files should be backed up at the end of each session during which those files were updated, rather than on a daily or other periodic basis.
- Your backup procedure for critical jobs must provide for the case when your primary computer system is "down" as well as for simple file errors. Your backup media must be readable on your backup machine. If your primary system has a hard disk and your secondary system has only diskette drives, file backups must be made to diskettes readable on the secondary system.

The automatic backup program described here is designed to be used with a batch file that runs a proprietary file-maintenance program and then runs DOBACK as soon as the file-maintenance session ends. (Record-keeping programs that I write myself include the functions of DOBACK.) DOBACK uses an assembled subroutine to force the user to insert the proper backup diskette into a specific drive before it backs up only the files that were modified during the session.

VLABEL.ASM

VLABEL.ASM (Listing 8-3) is an assembled subroutine to "read" the volume label on the disk in the named drive. That label is returned in the string-variable argument that must have a length of exactly eleven characters, or an error indication is returned instead. VLABEL reads the volume label on the default drive unless the first two characters in the string argument are "d:" where d is the alphabetic "drive code" used by DOS and is case-insensitive.

VLABEL is an assembled procedure using a string argument. The address passed for the string argument is not the address of that string in string space. Rather, it is the address of the *string descriptor* in data space. The string descriptor is a two-word entity: a positive integer giving the length of the string, followed by the offset address of the string in string space. Assembled procedures using string arguments must not change the string descriptor or the length of the string itself. Thus, it does not appear feasible to write assembled string functions (those returning a string).

The address of the string descriptor is passed on the stack and recovered in the usual fashion (line 47). The address of the string itself is usually loaded into an index register (lines 48–49) and the length of the string into the CX (count) register (line 50). In this routine, CX is checked for the only allowable value, and an error return is sent if it is not correct. In the general case, CX is always checked to make sure it contains a positive nonzero value before starting any REP moves controlled by CX, or you may overwrite every byte in DGROUP by error.

QBASIC will not allow fixed-length strings to be used as dummy variables when declaring or defining a compiled or assembled procedure. The dummy argument in the "DECLARE SUB VLABEL" statement must be a variable-length string variable, even though a fixed-length string is actually used in all programs calling the subroutine.

```
 1:            PAGE    ,105
 2:            TITLE   VLABEL
 3:            .MODEL  MEDIUM
 4:  ;****************************************************************
 5:  ;                           VLABEL.ASM                        *
 6:  ;    VLABEL is an assembled subroutine to be linked to Microsoft *
 7:  ; compiled BASIC programs.  It reads the volume label on the    *
 8:  ; designated disk drive.                                        *
 9:  ;    Call with:     CALL VLABEL(<string>)                       *
10:  ;    where <string> is a string variable exactly 11 bytes long. *
11:  ;    If the first two bytes of string are not <d:> (the drive code *
12:  ; followed by a colon), the default drive will be used.         *
13:  ;    On return from the subroutine, <string> will contain the requested *
14:  ; disk volume label padded with blanks.  If the disk has no label, or *
15:  ; if the input string is not the proper length, or if an invalid drive *
16:  ; code is given, <string> will be returned as all 0FFH [CHR$(255)] *
17:  ; bytes.                                                        *
18:  ;                  Written by M. L. Lesser, 8/14/86             *
19:  ;  Modified for Microsoft BC version 4.0 and MASM version 5.0, 12-6-87 *
20:  ;****************************************************************
21:
22:  .DATA
23:  FCB     DB      0FFH                    ;Use extended FCB format to
24:          DB      5 DUP(0)                ;   save space.
25:          DB      8                       ;Label attribute
26:  DRIVE   DB      0                       ;Drive code goes here
27:  FLABEL  DB      11 DUP(?)               ;Dummy file name
28:          DB      21 DUP(?)               ;Remaining FCB filler
29:
30:  .CODE
31:          PUBLIC VLABEL
32:  VLABEL  PROC
33:          PUSH    BP                      ;Usual save
34:          MOV     BP,SP
35:          PUSH    DS                      ;Additional "must save"
36:          PUSH    SI                      ;   registers used in
37:          PUSH    DI                      ;   subroutine
38:  ;   Get and save BASIC's DTA:
39:          MOV     AH,2FH
40:          INT     21H
41:          PUSH    BX                      ;DTA offset
42:          PUSH    ES                      ;DTA segment
43:          PUSH    DS                      ;Restore ES addressability
44:          POP     ES                      ;   to DGROUP
45:  ;   Locate address of string in string space, and check its length:
46:          CLD
47:          MOV     BX,6[BP]                ;Address of string descriptor
48:          MOV     SI,2[BX]                ;Address of string
49:          MOV     DI,SI                   ;Will need it for moving label
50:          MOV     CX,[BX]                 ;Length of string in CX
51:          CMP     CX,11                   ;Check for proper length
52:          JNZ     ERROR                   ;Error return
53:          LODSW                           ;If AH has colon, AL has drive
54:          CMP     AH,":"
55:          MOV     AH,0                    ;For "nocode" case
56:          JNZ     NOCODE                  ;  ("drive" code 0 is default)
```

Listing 8 - 3 (continued)

```
57: ;   If drive code in string, convert to DOS number:
58:         AND     AL,5FH                  ;Make code character uppercase
59:         SUB     AL,40H                  ;Convert to FCB drive code
60:         MOV     AH,AL                   ;  (1 = A, 2 = B, etc.)
61: ;   Load drive code in FCB:
62: NOCODE: MOV     DRIVE,AH
63: ;   Load FLABEL portion of FCB with question marks:
64:         PUSH    DI                      ;Save two registers
65:         PUSH    CX
66:         MOV     AL,'?'
67:         LEA     DI,FLABEL
68: REP     STOSB
69:         POP     CX                      ;Get them back
70:         POP     DI
71: ;   "Find first" file containing a label (there is only one!)
72: ;       and write the corresponding directory information in same FCB.
73:         LEA     DX,FCB                  ;Set DTA to FCB
74:         MOV     AH,1AH
75:         INT     21H
76:         MOV     AH,11H                  ;Find first
77:         INT     21H
78:         OR      AL,AL                   ;Will be zero if label found
79:         JNZ     ERROR                   ;Exit on no label found
80:         LEA     SI,FLABEL               ;Else move label to <string>
81: REP     MOVSB
82: ;   Restore divots:
83: DONE:   POP     DS                      ;Restore BASIC's DTA
84:         POP     DX
85:         MOV     AH,1AH
86:         INT     21H
87:         POP     DI                      ;Must return to BASIC with
88:         POP     SI                      ; these registers unchanged
89:         POP     DS
90:         POP     BP
91:         RET     2
92:
93: ERROR:  MOV     AL,0FFH                 ;Error return - fill <string> with 0FFH
94: REP     STOSB
95:         JMP     DONE
96:
97: VLABEL  ENDP
98:
99:         END
```

Listing 8 - 3

DOBACK.BAS

As written, DOBACK.BAS (Listing 8-4) backs up recently modified files
to a single diskette in the A drive, using XCOPY to make the actual copies.
Files that were not changed during the maintenance session just ended
are not recopied to the backup diskette. DOBACK requires a rather com-

```
 1:  '*************************************************************************
 2:  '                          DOBACK.BAS                                  *
 3:  '      DOBACK is designed to be used in a batch file for automatically  *
 4:  ' backing up any files changed by a program run on that same batch     *
 5:  ' file.  As written, DOBACK asks for a particular diskette to be       *
 6:  ' inserted in the A: drive.  If the diskette so inserted does not have *
 7:  ' the volume label passed to DOBACK in its command line, the process   *
 8:  ' is repeated.  When the label requirement is satisfied, DOBACK SHELLs *
 9:  ' XCOPY with the argument to copy all files changed by the running     *
10:  ' program to the backup diskette.  Both DOBACK.EXE and XCOPY.EXE must  *
11:  ' be in directories on the PATH environment list.                     *
12:  '      Call with:  DOBACK <label>/<files>                             *
13:  '                  where <label> is the volume label on the diskette to *
14:  '                        be inserted into the A: drive.               *
15:  '                  <files> is the description of the file set to be    *
16:  '                        backed up.                                   *
17:  '      WARNING:  There is no way to terminate DOBACK before the label  *
18:  '                matches except to reboot the system.                 *
19:  '                Written by M. L. Lesser, August 16, 1986            *
20:  '                Modified February 5, 1987, to use SYSTEM.PRO        *
21:  '                Modified for Microsoft BC version 4.0, 12-7-87      *
22:  '                Compiled with switches /O/E                         *
23:  '*************************************************************************
24:
25:  ' Setup
26:      DEFSTR F, L
27:      DEFINT I
28:      DIM LABEL, FILE, I
29:      DIM D.LABEL AS STRING*11                        'Fixed-length string
30:
31:  ' Separate <label> from <files>
32:      LET I = INSTR(COMMAND$,"/")
33:      LET FILE = MID$(COMMAND$,I+1)
34:      LET LABEL = LEFT$(COMMAND$,I-1)
35:      CALL COLORIT                                    'Set display attribute
36:
37:  ' Check label in A: drive:
38:  DOIT:
39:      PRINT
40:      PRINT "Insert diskette with label "_
41:            CHR$(34) LABEL CHR$(34) " in A: drive."
42:      PRINT TAB(10) "--Press <ENTER> when ready--"
43:      WHILE INKEY$ <> CHR$(13): WEND                  'Wait loop for <ENTER>
44:      LET D.LABEL = "A:"                              'Input string for VLABEL
45:      ON ERROR GOTO TRAP                              'May have
46:          CALL VLABEL(D.LABEL)                        '   "Disk not ready"
47:      ON ERROR GOTO 0                                 '   error
48:  ' Test for results:
49:      IF LEFT$(D.LABEL,1) = CHR$(255) THEN            'No label on diskette
50:          PRINT: PRINT "Diskette in drive A: has no label."
51:          GOTO DOIT
52:      ELSEIF RTRIM$(D.LABEL) <> LABEL THEN            'Wrong label on diskette
53:          PRINT: PRINT "Label on diskette in drive A: is:  ";
54:          PRINT RTRIM$(D.LABEL)
55:          GOTO DOIT                                   'Try again
56:      END IF
```

Listing 8 - 4 (continued)

```
57:     PRINT
58: ' Use SHELL to run XCOPY with FILE in command line:
59:     SHELL "XCOPY " + FILE + " A: /M"
60: END      'End of main routine
61:
62: TRAP:   'Error trap if "disk not ready" for reading label
63:     PRINT:
64:     PRINT "Cannot read diskette in A drive.  Check door"
65:     RESUME DOIT
66: '   End of source code
```

Listing 8 - 4

plex command line which it expects to get from the same batch file that ran the application modifying the files.

Figure 8-2 is an excerpt from the batch file that runs the proprietary file-maintenance program[3] I use for keeping miscellaneous record files not used often enough to warrant writing a special program. The text to the left of the forward slash is the volume label on the backup diskette; the text to the right is the "wild card" description of the files to be backed up, that will be passed to XCOPY by SHELL.

XCOPY is a convenient utility introduced with DOS version 3.2. It reads as many source files as available memory permits before writing to the target diskette. The output of XCOPY is a set of files that are identical to the copied source files.

DOBACK, as written, is limited to backing up file sets to a single diskette, since XCOPY cannot copy files to more than one disk at a time. If your file-maintenance program uses more than one subdirectory for its files, you probably should run DOBACK several times from the batch file, backing up each subdirectory's files to a different diskette.

If you are using an earlier version of DOS and don't have XCOPY, you can use BACKUP instead. BACKUP has some disadvantages: you

```
DOBACK PCFILES_BAK/C:\PCF\*.*
```

Figure 8 - 2
Sample command line for DOBACK

must back up the entire application file set each time to prevent keeping multiple versions of previously backed-up files, it copies only one file at a time, and the backup files must be RESTOREd to the same-named subdirectory they were copied from.

The advantage of using BACKUP is that it handles overflow to a series of backup diskettes. If your file set cannot be subdivided and is too big to back up on a single diskette, you should use the BACKUP utility instead of XCOPY. In that case, DOBACK will only check the label on the first diskette of the backup set, and you are on your own for the rest.[4]

DOBACK is a very straightforward program. Although the argument string variable for VLABEL is declared as a fixed-length string (line 29), and the result is returned to that location, VLABEL actually operates on a variable-length copy of the string produced by the QBASIC support. However, using a fixed-length string allows the drive code to be inserted with a LET statement (line 44), since all statements (except RSET) assigning values to fixed-length strings act as though they were LSET statements — left-justifying the new string and packing any unused low-order bytes of the resulting variable with <SP> symbols.

There are no input validity checks in DOBACK, since input is intended to come from a tested command in a batch file. Once in control, DOBACK is very insistent that its instructions be followed; there is no way the user can circumvent DOBACK except to reboot the system. I tested DOBACK from the command line during implementation by commenting out lines 45 and 47, so I could get my system back in the event of command-line input errors by leaving the door of the A drive open and waiting for the time-out error interruption.

Diskettes are fragile devices, and it is very embarrassing to find your backup diskette has been damaged when it becomes necessary to use it. It is a good idea to use DOS's COMP utility periodically to compare all the files on the backup diskette with their original counterparts.

Using RUN

The RUN <filespec> statement is used to load and execute another EXE file from within a compiled QBASIC program. When used in this manner, it includes an equivalent of END, closing all open files before loading the new program.

N.B.   The programs discussed in this section cannot be tested with the development environment, since QB.EXE implements RUN and CHAIN in a manner similar to BASICA: the target program must be available as a BASIC source file having the extension BAS.

COMMAND.ASM

RUN operates in overlay mode; it does not build a new Program Segment Prefix (PSP)[5] for the child program, but loads the new program on top of the original PSP. Thus, unless you can change the PSP copy of the parent program's "rest of the command line" before executing the RUN statement, the child's COMMAND$ will return the same value as did the parent's. The assembly-language subroutine COMMAND.ASM (Listing 8-5) allows the parent program to change the command-line input to the PSP before RUNning the child program.

As far as I know, RUN will load and execute any EXE file — except QBASIC programs that were compiled with QB version 2.01 to use the run-time module and linked with the /e (EXEPACK) switch. However, I have found proprietary EXE programs that do not react as expected to COMMAND. XCOPY is one of these, which is one reason DOBACK uses SHELL instead of RUN.

COMMAND uses an *undocumented interface* to locate the PSP when a program is running under DOS 2.x. An undocumented interface is one that was put into a system program for the convenience of the implementers, not for the convenience of the users. Many of those "reserved for DOS" interrupts, and the DOS INT 21H calls missing from the *DOS Technical Reference* manual, conceal undocumented interfaces. If you know what lies behind the interface, you can use it at your peril. The vendor of the system program has no obligation to keep undocumented interfaces unchanged in later versions of the program.

Now, many programmers knew about the undocumented interface behind AH=51H, INT 21H, in DOS version 2.x; it returned the segment address of the PSP in register BX. So lots of them used it. When Microsoft made the function a documented interface in DOS 3.0, but at AH=62H instead, existing programs using the old undocumented AH=51H interface would not run correctly under the new version. COMMAND checks for the DOS version number and uses the appropriate DOS call to get the PSP address (lines 27–33).

```
 1:          PAGE    ,105
 2:          TITLE   COMMAND
 3:          .MODEL  MEDIUM
 4: ;******************************************************************
 5: ;                          COMMAND.ASM                           *
 6: ;   COMMAND(<string>) is an assembled subroutine to be linked to *
 7: ; compiled Microsoft BASIC programs in order to insert "the rest of *
 8: ; the command line" in the Program Segment Prefix before starting *
 9: ; another compiled BASIC program with the "RUN <filename>" command. *
10: ;   Call with:  CALL COMMAND(<string>)                           *
11: ;        where <string> is the string expression to be returned by *
12: ;              COMMAND$ in the new program (COMMAND$ will convert any *
13: ;              lowercase letters in <string> to uppercase).      *
14: ;   If LEN(<string>) > 125, a null command line will be inserted *
15: ; instead.                                                       *
16: ;                    Written by M. L. Lesser, April 6, 1986      *
17: ;         Modified for Microsoft BC 4.0 and MASM 5.0, 12-7-87    *
18: ;******************************************************************
19:
20: .CODE
21:          PUBLIC COMMAND
22: COMMAND PROC
23:          PUSH    BP
24:          MOV     BP,SP
25:          PUSH    SI
26:          PUSH    DI
27: ; Check for DOS version:
28:          MOV     AH,30H
29:          INT     21H
30:          MOV     AH,51H              ;DOS call for PSP, version 2.x
31:          CMP     AL,2H               ;Is it version 2.x?
32:          JZ      GO                  ;If so, use AH=51H
33:          MOV     AH,62H              ;Else use AH=62H
34: ; Set ES to PSP segment address
35: GO:      INT     21H                 ;Put PSP segment address in BX
36:          MOV     ES,BX               ;Set ES to PSP segment
37: ; Insert string in command line in proper form:
38:          MOV     DI,80H              ;Command-line offset
39:          CLD
40:          MOV     BX,6[BP]            ;Address of string descriptor
41:          MOV     CX,[BX]             ;Length of string
42:          OR      CX,CX               ;Is it null string?
43:          JZ      NULL
44:          CMP     CX,7DH              ;Is it within length limit?
45:          JA      NULL                ;If not, replace with null
46:          MOV     SI,2[BX]            ;Address of first byte of string
47:          MOV     AL,CL
48:          INC     AL
49:          STOSB                       ;Store command-line byte count
50:          MOV     AL,' '              ;Insert leading <SP>
51:          STOSB
52:          REP     MOVSB               ;Move text of <string>
53: DONE:    MOV     AL,0DH              ;Add trailing <CR>
54:          STOSB
55:          POP     DI                  ;  and return
56:          POP     SI
```

Listing 8 - 5 (continued)

```
57:              POP      BP
58:              RET      2
59:   NULL:      XOR      AL,AL                    ;Forces null command line
60:              STOSB
61:              JMP      DONE
62:   COMMAND ENDP
63:
64:              END
```

Listing 8 - 5

COMPILE.BAS

When you find yourself in a repeated mistake pattern when entering commands at the console, you should write a utility to correct your errors before they occur. I have two bad habit patterns when using the QBASIC compiler: I forget to use the /e switch when recompiling an old program that includes error trapping, and I sometimes forget to copy the PQB.BI file to the default directory when it is needed. So I wrote COMPILE.BAS (Listing 8-6) to take care of both problems.

Any requested compile-time switches are separated from the <filespec> given on the command line so FINDFILE can be used to locate the source file (lines 28–32). Most of the rest of COMPILE is lightly edited from equivalent portions of DOLIB.BAS. The major exception is in copying PQB.BI to the default directory.

There are no "error interrupt" tests for the presence of PQB.BI in the default directory. If the file is needed, and there is an INCLUDE environment list, PQB.BI is copied by OPENing two BASIC files and copying the contents of one into the other (lines 63–77). The two BASIC file buffers are set at 2K (2,048 bytes) each, with the LEN clause (lines 70–71). This assures that the input file will be "block read" in its entirety before any attempt is made to write the output file. If your PQB.BI files grow to longer than 2K, increase the size of the BASIC buffers accordingly by increments of 512 bytes.

If you wrote your PQB.BI file with a word processor that hangs an end-of-file (EOF) symbol [Ctrl-Z, 1AH] on the end of its output file, you will find the newly copied PQB.BI file in the default directory to be 1 byte shorter than the original. Unlike BASICA and earlier QBASICs, QBASIC 4.0 does not append an EOF symbol when it writes a sequential file.

```
1:   '*************************************************************************
2:   '                        COMPILE.BAS                                   *
3:   '    COMPILE reads the source code of a QBASIC program.  If the header *
4:   ' file PQB.BI is required and an INCLUDE environment string exists,    *
5:   ' COMPILE will copy that file to the default directory.  If the        *
6:   ' program includes error trapping, COMPILE will add "/E" to any other  *
7:   ' appended switches before transferring control to the BC compiler.    *
8:   '    Call with:  COMPILE [<path>]<progname>[<switches>]                *
9:   '              where <path> is required if <progname>.BAS is not in a  *
10:  '                        directory on the PATH environment list         *
11:  '                  <switches> are any desired compile-time switches    *
12:  '                        except /E                                      *
13:  '  The QBASIC compiler BC.EXE must be in a directory on the PATH list  *
14:  '            Written by M. L. Lesser, February 23, 1987               *
15:  '          Modified for Microsoft BC version 4.0, 12/7/87             *
16:  '*************************************************************************
17:
18:      DEFSTR D,F,S,T
19:      DEFINT I
20:      DIM DIRECTORY, FILE, I, INCLUDE.FLAG, SWITCH, TEMP, TEXT
21:
22:      CALL COLORIT                           'Set display attribute
23:      LET FILE = COMMAND$
24:      IF LEN(FILE) = 0 THEN                  'Accepts only command-line input
25:          PRINT: PRINT "No input source file given";
26:          GOTO ERREND
27:      END IF
28:      LET I = INSTR(FILE,"/")                'Check for appended switches
29:      IF I THEN                              ' and separate if exist
30:          LET SWITCH = MID$(FILE,I)          'Appended compile switches
31:          LET FILE = LEFT$(FILE,I-1)         'Name of source file to compile
32:      END IF
33:      IF INSTR(FILE,".") = 0 THEN LET FILE = FILE + ".BAS"
34:      TEMP = FILE
35:      CALL FINDFILE(FILE)
36:      IF LEN(FILE) = 0 THEN
37:          PRINT: PRINT TAB(10) TEMP " not found";
38:          GOTO ERREND
39:      ELSE                                   'Read source file
40:          PRINT
41:          PRINT TAB(10) "Reading "; FILE
42:          OPEN FILE FOR INPUT AS #1
43:          WHILE NOT EOF(1)                   'Read entire file if necessary
44:              LINE INPUT #1, TEXT
45:              LET TEXT = UCASE$(TEXT)
46:              IF LEFT$(TEXT,1) = "'" THEN          'If a remark
47:                  IF INSTR(TEXT,"$INCLUDE") THEN ' and needs include
48:                      LET INCLUDE.FLAG = -1      ' file, set flag.
49:                  END IF
50:              ELSE         'Assumption: $INCLUDE before "ON ERROR GOTO"
51:                  IF INSTR(TEXT,"ON ERROR GOTO") THEN     'Add error trap
52:                      LET FILE = FILE + "/E"               ' switch,
53:                      GOTO DONE                            ' and exit loop
54:                  END IF
55:              END IF
56:          WEND
```

Listing 8 - 6 (continued)

```
57:    DONE:    CLOSE #1
58:         END IF
59:    ' Copy PQB.BI to default directory, if necessary:
60:         IF INCLUDE.FLAG THEN                         'If PQB.BI required
61:             LET DIRECTORY = ENVIRON$("INCLUDE")
62:         END IF
63:         IF LEN(DIRECTORY) <> 0 THEN
64:             PRINT TAB(10) "Copying PQB.BI to default directory"
65:             LET I = INSTR(DIRECTORY,";")                'Only checks one
66:             IF I THEN LET DIRECTORY = MID$(DIRECTORY,I-1)   ' include entry
67:             IF RIGHT$(DIRECTORY,1) <> "\" THEN
68:                 LET DIRECTORY = DIRECTORY + "\"
69:             END IF
70:             OPEN DIRECTORY + "PQB.BI" FOR INPUT AS #1 LEN=2048
71:             OPEN "PQB.BI" FOR OUTPUT AS #2 LEN=2048
72:             WHILE NOT EOF(1)
73:                 LINE INPUT #1, TEXT
74:                 PRINT #2, TEXT
75:             WEND
76:             CLOSE #1: CLOSE #2
77:         END IF
78:    ' Locate directory holding BC.EXE:
79:         LET TEMP = "BC.EXE"
80:         CALL FINDFILE(TEMP)
81:         IF LEN(TEMP) = 0 THEN
82:             PRINT: PRINT TAB(10) "Cannot find QBASIC compiler";
83:             GOTO ERREND
84:         END IF
85:    ' Set up command line for compilation:
86:         LET FILE = FILE + SWITCH
87:         PRINT TAB(10) "Compiling " FILE
88:         CALL COMMAND(FILE + ";")
89:         RUN TEMP
90:    END                                         'Normal program end
91:
92:    ERREND: 'Abnormal end of program
93:         PRINT " - Terminating program."
94:         END                                     'Abnormal program end
95:    '                 End of source code
```

Listing 8 - 6

Unlike SHELL, RUN does not use a new resident command processor, so it has no facility to hunt for the new EXE file; the complete path to that file must be included as part of the RUN string argument. COMPILE uses FINDFILE, again, to locate the compiler (lines 78– 84), after which it calls COMMAND to insert the BC argument in its "command line" (line 88).

If you attempt to compile COMPILE with itself, it will compile with the /e switch, even though COMPILE.BAS does not include error trapping. Why? Can COMPILE be modified to prevent this? How?

About CHAIN

There are two differences between CHAIN and RUN. The defining, but not particularly useful, difference allows a minimal data set to be passed from the parent to the child: any files left OPEN by the parent program are still OPEN for the child, and the values of any variables named in blank COMMON are available to the child. The difference that makes CHAIN essentially useless in the compiled environment is that both the parent and the child program must have been compiled and linked to run with the run-time module.

The only reason to use CHAIN is to execute program sets having more combined capability than could have been contained in a single program running in the same limited memory space. Except for programs using SHELL, programs compiled with the /o switch will run in considerably less memory than would be required for the same program compiled for the run-time module. If memory space is a limitation, you are usually better off coding the additional capability into the single program and compiling it with the /o switch, rather than attempting to use CHAIN. If you still can't fit your program into the desired space, but can split it into separate pieces, you can compile each piece with the /o switch and connect the pieces with RUN. The information that would have been in blank COMMON can be passed to the next program in a temporary file.

Notes

1. Unlike BASICA and earlier versions of QB.EXE, QBASIC no longer keeps its own cursor-position record. It will not overwrite a text display produced by a SHELLed program.
2. The major advantage of do-it-yourself utilities over proprietary equivalents is that you can write your own utilities to suit your own idiosyncrasies, rather than having to modify your practices to suit the idiosyncrasies of the utility vendor.
3. *PC-File III* version 4 (published by ButtonWare, Inc., P.O. Box 5786, Bellevue, WA 98006) is an inexpensive, easy-to-use file-maintenance program. It is written in Microsoft Business BASIC augmented with assembly-language subroutines.

4. Do not use the VLABEL subroutine in DOBACK if you are going to use the version of BACKUP supplied with PC-DOS 3.3. That BACKUP writes its own sequential volume label on each backup diskette. There is no way of identifying which set of backup diskettes belongs to which set of files from the volume labels.

5. See the chapter on "DOS Control Blocks and Work Areas" in the IBM *Disk Operating System Technical Reference* for a description of the contents of the Program Segment Prefix.

Chapter 9

Advanced String Handling

The characteristic that makes BASIC unique among programming languages is its automatic management of variable-length strings. A new "string" type, the *fixed-length string*, was introduced with QBASIC 4.0. Fixed-length strings are not managed by BASIC's automatic string-space manager, have limited utility, and are not discussed in this chapter.

The intrinsic difference between string usage in QBASIC and that in BASICA is in the maximum length of string variables permitted. Variable-length strings (henceforth called *strings* with no modifier) are managed through the use of a string descriptor, constructed when the string variable is declared. BASICA uses a 1-byte length symbol in its string descriptor, limiting its maximum string length to 255 characters; QBASIC uses a 2-byte integer, allowing strings of up to 32,767 bytes. This tremendous increase in allowable string length permits QBASIC strings to be used in ways impossible under the interpreter. One is to use long strings as list structures — to be searched very rapidly with the built-in INSTR function.

After a review of QBASIC's string-management system, the remainder of this chapter describes the use and structure of a utility to search QBASIC source-code files for "undeclared" variables. A data-entry and verification program, LOADKEY, is used to construct a reference file of the QBASIC keywords that will be read by the variable-checking utility. That utility, VARCHK, is programmed in two modules: the compiled module is linked to an assembled module providing INSTR-like wild-card facilities for locating the beginning and end of "tokens" in a text stream.

QBASIC String Management

As described in the previous chapter, the entity directly related to the name of a string variable is a 4-byte string descriptor: an integer giving the length of the string followed by a 2-byte word giving the offset (from the base of DGROUP) of the address in string space containing the first byte of the value of that string.

When a simple string variable is declared, data space for the string descriptor is allocated during compile time. Declared static string arrays are arrays of string descriptors, all allocated in data space. When a dynamic string array is declared, only space for an array descriptor is allocated in data space; the actual string array will be allocated in the top of string space during run time, when the dynamic array DIM statement is executed.

Initially, all string descriptors point to *null* strings, each of zero length with a dummy string-space address. When a value is assigned to a string variable during run time, that value (along with some internal bookkeeping code) is written into string space at the first available location (starting from the bottom of string space), and the proper length and address data are written into the corresponding string descriptor. If any previously assigned string value is modified, the old value in string space is marked as invalid, a new value is written at the current top of used string space, and the corresponding string descriptor is updated accordingly.

Eventually, there may not be any more string space available when it becomes time to write a new value, so the string-space manager reclaims the invalid string space by moving all still-valid string values to the bottom of string space, changing their descriptors accordingly, and resetting the current "top of used string space" to the end of the still-valid values. The technical term for this reclamation process is *garbage collection*.

```
defstr s
defint i
for i = 1 to 10
    let s = space$(10000)
    print i, hex$(sadd(s))
next i
```

Figure 9 - 1

STRING.BAS, demonstrating automatic garbage collection

Figure 9-1 shows STRING.BAS, a small demonstration program to illustrate automatic garbage collection — that initiated by the string-space manager. The result of running STRING.BAS, compiled in the BC default mode, is shown in Figure 9-2. The first column of numbers is just the iteration number; the second column is the DGROUP offset (in hex) of the first byte of the newly written string value — returned by the built-in SADD function. Since there is only one string variable involved, each time the string is written the earlier version is marked invalid, until there is no longer room in string space for the new value. Automatic garbage collection took place before writing the string for the sixth time, and the starting addresses for the next five values repeat.

```
 1    2080
 2    4798
 3    6EB0
 4    95C8
 5    BCE0
 6    2080
 7    4798
 8    6EB0
 9    95C8
10    BCE0
```

Figure 9 - 2

Running STRING

If you were to run STRING.BAS under the development environment, you would get similar results, although the starting addresses would be higher because more of data space is used by the development environment for its own machinations. If you were to compile STRING.BAS with the /o switch and run the stand-alone version, the increase in available string space would postpone automatic garbage collection until the seventh attempt to write the string.

QBASIC manages what I have called "string space" as two allocatable data areas (sometimes called "heaps") having a movable boundary between them, and using two different manager functions. While the string-space manager is taking care of the space available for strings, a "run-time heap" manager is managing any portion of string space temporarily devoted to dynamic string arrays and BASIC file buffers. If there is nothing for the run-time heap manager to manage, the string-space manager "owns" all of string space.

Each time your program DIMs a dynamic string array or OPENs a file, the newly created entity is assigned space in string space, starting at the top and working down. The run-time heap manager takes this portion of string space away from the string-space manager by lowering the boundary between its domain and that of the string-space manager. Each time the program ERASEs a dynamic string array or CLOSEs a file, the run-time heap manager deallocates the space used, making that space available for its own use in later allocations. The run-time heap manager will turn unused space over to the string-space manager by moving the boundary up only if the program forces garbage collection by executing the FRE() function with any argument other than -2, or by executing a SHELL statement.

Data Entry and Verification

The variable-checking utility, VARCHK, parses a QBASIC source-code file by separating the text into a series of *tokens* — sequences of characters having a collective meaning. As does a compiler, VARCHK must distinguish between those tokens that are language keywords and those that represent variable names. Unlike a compiler, VARCHK does not contain a list of the keywords built into its source code; it reads a file containing one record for each keyword, loading those tokens into a single-string list.

Thus, compiler updates that add capabilities establishing new keywords can sometimes be accommodated merely by adding those words to the keyword file. Of course, if the new capability includes the ability to declare a new class of variables (or equivalent), the VARCHK source code must be modified accordingly.

One way to construct the necessary keyword file would be to write it with a text editor — one keyword per record. While this might be the easiest way, it is also the method most prone to possible error. Proofreading a file to check for typos, omissions, and other errors is a very unsatisfactory procedure. As many years of dealing with punch-card input to automatic computer systems demonstrated, the only way to assure a high probability of accurate data input is to repeat the input process, comparing the second set of entries with those entered the first time. This double-entry technique is called *verification*.

LOADKEY.BAS

LOADKEY.BAS (Listing 9-1) illustrates some of the requirements of a program to perform both the data input and data verification processes. On program entry, the user is asked whether the session is to start with Input or with Verification. It is not necessary to enter and verify the entire file in a single session.

The data-entry phase (lines 37–55) writes the keyed input words, one word per record, into the KEYBAS.TMP file in the default directory. Input continues until the entered string is null (Enter key with no entry). This portion of the program is quite straightforward, and I will not describe it further.

The verification phase (the remainder of the program) reads the keywords previously written in the KEYBAS.TMP file one at a time and compares each word with the word just entered from the keyboard. If the two versions match, the word is appended to the KEYBAS.SVE file in the default directory. (If there is no KEYBAS.SVE in the default directory, one will be created.) If there is a mismatch, the PC beeps to attract the user's attention, and the user is asked for further instructions.

There are two general design considerations demonstrated in the verification code. The first is designing sequential file usage for best performance when information is being read from one file, processed, and then written to a second file (a process sometimes referred to as a *filter*). As described in the next chapter, DOS sequential files are organized to

```
1:  '**********************************************************************
2:  '                         LOADKEY.BAS                                 *
3:  '      LOADKEY is a data-entry and verification program used to enter *
4:  ' QBASIC keywords for use with CHKVAR.  Upon entry, LOADKEY writes the*
5:  ' words to a temporary KEYBAS.TMP file in the default directory.      *
6:  '      Verified words will be appended to the KEYBAS.SVE file if it is *
7:  ' in the default directory.  Entering and verifying the keywords can  *
8:  ' be done in sequential stages if desired.                           *
9:  '      When all keywords have been entered and verified, copy KEYBAS.SVE *
10: ' to a directory in the PATH environment list for use by CHKVAR.     *
11: '              Written by M. L. Lesser, March 10, 1987               *
12: '              Modified for Microsoft BC version 4.0, 12-12-87        *
13: '                   Compiled with /O/E switches                      *
14: '**********************************************************************
15:     DEFSTR O,P,T,W
16:     DEFINT C,R
17:     DIM OLDWORD, PASS, TEXT, WORD
18:     COMMON /CURSOR/ ROW.T, COL.T, ROW.B, COL.B, ROW, COL
19:     CALL COLORIT
20: ' Full-screen window:
21:     LET ROW = 2: ROW.T = 1: COL.T = 1: ROW.B = 25: COL.B = 80
22: ' Sign on:
23:     CALL CWINDOW("Loading QBASIC Keywords into KEYBAS.SVE File")
24:     CALL DWINDOW("")
25:     LET COL = 10
26:     LET TEXT = "Press " + CHR$(34) + "V" + CHR$(34) _
27:                  + " to verify existing KEYBAS.TMP file."
28:     CALL DWINDOW(TEXT)
29:     LET TEXT = "Press " + CHR$(34) + "<ESC>" + CHR$(34) _
30:                  + " to exit to DOS"
31:     CALL DWINDOW(TEXT)
32:     CALL DWINDOW("Press any other key to enter new keywords.")
33:     WHILE INKEY$ <> "": WEND                    'Flush type-ahead buffer
34:     LET PASS = UCASE$(INPUT$(1))
35:     IF PASS = CHR$(27) THEN GOTO QUIT          'Requested end
36:     IF PASS = "V" THEN GOTO VERIFY
37: ' Entering new keywords into KEYBAS.TMP
38:     CLS
39:     LET ROW = 2
40:     CALL CWINDOW("Entering keywords into KEYBAS.TMP file")
41:     CALL DWINDOW("")
42:     OPEN "KEYBAS.TMP" FOR OUTPUT AS #1 LEN=5120        '5K buffer
43:     LET COL = 5
44:     CALL DWINDOW("Enter each of the keywords separately.")
45:     CALL DWINDOW("Press <RETURN> with no entry when finished")
46:     LET ROW.T = ROW + 2: COL = 10        'Instructions won't scroll
47: ENTRY:                                   'Start of bottom-tested loop
48:     CALL DWINDOW("Enter the next keyword:  ")
49:     LINE INPUT; WORD
50:     LET WORD = UCASE$(WORD)
51:     IF WORD <> "" THEN
52:         PRINT #1, WORD
53:         GOTO ENTRY
54:     END IF
55:     CLOSE #1
56: ' Verifying entries in KEYPAS.TMP and writing to KEYPAS.SVE
```

Listing 9 - 1 (continued)

```
57:   VERIFY:
58:   ' Verify signon:
59:        CLS
60:        LET ROW = 2: ROW.T = 1
61:        CALL CWINDOW("Verifying keywords in KEYBAS.TMP file")
62:        CALL DWINDOW("")
63:        LET COL = 5
64:        CALL DWINDOW("KEYBAS.TMP file must be in default directory")
65:        CALL DWINDOW("Terms will be appended to KEYBAS.SVE in default" _
66:                        + " directory")
67:        CALL DWINDOW("")
68:        LET COL = 10
69:        LET TEXT = "Press " + CHR$(34) + "<ESC>" + CHR$(34) _
70:                        + " to exit to DOS"
71:        CALL DWINDOW(TEXT)
72:        CALL DWINDOW("Press any other key to verify keywords.")
73:        WHILE INKEY$ <> "": WEND
74:        IF INPUT$(1) = CHR$(27) THEN GOTO QUIT
75:        ON ERROR GOTO TRAP                             'Trap error if
76:            OPEN "KEYBAS.TMP" FOR INPUT AS #1 LEN=5120 'KEYBAS.TMP not in
77:        ON ERROR GOTO 0                                'default directory
78:        OPEN "KEYBAS.SVE" FOR APPEND AS #2 LEN=5120
79:   ' Re-enter words for verification:
80:        LET ROW.T = 3: ROW = 3: COL = 5               'Keep sign-on
81:        CALL CLEARIT
82:        CALL DWINDOW("")
83:        CALL DWINDOW("Verify the list by re-entering the keywords:")
84:        LET ROW.T = ROW + 2                    'Prevent scrolling instructions
85:        WHILE NOT EOF(1)               'Read old words as long as there are any
86:            INPUT #1, OLDWORD
87:   AGAIN:   LET COL = 10
88:            CALL DWINDOW("Enter the next keyword:  ")
89:            LINE INPUT; WORD
90:            LET WORD = UCASE$(WORD)
91:            IF WORD <> OLDWORD THEN                     'Doesn't verify
92:                BEEP
93:                LET TEXT = "The old word you entered was " + CHR$(34) _
94:                            + OLDWORD + CHR$(34)
95:                CALL DWINDOW(TEXT)
96:                LET TEXT = "The new word you entered was " + CHR$(34) _
97:                            + WORD + CHR$(34)
98:                CALL DWINDOW(TEXT)
99:                LET COL = 15
100:               LET TEXT = "Press " + CHR$(34) + "O" + CHR$(34) _
101:                           + " to keep the old word"
102:               CALL DWINDOW(TEXT)
103:               LET TEXT = "Press " + CHR$(34) + "N" + CHR$(34) _
104:                           + " to substitute the new word"
105:               CALL DWINDOW(TEXT)
106:               LET TEXT = "Press " + CHR$(34) + "I" + CHR$(34) _
107:                           + " to insert new word in the list"
108:               CALL DWINDOW(TEXT)
109:               LET TEXT = "Press " + CHR$(34) + "E" + CHR$(34) _
110:                           + " to erase the new word and reenter it."
111:               CALL DWINDOW(TEXT)
112:   RETRY:      WHILE INKEY$ <> "": WEND
```

Listing 9 - 1 (continued)

```
113:                    LET PASS = UCASE$(INPUT$(1))
114:                    LET COL = 20
115:                    IF PASS = "O" THEN
116:                        CALL DWINDOW("O - Old word used.")
117:                        PRINT #2, OLDWORD
118:                    ELSEIF PASS = "N" THEN
119:                        CALL DWINDOW("N - Old word replaced with new word.")
120:                        PRINT #2, WORD
121:                    ELSEIF PASS = "I" THEN
122:                        CALL DWINDOW("I - New word inserted into list.")
123:                        PRINT #2, WORD
124:                        GOTO AGAIN
125:                    ELSEIF PASS = "E" THEN
126:                        CALL DWINDOW("E - New word ignored.")
127:                        GOTO AGAIN
128:                    ELSE                        'Illegal entry
129:                        CALL DWINDOW(PASS + " - Unrecognized entry; try again")
130:                        GOTO RETRY
131:                    END IF                  'End of mismatched word
132:                ELSE                        'Word matched
133:                    PRINT #2, OLDWORD
134:                END IF                      'End of this word entry
135:        WEND
136:        CLOSE
137:        KILL "KEYBAS.TMP"
138:        CALL DWINDOW("")
139:        CALL DWINDOW("All items verified")
140:        IF ROW >= 25 THEN CALL DWINDOW("")
141: END
142:
143: QUIT:    'Requested end
144:        CALL DWINDOW("")
145:        CALL CWINDOW("Program terminated by user")
146:        PRINT
147: END
148:
149: TRAP:    'Unable to open KEYBAS.TMP
150:        CALL DWINDOW("")
151:        CALL DWINDOW("Cannot find KEYBAS.TMP.  Terminating program")
152:        PRINT
153: END
154: '        End of source code
```

Listing 9 - 1

optimize reading and writing in large blocks. Performance is at its minimum in filters where one record at a time is read from the input file and then written to the output file with both files on the same real disk drive. Thus, to maximize performance (and to minimize wear and tear on drives and diskettes), you should block sequential file input and output when writing filters. Fortunately, QBASIC 4.0 added the capability for blocking sequential file reads and writes automatically, by allowing the sequential file buffers to be set at (almost) any desired length. I have used 5K file buffers in this program (lines 42, 76, and 78), considerably longer than is required for any of the files used.

The second design decision relates to the user interface. Unskilled keyboard operators watch the display and expect to be prompted for every entry. Skilled keyboard operators do not watch the display; rather, they keep their attention on the source copy. They will continue to enter the source copy into the type-ahead buffer while the system processes the previous entry. If the data-entry program is to be useful for skilled operators, it must allow this mode — interrupting the operator only when an error has been detected.

The prompt is displayed for every entry word (lines 88–89). If the words match, another prompt is displayed. If the words do not match, the following sequence occurs:

- The user's attention is attracted by a BEEP (line 92).
- Both the newly entered and previously entered words are displayed, identified as to which is which (lines 93–98).
- A menu prompt giving the available operator options is displayed (lines 99–111).
- The type-ahead buffer is cleared of any portion of the "following" entry before accepting the operator option (line 112).
- The result of the operator decision is displayed before returning to the "normal" verification process (lines 113 – 131).

A word about the operator choices: the operator can keep either of the two words displayed (O or N); can insert the new word into the list at this point (I); or can "erase" the new word (E), restarting the process of verification as though that entry had never been made. The last option is to allow a previously written KEYBAS.TMP file to be verified at a later time. Entering a null "new word" will display the starting point of KEYBAS.TMP.

The Keyword List

The keywords currently recognized by QBASIC 4.0 are given in Appendix B of the *BASIC Language Reference* manual furnished with the compiler. (Any changes or additions for versions after 4.0 will be found in the README.DOC file on one of the distribution diskettes.) I entered the keyword list with LOADKEY, entering and verifying one column at a time rather than attempting the entire list at once.

Since the compiler recognizes two variables having the same name other than for differing trailing type-designation symbols as separate variables, it was necessary to design VARCHK to attach any trailing type-designation symbol to the variable name as it is encountered. Since both keywords and variables are picked up by the same scanning process, similar keywords, such as VARPTR and VARPTR$, are separated by the same mechanism.

BASICA programmers have learned several bad habits in the attempt to save memory space, and the compiler supports them. For example, the compiler knows what to do with the statement

```
PRINT#1,USING" ####";NUMBER
```

even if you have to struggle to understand what was intended. I added seven more keywords to the list — CLOSE#, FIELD#, GET#, INPUT#, PRINT#, PUT#, and WRITE# — to take care of such poor programming style. I didn't bother to enter them in their proper alphabetical location in the list; I just hung them on the end. VARCHR is not sensitive to the order in which the keywords appear in the list. So, if new keywords are added for later versions of the compiler, you can hang them on the end of your existing KEYBAS.SVE file with LOADKEY.

Checking for Undeclared Variables

The utility VARCHK scans a QBASIC source-code file looking for "undeclared" variables, taking into account variable scope. VARCHK considers that a variable has been "declared" if it is first named in a (usually nonexecutable) statement that allocates memory space but does not assign a value to that variable. VARCHK distinguishes between similarly named simple and array variables, and between variables that would be similarly named except for being of different types as indicated by a trailing type-defining symbol in the name.

N.B. The compiler recognizes two variable (or symbolic constant) names as being the same if the only difference is the addition of a type-defining symbol and that symbol corresponds to the implicit type declaration of that variable. (The implicit type declaration of a symbolic constant is established by its value, not by the DEF<typ> statements.) VARCHK will consider these as two separate names and will report the one not explicitly declared.

The scope of variables declared in DIM or COMMON statements in the main portion of the program is either "global" or "main," depending on whether or not the declaring statement included the SHARED keyword. Scope of variables declared in formal parameter lists is always local, as are variables declared with the STATIC, DIM, or SHARED keywords in compiled procedures, or with STATIC in multiline defined functions. (The scope of variables declared in DIM statements inside of multiline function definitions is a special case.) The names of all variables found that either have not been declared, or have been declared but do not have scope over the program substructure being scanned, are displayed showing the line number on which they occur.

Now, there is nothing wrong with using undeclared variables in a BASIC program. The problems are with unintentional undeclared variables due to typos in the source code, and with undeclared local variables in compiled subroutines that should have been declared SHARED. The compiler cannot catch these common sources of hard-to-find bugs, so I built VARCHK to fill the need.

VARCHK does not check for conditions the compiler or linker will find. Thus, it ignores labels and subroutine names in CALL statements. While I have attempted to design VARCHK for all "reasonable" programming style conventions the compiler will accept, there are several limitations I know about. These are discussed in the "Limitations" subsection near the end of this chapter. There may be other limitations I have missed. If any of these are important to your style of programming, you will have to correct the code.

VARCHK is built from two modules: the assembled module CTYPE.ASM and the compiled module VARCHK.BAS. After compiling VARCHK and assembling CTYPE, the two modules are linked together and to the libraries.

```
        Checking C:\SOURCE\FILL_2.BAS for undeclared variables
   15: Start of FILLCHAR procedure definition
   16: I
   17: I
   18: I
   19: End of procedure definition
        All source text analyzed
```

Figure 9 - 3
Running VARCHK

Figure 9-3 shows the results of analyzing FILL_2.BAS (Listing 4-3) with VARCHK. You might compare this output with the original listing.

CTYPE.ASM

VARCHK separates tokens in a text stream by using the appropriate procedure in the CTYPE.ASM module (Listing 9-2). These routines are a set of INSTR-like functions, each of which locates the first character in a string argument belonging to a specified "class" (e.g., alphabetic, numeric, etc.), returning the position as an integer.

The character classes are identified by the presence of a particular bit in the 1-byte table entry corresponding to the character. I have coded these classes into 7 bits of the byte (lines 32–38), leaving a little room for expansion. The complete character classification table is given in lines 46–75.

The character classes used in CTYPE.ASM were selected to be useful in parsing BASIC source code. For example, the ampersand (&) and decimal point (.) are coded as "numeric," since BASIC source-code representations of numeric values can begin with an ampersand or a decimal point. (Starting with QBASIC 4.0, the ampersand is also a type-defining suffix — denoting type LONG.) I have also taken advantage of the fact that the QBASIC compiler refuses to recognize certain ASCII symbols (returning the severe error message "Invalid character" when it finds one in its parsing scan) and have coded those symbols as class zero.

```
 1:          PAGE    ,105
 2:          TITLE   CTYPE
 3:          .MODEL  MEDIUM
 4:  ;*********************************************************************
 5:  ;                            CTYPE.ASM                              *
 6:  ;    CTYPE is a module of integer functions used by the QBASIC program *
 7:  ; VARCHK.BAS to simplify finding "tokens" in QBASIC source-code files. *
 8:  ; All the functions are declared in the same manner:               *
 9:  ;              DECLARE FUNCTION <name>% (A$)                        *
10:  ;        where <name> is the name of the particular function.      *
11:  ;                                                                   *
12:  ;    Each function returns the location of the first byte in the    *
13:  ; string argument that matches the attribute searched for by <name>. *
14:  ; If the attribute is not found in the string, the function returns a *
15:  ; zero.                                                             *
16:  ;        ISALPHA searches for an alphabetic character              *
17:  ;        ISNUM   searches for a numeric character (includes "&","."). *
18:  ;        STARTOK searches for an alphanumeric character            *
19:  ;        ENDTOK  searches for any BASIC token delimiter, including  *
20:  ;                operators, white space, and type-defining symbols  *
21:  ;        ISTYPE  searches for a type-defining symbol               *
22:  ;                ("$","%","&","!","#")                             *
23:  ;        ISMARK  searches for a quotation mark, apostrophe, underscore *
24:  ;        ISPRINT searches for a non-white space character          *
25:  ;                                                                   *
26:  ;        Written by M. L. Lesser, September 15, 1986               *
27:  ;        Modified for Microsoft BC 4.0 and MASM 5.0, 12-13-87       *
28:  ;*********************************************************************
29:
30:  ; Values of bit coding used for character attribute table:
31:  ; Symbols not used in BASIC source code are coded as 0H
32:          ALPHA   EQU     80H             ;Alphabetic characters
33:          NUM     EQU     40H             ;Numeric characters (in BASIC)
34:          SEPAR   EQU     20H             ;"," " ":" ";" "(" ")" "[" "]"
35:          TYPEDEF EQU     10H             ;BASIC variable type symbols
36:          MARKER  EQU     08H             ;Quote, apostrophe, underscore
37:          OPER    EQU     04H             ;Operators
38:          WHITE   EQU     02H             ;<HT> <LF> <CR> <SP>
39:          DELIM   EQU     SEPAR + MARKER + OPER + WHITE + TYPEDEF
40:          ALPHANUM EQU    ALPHA + NUM
41:          NONWHITE EQU    0FFH - WHITE
42:
43:  .DATA
44:  ATTRIB  DB      ?                       ;Search attribute used
45:  ; 128-byte translate table of ASCII character attributes:
46:  TABLE   DB      9 DUP(0)                ;<NUL> through <BS>
47:          DB      2 DUP(WHITE)            ;<HT> <LF>
48:          DB      2 DUP(0)                ;<VT> <FF>
49:          DB      WHITE                   ;<CR>
50:          DB      18 DUP(0)               ;<SO> through <US>
51:          DB      WHITE                   ;<SP>
52:          DB      TYPEDEF                 ; '!'
53:          DB      MARKER                  ; '"' (double quotes)
54:          DB      3 DUP(TYPEDEF)          ; '#' '$' '%'
55:          DB      TYPEDEF + NUM           ; '&'
```

Listing 9 - 2 (continued)

```
56:          DB      MARKER                    ; ''' (apostrophe)
57:          DB      2 DUP(SEPAR)              ; '(' ')'
58:          DB      2 DUP(OPER)               ; '*' '+'
59:          DB      SEPAR                     ; ','
60:          DB      OPER                      ; '-'
61:          DB      NUM                       ; '.'
62:          DB      OPER                      ; '/'
63:          DB      10 DUP(NUM)               ; '0' through '9'
64:          DB      2 DUP(SEPAR)              ; ':' ';'
65:          DB      3 DUP(OPER)               ; '<' '=' '>'
66:          DB      2 DUP(0)                  ; '?' '@'
67:          DB      26 DUP(ALPHA)             ; 'A' through 'Z'
68:          DB      SEPAR                     ; '['
69:          DB      OPER                      ; '\'
70:          DB      SEPAR                     ; ']'
71:          DB      OPER                      ; '^'
72:          DB      MARKER                    ; (underscore)
73:          DB      0                         ; '`'
74:          DB      26 DUP(ALPHA)             ; 'a' through 'z'
75:          DB      5 DUP(0)                  ; '{' '|' '}' '~' <DEL>
76:
77:  .CODE
78:  ;   Local routine used by all called subroutines in module:
79:  DUMMY   PROC               ;Dummy Far Proc for correct RETurn
80:  FINDIT:                    ;"Near" label for jump target
81:          PUSH    BP                        ;Save BASIC's stack frame
82:          MOV     BP,SP                     ;Stack frame for this module
83:          PUSH    SI                        ;Used to scan string
84:          MOV     BX,6[BP]                  ;Address of string descriptor
85:          MOV     CX,[BX]                   ;String length
86:          OR      CX,CX                     ;Check for null string
87:          JZ      NONE                      ;Return zero if null
88:          CLD                               ;Will scan string "up"
89:          MOV     SI,2[BX]                  ;Address of string itself
90:          PUSH    CX                        ;Save length for later
91:          LEA     BX,TABLE                  ;Address of look-up table
92:  AGAIN:  LODSB                             ;Next byte of string in AL
93:          AND     AL,7FH                    ;Force to 7-bit character code
94:          XLAT                              ;Substitute character attribute
95:          TEST    AL,ATTRIB                 ;Test for desired attribute
96:          JNZ     OK                        ;Quit loop if found
97:          LOOP    AGAIN                     ;Or continue until end of string
98:  ;  If attribute not found in string, loop exit will be to here:
99:          POP     AX                        ;Clear stack of PUSHed old CX
100: NONE:   XOR     AX,AX                     ;Set zero return
101:         JMP SHORT DONE                    ;Will return zero
102: OK:     POP     AX                        ;Original length of string
103:         SUB     AX,CX                     ;"Found" byte location less 1
104:         INC     AX                        ;Location of "found" byte
105: DONE:   POP     SI                        ;Restore divots
106:         POP     BP
107:         RET     2                         ;  and return to caller
108: DUMMY   ENDP
109:
110: ; Public procedures
```

Listing 9 - 2 (continued)

```
111:           PUBLIC   ISALPHA
112: ISALPHA PROC
113:           MOV      ATTRIB,ALPHA          ;Set search argument
114:           JMP      FINDIT                ;Do routine
115: ISALPHA ENDP
116:
117:           PUBLIC   ISNUM
118: ISNUM   PROC
119:           MOV      ATTRIB,NUM
120:           JMP      FINDIT
121: ISNUM   ENDP
122:
123:           PUBLIC   STARTOK
124: STARTOK PROC
125:           MOV      ATTRIB,ALPHANUM
126:           JMP      FINDIT
127: STARTOK ENDP
128:
129:           PUBLIC   ENDTOK
130: ENDTOK  PROC
131:           MOV      ATTRIB,DELIM
132:           JMP      FINDIT
133: ENDTOK  ENDP
134:
135:           PUBLIC   ISTYPE
136: ISTYPE  PROC
137:           MOV      ATTRIB,TYPEDEF
138:           JMP      FINDIT
139: ISTYPE  ENDP
140:
141:           PUBLIC   ISMARK
142: ISMARK  PROC
143:           MOV      ATTRIB,MARKER
144:           JMP      FINDIT
145: ISMARK  ENDP
146:
147:           PUBLIC   ISPRINT
148: ISPRINT PROC
149:           MOV      ATTRIB,NONWHITE
150:           JMP      FINDIT
151: ISPRINT ENDP
152:
153:           END
```

Listing 9-2

If you were creating a word processor, you would need a different set of character classifications and CTYPE functions, to distinguish between upper- and lowercase alphabetical characters, punctuation marks, etc. A good example for a more general set is the classification of the ASCII character set used in the C library *ctype* macros and functions.[1]

```
 1:   '*****************************************************************************
 2:   '                           VARCHK.BAS                                       *
 3:   '      VARCHK reads a QBASIC source-code file and displays "undeclared"       *
 4:   ' variable usage by name and pseudo line number.                              *
 5:   '      Command-line call is:  VARCHK [<path>]<filename>                        *
 6:   '         where [<path>] is required only if <filename>.BAS is not in a        *
 7:   '            directory listed in the PATH environment string.                  *
 8:   '      The file KEYBAS.SVE, containing all the QBASIC keywords, must be         *
 9:   ' available in a directory in the PATH environment string.                     *
10:   '            Written by M. L. Lesser, March 11, 1987                           *
11:   '            Rewritten for Microsoft BC version 4.0, 12-14-87                  *
12:   '         After compilation, link to the assembled module CTYPE.OBJ            *
13:   '*****************************************************************************
14:       DEFSTR A-Z
15:       DEFINT I-N
16:       TYPE FLAGS
17:           HEADER AS INTEGER
18:           LCONT  AS INTEGER
19:           LSTART AS INTEGER
20:       END TYPE
21:       TYPE POINTER
22:           ENDD   AS INTEGER
23:           START  AS INTEGER
24:       END TYPE
25:       CONST NTYPES = 64
26:
27:   ' CTYPE function declarations:
28:       DECLARE FUNCTION ISNUM% (A$)
29:       DECLARE FUNCTION STARTOK% (A$)
30:       DECLARE FUNCTION ENDTOK% (A$)
31:       DECLARE FUNCTION ISTYPE% (A$)
32:       DECLARE FUNCTION ISMARK% (A$)
33:       DECLARE FUNCTION ISPRINT% (A$)
34:
35:   ' Global and Main variables:
36:       DIM FILE, FILENAME, I, STATE, TEMP
37:       DIM SHARED FLAG AS FLAGS, LEFT.PAREN, MARK AS POINTER,  _
38:                  TEXT, TOKEN, TYPES(NTYPES), TYPE.LIST(NTYPES), _
39:                  VAR.GLOB, VAR.KEY, VAR.LOC, VAR.MAIN, VAR.PROC
40:
41:   ' Defined function:
42:   DEF FNSYMBOL
43:   ' Returns next non-white-space symbol in TEXT; if no remaining printable
44:   ' symbol, returns null string (will not check any "continued" line):
45:       IF ISPRINT(TEXT) THEN
46:           LET FNSYMBOL = MID$(TEXT,ISPRINT(TEXT),1)
47:       ELSE
48:           LET FNSYMBOL = ""
49:       END IF
50:   END DEF
51:
52:   ' Program starts here:
53:   ' Get name of source-code file; <ext> will be forced to BAS:
54:       LET FILE = COMMAND$
55:       IF LEN(FILE) = 0 THEN                      'No <filename> on command line
56:           INPUT "Enter [<path>]<filename> to check:  ", FILE
```

Listing 9 - 3 (continued)

```
57:      END IF
58:      LET I = INSTR(FILE,".")
59:      IF I THEN LET FILE = LEFT$(FILE,I-1)        'Remove any <.ext>
60:      LET FILE = FILE + ".BAS"                    ' and force to .BAS
61:      LET FILENAME = UCASE$(FILE)                 'For display header
62:      CALL FINDFILE(FILE)
63:      IF LEN(FILE) = 0 THEN
64:          PRINT: PRINT TAB(10) "Cannot find " CHR$(34) FILENAME CHR$(34);
65:          PRINT " - Terminating Program"
66:          END
67:      ELSE
68:          OPEN FILE FOR INPUT AS #1
69:      END IF
70: ' Set up string with BASIC keywords (from KEYBAS.SVE file):
71:      LET VAR.KEY = CHR$(0)
72:      LET FILE = "KEYBAS.SVE"
73:      CALL FINDFILE(FILE)
74:      IF LEN(FILE) = 0 THEN
75:          PRINT: PRINT TAB(10) "Cannot find KEYBAS.SVE file";
76:          PRINT " - Terminating Program"
77:          END
78:      ELSE
79:          OPEN FILE FOR INPUT AS #2
80:          WHILE NOT EOF(2)
81:              INPUT #2, TEMP
82:              LET VAR.KEY = VAR.KEY + TEMP + CHR$(0)
83:          WEND
84:          CLOSE #2
85:      END IF
86: ' Sign on:
87:      CALL COLORIT                                'Set preferred display colors
88:      LOCATE 2,10
89:      PRINT "Checking " FILENAME " for undeclared variables"
90:      PRINT
91:      LET VAR.MAIN = CHR$(0)                      'Initialize declared variable
92:      LET VAR.GLOB = CHR$(0)                      '   lists
93:      LET VAR.PROC = CHR$(0)
94:      LET TYPES(0) = MKI$(0)                      'Initialize TYPES array
95:
96: ' Code analysis starts here:
97: MAIN:                       'Analyze main segments of source code
98:      LET STATE = "MAIN"
99:      LET VAR.LOC = CHR$(0)
100:     CALL GETTOK                                 'Get next token
101: ' Check for variable declaration:
102:     IF FLAG.LSTART THEN
103:         SELECT CASE TOKEN
104:             CASE "DECLARE"
105: ' Declared function and called subroutine names put in VAR.PROC:
106:             CALL GETTOK                          'Either "SUB" or "FUNCTION"
107:             CALL GETTOK                          'Name of procedure
108:             LET VAR.PROC = VAR.PROC + TOKEN + CHR$(0)
109:             IF ISTYPE(RIGHT$(TOKEN,1)) THEN      'Type-defined function
110:                 LET TOKEN = LEFT$(TOKEN,LEN(TOKEN)-1)
111:                 LET VAR.PROC = VAR.PROC + TOKEN + CHR$(0)
112:             END IF
```

Listing 9 - 3 (continued)

```
113:                   CALL DELETE                'Delete rest of statement
114:               CASE "CONST"                   'Symbolic constant in VAR.GLOB
115:                   CALL VAR.LIST("GLOBAL")
116:               CASE "DIM"                     'Variable declaration
117:                   CALL GETTOK
118:                   IF TOKEN = "SHARED" THEN       'Add remaining tokens
119:                       LET STATE = "GLOBAL"       ' to global list
120:                   ELSE
121:                       CALL PUTTOK            'Return last token to TEXT
122:                   END IF
123:                   CALL VAR.LIST(STATE)
124:               CASE "COMMON"
125:                   CALL GETTOK
126:                   IF TOKEN = "SHARED" THEN
127:                       LET STATE = "GLOBAL"
128:                   ELSE
129:                       CALL PUTTOK
130:                   END IF
131:                   IF FNSYMBOL = "/" THEN CALL GETTOK        'named COMMON
132:                   CALL VAR.LIST(STATE)
133: ' State transfers:
134:               CASE "DEF"                      'May be a defined function
135:                   CALL GETTOK
136:                   LET TEMP = TOKEN            'Save for possible display
137:                   IF LEFT$(TOKEN,2) = "FN" THEN GOTO FUNCT
138:               CASE "FUNCTION"                 'Declared function definition
139:                   GOTO PROCEDURE
140:               CASE "SUB"                      'Called subroutine definition
141:                   GOTO PROCEDURE
142:               CASE "TYPE"                     'Store defined-type names
143:                   GOTO TYPEDEF
144:               CASE ELSE                       'Required dummy
145:           END SELECT
146:       END IF
147:       CALL CHKTOK(STATE)
148:       GOTO MAIN                'End of MAIN state
149:
150: FUNCT:                   'Analyze defined functions in source code:
151:       LET VAR.LOC = CHR$(0)
152:       LET STATE = "FUNCTION"
153: ' Check for formal parameter list:
154:       IF FNSYMBOL = "("  THEN CALL PARAM.LIST
155:       IF FNSYMBOL = "=" THEN
156: ' Process single-statement function:
157:           PRINT "Single-line "; TOKEN " definition  ";
158:           CALL GETTOK                        'First token in function def
159:           WHILE NOT FLAG.LSTART              'For the rest of this statement
160:               CALL CHKTOK("FUNCTION")
161:               CALL GETTOK
162:           WEND
163: ' Replace first token of next statement
164:           CALL PUTTOK
165:           GOTO MAIN                          ' and return to MAIN state
166:       END IF                    'End of single-statement function
167: ' Analyze multiline function:
168:       PRINT "Start of "; TEMP " definition";
```

Listing 9 - 3 (continued)

```
169:    MULTI.FUNC:
170:        CALL GETTOK
171:        IF FLAG.LSTART THEN            'Function declarations
172:            SELECT CASE TOKEN
173:                CASE "END"                    ' Check for end of definition
174:                    CALL GETTOK
175:                    IF TOKEN = "DEF" THEN
176:                        PRINT "End of defined function";
177:                        GOTO  MAIN
178:                    ELSE
179:                        CALL PUTTOK
180:                    END IF
181:                CASE "STATIC"                 'STATIC statement adds
182:                    CALL VAR.LIST("LOCAL")    ' tokens to local list
183:                CASE "DIM"                    'DIM statement has
184:                    CALL VAR.LIST(STATE)      ' special scope problem
185:                CASE ELSE
186:            END SELECT
187:        END IF
188:        CALL CHKTOK(STATE)
189:        GOTO MULTI.FUNC               'End of FUNCTION state
190:
191:    PROCEDURE:              'Analyze procedure definitions
192:        LET VAR.LOC = CHR$(0)
193:        LET STATE = "LOCAL"
194:        CALL GETTOK                          'Name of procedure
195:        PRINT "Start of "; TOKEN " procedure definition";
196:    ' Add TOKEN to VAR.PROC list in case this is first declaration:
197:        LET VAR.PROC = VAR.PROC + TOKEN + CHR$(0)
198:        IF ISTYPE(RIGHT$(TOKEN,1)) THEN
199:            LET VAR.PROC = VAR.PROC + LEFT$(TOKEN,LEN(TOKEN)-1) + CHR$(0)
200:        END IF
201:    ' Check for formal parameter list:
202:        IF FNSYMBOL = "(" THEN CALL PARAM.LIST
203:        CALL GETTOK
204:        IF TOKEN <> "STATIC" THEN CALL PUTTOK
205:    PROC.1:                  'Analyze internal statements
206:        CALL GETTOK
207:    ' Check for end of subroutine definition:
208:        IF FLAG.LSTART THEN
209:            IF TOKEN = "END" THEN
210:                CALL GETTOK
211:                IF TOKEN = "SUB" OR TOKEN = "FUNCTION" THEN
212:                    PRINT "End of procedure definition";
213:                    GOTO MAIN
214:                ELSE
215:                    CALL PUTTOK
216:                END IF
217:    ' Check for variable declaration statements:
218:            ELSEIF TOKEN = "STATIC" OR TOKEN = "SHARED" _
219:                OR TOKEN = "DIM" THEN
220:                CALL VAR.LIST(STATE)
221:            END IF
222:        END IF
223:        CALL CHKTOK(STATE)
224:        GOTO PROC.1            'End of PROCEDURE state
```

Listing 9 - 3 (continued)

```
225:
226:    TYPEDEF:                        'Store TYPE components in TYPES lists
227:         CALL GETTOK                              'Type name
228:         PRINT "Defining type "; TOKEN;
229:         LET I = CVI(TYPES(0)) + 1
230:         IF I > NTYPES THEN                            'Array full
231:             PRINT: PRINT TAB(10) "TOO MANY DEFINED TYPES"
232:                     PRINT TAB(10) "--TERMINATING PROGRAM--"
233:                     END                      'Abnormal end
234:         END IF
235:         LET TYPES(I) = TOKEN
236:         LET TYPES(0) = MKI$(I)
237:    TYPER:   CALL DELETE                          'Delete rest of statement
238:             CALL GETTOK                          'Name of field in record
239:             IF TOKEN = "END" THEN
240:                 PRINT "End of type definition";
241:                 CALL DELETE
242:                 GOTO MAIN                        'Normal exit from state
243:             END IF
244:             LET TYPE.LIST(I) = TYPE.LIST(I) + TOKEN + CHR$(0)
245:         GOTO TYPER
246:    ' End of TYPDEF state
247:
248:    ' Called subroutines in alphabetic order:
249:    SUB CHKTOK(STATE) STATIC           'Check for undeclared variable:
250:         CALL EMERGEX
251:    ' Test for line number or label
252:        IF FLAG.LSTART THEN
253:            IF ISNUM(LEFT$(TOKEN,1)) THEN   'We have a line number
254:                LET TOKEN = ""                 'Delete TOKEN and force
255:                LET TEXT = ":" + TEXT          '  line start on next TOKEN
256:            ELSEIF FNSYMBOL = ":" THEN         'We have a line label
257:                LET TOKEN = ""                 'Delete token
258:            END IF                  'End of label test
259:        END IF
260:    ' Test for subroutine call:
261:        IF TOKEN = "CALL" THEN
262:            CALL GETTOK                         'Name of subroutine
263:            LET TOKEN = ""                      'Throw it away
264:    ' Test for defined function call:
265:        ELSEIF LEFT$(TOKEN,2) = "FN" THEN
266:            LET TOKEN = ""
267:    ' Test for commands that are followed only by label names
268:    '    and for DEF<type>s (all eliminate rest of statement)"
269:        ELSEIF TOKEN = "GOSUB" OR TOKEN = "GOTO" _
270:               OR TOKEN = "RESUME" OR TOKEN = "RESTORE" _
271:               OR TOKEN = "DEFINT" OR TOKEN = "DEFLNG" OR TOKEN = "DEFSTR" _
272:               OR TOKEN = "DEFSNG" OR TOKEN = "DEFDBL" THEN            _
273:            CALL DELETE
274:    ' Test for use of UBOUND and LBOUND functions:
275:        ELSEIF TOKEN = "LBOUND" OR TOKEN = "UBOUND" THEN
276:            CALL GETTOK                         'Next token is array name
277:            LET TOKEN = TOKEN + "()"
278:    ' Test for ERASE statement--terms in rest of statement are array names,
279:    '    but do not carry the parens that are the array identifier:
280:        ELSEIF TOKEN = "ERASE" THEN
```

Listing 9 - 3 (continued)

```
281:              CALL GETTOK
282:              WHILE NOT FLAG.LSTART
283:                  LET TOKEN = TOKEN + "()"
284:                  GOSUB TESTIT                      'Test immediately
285:                  CALL GETTOK
286:              WEND
287:                  CALL PUTTOK
288:          END IF
289: ' Eliminate token if it is a number:
290:          IF ISNUM(LEFT$(TOKEN,1)) THEN LET TOKEN = ""
291: ' Eliminate token if it is a keyword:
292:          IF INSTR(VAR.KEY,CHR$(0)+TOKEN+CHR$(0)) THEN LET TOKEN = ""
293: ' Eliminate token if it is a procedure name:
294:          IF INSTR(VAR.PROC,CHR$(0)+TOKEN+CHR$(0)) THEN LET TOKEN = ""
295: ' Check for token being an array:
296:          IF TOKEN <> "" THEN
297:              IF (FNSYMBOL = "(" OR FNSYMBOL = "[") THEN
298:                  LET TOKEN = TOKEN + "()"
299:              END IF
300:          END IF
301: ' If TOKEN still exists, see if it is in a variable list:
302:          IF TOKEN <> "" THEN GOSUB TESTIT
303: EXIT SUB                      'Normal exit from CHKTOK
304:
305: TESTIT:            'Internal GOSUB subroutine to test if variable in list
306: ' Eliminate token if it is declared as local variable:
307:          IF INSTR(VAR.LOC,CHR$(0)+TOKEN+CHR$(0)) THEN LET TOKEN = ""
308: ' Eliminate token if it is declared as global variable:
309:          IF INSTR(VAR.GLOB,CHR$(0)+TOKEN+CHR$(0)) THEN LET TOKEN = ""
310: ' Test STATE to see if main variables have local scope:
311:          IF STATE = "MAIN" OR STATE = "FUNCTION" THEN
312:              IF INSTR(VAR.MAIN,CHR$(0)+TOKEN+CHR$(0)) THEN LET TOKEN = ""
313:          END IF
314: ' If still there, print token name after latest pseudo line number:
315:          IF TOKEN <> "" THEN PRINT TOKEN SPACE$(2);
316: RETURN                       'End of GOSUB subroutine
317: END SUB                      'End of CHKTOK subroutine
318:
319: SUB DELETE STATIC        'Delete remainder of current statement
320:      CALL GETTOK
321:      WHILE NOT FLAG.LSTART
322:          CALL GETTOK
323:      WEND
324:      CALL PUTTOK
325:      LET TOKEN = ""
326: END SUB                      'End of DELETE subroutine
327:
328: SUB GETTOK STATIC                'Finds next token in source code
329: DIM LINE.NUM, OLDTEXT, SYMBOL, TEMP
330: GETTOK.1:                        'Restart point for REM token
331:      LET FLAG.LSTART = 0                'Turn off line-start flag
332:      WHILE STARTOK(TEXT) = 0           'If no alphanum symbol in string
333:          IF FLAG.HEADER THEN           '  tack on next line
334:              GOSUB HEADLINE
335:          ELSE
336:              GOSUB NEWLINE
```

Listing 9 - 3 (continued)

```
337:          END IF
338:       WEND
339:       LET MARK.START = STARTOK(TEXT)
340:       LET I = INSTR(TEXT,":")              'Look for statement-end symbol
341:       IF I AND (I < MARK.START) THEN       '  If found and ahead of token
342:          LET FLAG.LSTART = -1              '      set line-start flag
343:       END IF
344:       LET TEXT = MID$(TEXT,MARK.START)     'Clean off leading separators
345:       IF ENDTOK(MID$(TEXT,2)) = 0 THEN     'Token is at end of string
346:          LET TOKEN = TEXT
347:          LET TEXT = ""
348:       ELSE
349:          LET MARK.ENDD = ENDTOK(MID$(TEXT,2))     'Mark end of TOKEN,
350:          IF MARK.ENDD+1 = ISTYPE(TEXT) _          'If type-def mark is
351:             THEN LET MARK.ENDD = MARK.ENDD + 1 '  delimiter, include it
352:          LET TOKEN = LEFT$(TEXT,MARK.ENDD)
353:          LET TEXT = MID$(TEXT,MARK.ENDD + 1)
354:          IF TOKEN = "REM" THEN                 'Check for included PQB.BI file
355:             IF INSTR(TEXT,"$INCLUDE") <> 0 THEN GOSUB HEADER
356:             LET TEXT = ""                      'Delete remainder of line
357:             LET FLAG.LCONT = 0                 'Turn off line-continuation flag
358:             GOTO GETTOK.1                      'And get token from next line
359:          END IF
360:       END IF
361:       EXIT SUB                'Nominal end of GETTOK subroutine
362:
363: ' Embedded GOSUB subroutines used by GETTOK:
364: NEWLINE:                              'Reads new line from source-code file
365: ' If no more source code to read, display message and terminate program:
366:       IF EOF(1) THEN
367:          PRINT: PRINT
368:          PRINT TAB(10) "All source text analyzed"
369:          END                                'Normal program end
370:       END IF
371: ' Else read next physical line and set line-start flag:
372:       LINE INPUT #1, TEXT                   'Read next line
373:       IF NOT FLAG.LCONT THEN                'If not continuation line
374:          LET TEXT = ":" + TEXT              '  insert statement-end mark
375:       END IF
376:       LET LINE.NUM = LINE.NUM + 1           'Next pseudo line number
377: ' If no tokens have been displayed since reading last line, overwrite
378: '      previous line number on display:
379:       IF POS(0) < 10 THEN LOCATE ,1 ELSE PRINT
380:       PRINT USING "#####"; LINE.NUM;
381:       PRINT ": ";
382:       GOSUB CLEANUP                         'Delete extraneous material
383: RETURN                      'End of NEWLINE GOSUB subroutine
384:
385: CLEANUP:                                'Clean off quoted strings, remarks, etc.
386:       LET FLAG.LCONT = 0                    'Turn off line-continuation flag
387:       LET TEXT = UCASE$(TEXT)               'Make all caps
388: ' Delete quoted strings and any text following apostrophe or underscore:
389:       WHILE ISMARK(TEXT) <> 0               'Check for quote, apostrophe, or
390:          LET MARK.START = ISMARK(TEXT)      '  underscore in TEXT
391:          LET OLDTEXT = ""
392:          LET SYMBOL = MID$(TEXT,MARK.START,1)
```

Listing 9 - 3 (continued)

```
393:    ' If first marker found is double quote, find next quote (if any) and
394:    '     save text after second qoute:
395:            IF SYMBOL = CHR$(34) THEN
396:                LET MARK.ENDD = INSTR(MARK.START+1,TEXT,CHR$(34))
397:                IF MARK.ENDD THEN LET OLDTEXT = MID$(TEXT,MARK.ENDD+1)
398:            ELSEIF SYMBOL = "_" THEN          'If marker is underscore
399:                LET FLAG.LCONT = -1          '  set continuation flag
400:            ELSEIF SYMBOL = "'" THEN
401:    ' If marker is an apostrophe, check if PQB.BI is included:
402:                IF INSTR(MARK.START+1,TEXT,"$INCLUDE") THEN GOSUB HEADER
403:            END IF
404:            LET TEXT = LEFT$(TEXT,MARK.START-1) + OLDTEXT    'Delete remark
405:        WEND                                 'Repeat as required
406: RETURN                    'End of CLEANUP GOSUB subroutine
407:
408: HEADER:          'Set UP header file to be read by HEADLINE:
409:        LET TEMP = ENVIRON$("INCLUDE")
410:        PRINT "Including PQB.BI file";
411:        IF RIGHT$(TEMP,1) <> "\" THEN LET TEMP = TEMP + "\"
412:        LET TEMP = TEMP + "PQB.BI"
413:        OPEN TEMP FOR INPUT AS #2
414:        LET FLAG.HEADER = -1          'Turn on flag for GETTOK
415: RETURN                    'End of HEADER GOSUB subroutine
416:
417: HEADLINE:              'Read line of text from PQB.BI file
418: ' If no more source code to read, close file and turn off flag:
419:        IF EOF(2) THEN
420:            CLOSE #2
421:            LET FLAG.HEADER = 0
422:            GOSUB NEWLINE
423:        ELSE                     'Read next line from file
424:            LINE INPUT #2, TEXT              'Read next line
425:            IF NOT FLAG.LCONT THEN           'If not continuation line
426:                LET TEXT = ":" + TEXT       ' insert statement-end mark
427:            END IF
428:            GOSUB CLEANUP                    'Delete extraneous material
429:        END IF
430: RETURN                    'End of HEADLINE GOSUB subroutine
431: END SUB                   'End of GETTOK called subroutine
432:
433: SUB PARAM.LIST STATIC            'Insert variables into VAR.LOC
434:        LET LEFT.PAREN = 1
435:        WHILE LEFT.PAREN
436:            CALL GETTOK
437:            IF FNSYMBOL = "(" OR FNSYMBOL = "[" THEN
438:                LET LEFT.PAREN = LEFT.PAREN + 1
439:                LET TEXT = MID$(TEXT,ISPRINT(TEXT)+1)    'Clean off "("
440:                LET TOKEN = TOKEN + "()"              'Assume array variable
441:            END IF
442:            WHILE FNSYMBOL = ")" OR FNSYMBOL = "]"        'May have multiple
443:                LET LEFT.PAREN = LEFT.PAREN - 1          '  right parens
444:                LET TEXT = MID$(TEXT,ISPRINT(TEXT)+1)
445:            WEND
446:    ' Clean off numeric token:
447:            IF ISNUM(LEFT$(TOKEN,1)) THEN LET TOKEN = ""
448:            IF LEN(TOKEN) THEN                                'Add to local
```

Listing 9 - 3 (continued)

```
449:                 LET VAR.LOC = VAR.LOC + TOKEN + CHR$(0)      ' variable list
450:           END IF
451:       WEND
452:   END SUB                    'End of PARAM.LIST subroutine
453:
454:   SUB PUTTOK STATIC              'Put back "unused" TOKEN
455:       IF FLAG.LSTART THEN                      'If this was first token in line
456:           LET TOKEN = ":" + TOKEN             'Insert statement-end mark
457:           LET FLAG.LSTART = 0                 '  and turn off line-start flag
458:       END IF
459:       LET TEXT = TOKEN + " " + TEXT          '<SP> is separator
460:       LET TOKEN = ""
461:   END SUB                    'End of PUTTOK subroutine
462:
463:   SUB VAR.LIST(CLASS) STATIC          'Add token to appropriate variable.list
464:   DIM I, J, K
465:   SHARED STATE
466:       CALL GETTOK
467:       WHILE NOT FLAG.LSTART                      'For single statement
468:           IF ISNUM(LEFT$(TOKEN,1)) THEN          'Ignore numeric tokens
469:           ELSEIF TOKEN = "AS" THEN               'Type definition
470:               GOSUB DEF.TYPE
471:           ELSE
472:               LET TEMP = TOKEN                      'Save for defined type
473:               GOSUB DIM.ARRAY                  'Check for array variable
474:   '   Add token to proper variable list:
475:               GOSUB LIST.TOK                      'Put in proper list
476:           END IF
477:           CALL GETTOK
478:       WEND
479:       CALL PUTTOK                          'Replaces divots
480:   EXIT SUB                 'Return point from VAR.LIST
481:
482:   ' Embedded GOSUB subroutines used only by VAR.LIST:
483:   DEF.TYPE:                'Adds "record" names to variable list:
484:       CALL GETTOK                          'Variable type
485:       FOR I = 1 TO CVI(TYPES(0))          'Read TYPES array until
486:           IF TOKEN = TYPES(I) THEN          '  matches type name
487:               LET K = 1
488:               LET J = INSTR(K,TYPE.LIST(I),CHR$(0))
489:               WHILE J
490:                   LET TOKEN = TEMP + "." + MID$(TYPE.LIST(I),K,J-K)
491:                   GOSUB LIST.TOK
492:                   LET K = J + 1          'Start of next field name
493:                   LET J = INSTR(K,TYPE.LIST(I),CHR$(0))
494:               WEND
495:           END IF
496:       NEXT I
497:   RETURN                 'End of DEF.TYPE GOSUB subroutine
498:
499:   DIM.ARRAY:      'Check for declared variable being an array
500:       IF FNSYMBOL = "(" OR FNSYMBOL = "[" THEN
501:           LET SAVE.TOK = TOKEN + "()"          'Mark as array
502:           LET TEXT = MID$(TEXT,ISPRINT(TEXT)+1)     'Step over symbol
503:           IF FNSYMBOL = ")" OR FNSYMBOL = "]" THEN
504:   ' Array is in COMMON variable list
```

Listing 9 - 3 (continued)

```
505:            ELSE
506: ' Array has dimension values, either constants or variables
507:               LET LEFT.PAREN = 1
508:               WHILE LEFT.PAREN
509:                  CALL GETTOK
510:                  CALL CHKTOK(STATE)
511:                  IF FNSYMBOL = "(" OR FNSYMBOL = "[" THEN
512: ' Dynamic array element was dimensioned with an array element
513:                     LET LEFT.PAREN = LEFT.PAREN + 1
514:                  ELSE
515:                     WHILE FNSYMBOL = ")" OR FNSYMBOL = "]"
516:                        LET LEFT.PAREN = LEFT.PAREN - 1
517:                        LET TEXT = MID$(TEXT,ISPRINT(TEXT)+1)
518:                     WEND
519:                  END IF
520:               WEND
521:            END IF
522:            LET TOKEN = SAVE.TOK
523:         END IF
524: RETURN                      'End of DIM.ARRAY GOSUB subroutine
525:
526: LIST.TOK:                   'Put token in proper variable list
527:    IF CLASS = "GLOBAL" THEN
528:       LET VAR.GLOB = VAR.GLOB + TOKEN + CHR$(0)
529:    ELSEIF CLASS = "MAIN" THEN
530:       LET VAR.MAIN = VAR.MAIN + TOKEN + CHR$(0)
531:    ELSEIF CLASS = "LOCAL" THEN
532:       LET VAR.LOC = VAR.LOC + TOKEN + CHR$(0)
533:    ELSEIF CLASS = "FUNCTION" THEN
534: ' If token has not previously been declared static, put in VAR.MAIN:
535:       IF INSTR(VAR.LOC,CHR$(0)+TOKEN+CHR$(0)) = 0 THEN
536:          LET VAR.MAIN = VAR.MAIN + TOKEN + CHR$(0)
537:       END IF
538:    END IF
539: RETURN                      'End of LIST.TOK GOSUB subroutine
540: END SUB                     'End of VAR.LIST subroutine
541: '          End of VARCHK.BAS source code
```

Listing 9 - 3

VARCHK.BAS

VARCHK.BAS (Listing 9-3) is structured as a "state" machine for ease of implementation. Each state is written as an infinite GOTO loop, analyzing the source code in a specific substructure segment. The states test tokens for special cases not common to all three states, including tests for those keywords that cause switching to another state. A conditional GOTO transfers control to another state when the appropriate tokens are found. All states other than MAIN return to the beginning of the MAIN state on exit. Routines common to more than one state are written as called subroutines.

The MAIN state (lines 97–148) is in control while VARCHK is analyzing text from the main segment of a QBASIC program. The MAIN state remains in control until transfer out occurs when a "DEF FN<name>" token pair, a FUNCTION token, a SUB token, or a TYPE token is encountered.

The FUNCT state (lines 150–189) is in control during the analysis of a defined function. The FUNCT state automatically transfers back to MAIN if the definition is for a single-line function; the MULTI.FUNC substate loops until the token pair "END DEF" is found.

PROCEDURE (lines 191–224) is in control during the analysis of a compiled called subroutine or declared function definition. The PROCEDURE state remains in control until either an "END FUNCTION" or "END SUB" token pair is read.

TYPEDEF (lines 226–245) was added for QBASIC 4.0 to analyze the new record TYPE definitions. Note that the "TYPE <name>" statement does not *declare* a variable; it merely sets up a "new" variable type that can be declared by a following DIM (or equivalent) statement.

As far as VARCHK is concerned, the "TYPE <name>" statement requires adding <name> to a list of defined types and then saving all the members of the <name> record type to be appended to any record variable declared as type <name>. The TYPEDEF state handles this chore in a somewhat clumsy manner, but it was the best I could think of at the time. I set up two string arrays, TYPES and TYPE.LIST, each having a maximum subscript of 64 (you can change this number by changing the value of the NTYPES constant in line 25). As each TYPE statement is evaluated, <name> is loaded into the next available slot in the TYPES array, and all of <name>'s member names, separated by CHR$(0) symbols, are listed in a single string in the corresponding element of the TYPE.LIST array.

String Processing

The VARCHK parsing process consists of reading each source-code text line from the file being analyzed into the global string variable TEXT, and then destructively parsing TEXT. Each successive token is deleted from the head of TEXT and its value is assigned to the string variable TOKEN for examination.

The conventions to scan and manage the input text strings are established in the called subroutine GETTOK (lines 328–431). GETTOK removes the next token from the global string variable TEXT (lines 328–361). If there isn't another token in TEXT, GETTOK calls on the embedded GOSUB subroutine NEWLINE (lines 364–383) to read another text line. When NEWLINE reads in the next record from the source-code file, LINE.NUM is incremented. If there has been no further output to the display since the last time LIN.NUM was incremented, the new displayed value overwrites the old; otherwise, the new value is displayed on the next row of the display (lines 377–381). In turn, NEWLINE calls on the GOSUB subroutine CLEANUP (lines 385–406) to delete comments and quoted strings.[2] If a $INCLUDE is found buried in a remark, the PQB.BI file is OPENed by HEADER (lines 408– 415) and FLAG.HEADER is set. Then, the next time GETTOK needs a new line of TEXT, PQB.BI is read by HEADLINE (lines 417–430) until all the declarations have been processed.

Keywords requiring the remainder of the tokens in the statement to be deleted force a call to the subroutine DELETE (lines 319– 326). DELETE operates by repeatedly calling GETTOK until FLAG.LSTART shows that one too many tokens have been retrieved. PUTTOK (lines 454–461) replaces the last-retrieved TOKEN at the head of TEXT.

Some tokens are eliminated merely by being passed through the appropriate "state" mechanism. Any TOKEN making it through those mazes is tested for "undeclared" status in the CHKTOK subroutine (lines 249–317). If TOKEN is numeric, or if it is contained in any valid list, it is set to null. The first list searched is VAR.KEY — a list of keywords. The next list is VAR.PROC, a list of declared functions and subroutines. If TOKEN is still non-null and the next printable symbol in TEXT is a left parenthesis or left bracket,[3] TOKEN is marked as an array before the declared-variable lists are searched by calling the embedded GOSUB subroutine TESTIT (lines 305 – 316). VAR.LOC is a list of variables currently declared local, VAR.GLOB contains the variables declared as global, and VAR.MAIN contains variable names having scope only over the main and defined function substructures in the program. VAR.MAIN is not searched if VARCHK is in the PROCEDURE state.

All lists have the same form. Each list is a single string having a <NUL> — CHR$(0) — as the initial byte, followed by all the tokens in the list, each separated by a <NUL>. VAR.KEY is constructed from the

KEYBAS.SVE file (lines 70–85) and has a length of 1,273 bytes for QBASIC 4.0. VAR.LOC is reset to the initial <NUL> 1-byte string when entering any source-code state that may declare a variable (lines 99, 151, 192).

The lists are searched for the existence of TOKEN with the BASIC built-in INSTR function. Keeping the lists in single strings, to be searched by the INSTR function, is most certainly the easiest list-search algorithm to program. It may well be the best performing.

If a token makes it through all the mazes without being nulled, it is displayed opposite the pertinent line number as an undeclared variable.

Variable Declarations

Tokens found in DECLARE statements (valid only when in the MAIN state) are placed in the VAR.PROC list (lines 104– 113). Tokens that are the <name> of a procedure defined within the source code are also placed in the VAR.PROC list (lines 196– 200), in case the procedure definition also serves as its declaration. Duplicate entries in a string list take up a little room in string space, but are immaterial to the action of the program.

Tokens found in function or procedure definition formal parameter lists always declare local variables and are handled by the PARAM.LIST subroutine (lines 433–452).

Named variables found in DIM, COMMON, CONST, STATIC, or SHARED statements are analyzed in the VAR.LIST subroutine (lines 463–540) and placed in the proper list based on the value of the STATE variable established by the scanning state. VAR.LIST is complicated by the existence of defined types and by a compiler anomaly when declaring local arrays in defined functions. These problems are handled by the embedded subroutines, DEF.TYPE (lines 483–497) and LIST.TOK (lines 526–539).

The declaration of a defined type (which may be one of the five intrinsic variable types) is recognized by finding the token "AS" (line 469). DEF.TYPE reads the following token and checks to see if it is one of those listed in the TYPES array. If not, the program assumes it is an intrinsic type and continues. (Undefined nonintrinsic types will be caught by the compiler.) If type <name> is found in the TYPES array, the variable name (now in TEMP) will be added to the appropriate variable list, followed by the enhanced name of each member of type <name>.

The GOSUB subroutine LIST.TOK takes care of the local-array-declaration anomaly. Declaring an array with a DIM statement within a multiline function definition usually makes it a main variable. However, if the DIM statement is preceded by a declaration of the same array variable with a STATIC statement, the array is a local variable. Although both the compiler and VARCHK will accept the notion of a local array variable, it is a poor construct to use in function definitions. This STATIC array is *dynamic*, and the DIM statement is executable. So if you use the defined function more than once, you will get a run-time "Redimensioned array" error interrupt the second time you call it.

Arrays DIMensioned in compiled procedures (the PROCEDURE state) are always local, irrespective of whether the same array was earlier declared in a STATIC statement. However, declaring the array STATIC also makes the DIM an executable statement, with the same unfortunate effect as when done in a function definition.

There is a special problem with dynamic array variables dimensioned with a variable: although the array name is to be added to the appropriate variable list, the dimensioning variable(s) must be passed through CHKTOK. DIM.ARRAY (lines 499–524) takes care of the case where a dynamic array is dimensioned by an array element with variable subscript(s). I'm a little doubtful, but it may even handle dimensioning with an array element whose subscript is an array element with a variable subscript, etc. I leave testing such esoteric cases to the interested reader.

VARCHK Limitations

I have designed VARCHK primarily for my own programming style conventions, with a few attempts to allow for cases I never use. However, you should understand the limitations built into the design, so you can change them if you desire.

The only $INCLUDE file VARCHK looks for is PQB.BI. If you wish to use other $INCLUDE files, including nested $INCLUDE files, you must change the appropriate portions of GETTOK, CLEANUP, and HEADER.

VARCHK will not recognize arrays if the array name and its subscript(s) are on two physical lines, separated by a continuation symbol, although the compiler allows such poor programming style.

There is a scope problem associated with CONST statements that VARCHK cannot handle. Symbolic constants first defined in the MAIN state are global and are so treated by both VARCHK and the compiler. Symbolic constants defined in procedure definitions or in defined functions are local (even if also defined in the MAIN state), but there is a compiler anomaly. A global symbolic constant can be used within a compiled procedure or defined function, after which it can be "redefined" locally for the rest of that procedure or function with another CONST statement. VARCHK cannot handle this case, so it treats all symbolic constants first defined in procedures or defined functions as undeclared variables.

In one sense, random-file FIELD variables could be considered to have been "declared" in the defining FIELD statement. However, there is a scope problem associated with FIELD variables when used in called subroutines (discussed in the next chapter), so it probably is a safer programming style to declare FIELD variables explicitly in DIM or COMMON statements before using them in FIELD statements. VARCHK treats FIELD variables first named in FIELD statements as undeclared variables.

Notes

---

1. The character classification system used in C is shown in Appendix A of W. David Schwaderer's book, *C Wizard's Programming Reference*, Wiley, New York, 1985, pp. 169–170. Although Schwaderer shows nine "class" symbols, there is enough redundancy to code these into a table of bytes.

2. If COMPILE.BAS (Listing 8-6) had been written to remove embedded quoted strings from its input text lines before scanning for "ON ERROR GOTO," it would not falsely compile itself with the /e switch. Note that NEWLINE takes care of the sloppy coding allowed by the compiler — quoted strings do not need the closing quotation mark if they continue to the end of the physical line.

3. The compiler will allow array dimensions to be surrounded by either parentheses or square brackets. Parentheses are required for argument lists and formal parameter lists.

Chapter 10

File Handling

The major differences in file usage between QBASIC and BASICA stem from architectural differences between the two implementations. The first is in file-buffer management. The file buffers in QBASIC programs are created and released by the executing program; the maximum number of files allowed to be open simultaneously is established at system boot time by a FILES= statement in the CONFIG.SYS file. The BASICA file buffers are established in the interpreter's work area when the interpreter itself is loaded; the operator must call the interpreter with the proper switches if more than three files are to be open simultaneously or if any random file is to have a record length of greater than 128 bytes.

The second difference is in the allowable length of sequential-file buffers. In BASICA (and in all versions of QBASIC prior to version 4.0), sequential file buffers contain 128 bytes, requiring the use of large string arrays for intermediate storage if one wishes to increase disk-use efficiency by blocking reads and writes. Starting with QBASIC 4.0, the default length of a sequential-file buffer is 512 bytes (one disk sector), and the programmer can perform automatic file blocking by specifying larger sequential-file buffers.

The final difference is the increased facility for "fielding" random-file records. In addition to the classic FIELD statement, QBASIC (starting with version 4.0) allows the use of the TYPE statement to build arbitrary record structures, thereby removing some of the restrictions associated with using the string structures implicit in the FIELD statement.

The basic concepts of QBASIC file management (which calls on the DOS file manager) are reviewed in this chapter. The QBASIC usage is illustrated with a pair of financial record-keeping programs. One keeps the data for each account in its own random file, accessing any account through two-level menus maintained in self-extending sequential files. The other lists the data in the account files.

DOS File Management

QBASIC uses DOS's *handle* functions in managing its files. Unless you use a FILES= command in your CONFIG.SYS file to increase the number, DOS allows a maximum of eight files or devices to be open simultaneously in handle mode. Three DOS handle "files" are devoted to DOS's default devices (CON, PRN, and AUX) — not used by QBASIC. This leaves a maximum of five simultaneously open files for your program, including any used for redirection, for a CHAIN command, and for devices either your program or the QBASIC support system might have opened as files.

N.B.   For reasons known only to its implementers, QBASIC reopens the LPT1 device when the first LPRINT statement is executed, rather than using the already open DOS printer handle. Thus, programs using LPRINT statements are limited to four simultaneously open files.

All information stored on DOS disks is organized into 512-byte *sector records*. Thus, all information transmitted between disk storage and "internal" RAM memory must be in units of 512 bytes per transfer. QBASIC transfers data between its buffers and disks on a *physical record* basis (the record size given by the LEN clause in an OPEN statement) by calling on DOS to make the translation.

DOS takes care of the translation between the program's physical records and its own 512-byte sector records by reading or writing the physical records one sector at a time. DOS manages physical records that do not start on a sector boundary, or do not fill a complete sector, by using a DOS sector buffer (within resident DOS) as a staging area. The number of DOS sector buffers available may be as few as two, unless specified otherwise with a BUFFERS= command in the CONFIG.SYS file.

Although DOS reads and writes disk files one sector at a time, DOS *allocates* disk space to files on a *cluster* basis. The number of contiguous sectors making up a cluster varies with the type of disk. DOS maintains the status of a disk's clusters in a File Allocation Table (FAT) stored on each disk. The size of the FAT, and hence the number of disk sectors required to store it, depends on the type of disk.

The File Allocation Table has an entry for each cluster the disk contains, where the location (cluster number) of each entry in the table corresponds to the physical location of that cluster on the disk. All unallocated clusters are marked by a zero entry in the FAT. The starting cluster number for each file on the disk is contained in that file's directory entry. FAT entries for the file contain either the cluster number of the *next* cluster in that file, or a symbol indicating that this is the last cluster in the file. When a file being written fills its current cluster, DOS assigns the next available (zero-entry) cluster number to that file. Files become *fragmented* when the next available cluster is not the next contiguous cluster.

DOS can read the information contained in the directories and the File Allocation Table only by reading the appropriate sector into one of its sector buffers. The sector buffers are managed by a least recently used (LRU) algorithm. This is not a "true" LRU algorithm, since it is weighted to favor FAT sectors — in an attempt to keep the FAT in a buffer until needed to locate the next cluster in the file. Each time a sector buffer is used, the LRU priorities of the sector buffers are updated.

DOS keeps data on each sector buffer, giving the file handle it belongs to, the disk location corresponding to its contents, whether or not it has been modified since having been read from the disk, and its LRU priority. When a sector buffer must be made available, that buffer with the lowest priority is released, writing its contents to the disk if they have been modified since originally read. In general, it takes at least two sector buffers to read or write a file longer than a single cluster — one for the FAT and one for the sector being accessed.

DOS maximizes disk performance when sequentially reading or writing long files that have physical record lengths (QBASIC buffer size) that are multiples of 512 bytes. The DOS sector buffer is used only when transferring the first sector of each physical record; the remaining sector transfers are directly between the disk sector and the QBASIC buffer — saving the additional processing time for the internal memory-to-memory transfer between buffers. If you are reading an input sequential file, processing its data, and then writing an output file, performance is maximized and head movement is minimized if each QBASIC file buffer is long enough to contain its complete file.

In order to write a record of less than sector length to an existing portion of a file, DOS must first bring the sector containing the old value of the record into a DOS sector buffer before the new record can be "inserted" into it. The worst disk performance occurs when writing a random record to an existing file when that record fills a portion of each of two sectors, spanning two clusters. DOS may have to write the contents of three sector buffers to the disk to free up room for the FAT and the two sectors required for the record, and then read the necessary three sectors from the disk before it can write the record, thus producing up to six "unnecessary" disk accesses with several intervening disk seeks.[1] Unecessary disk accesses can be minimized if all random record lengths are powers of two.

When DOS closes a file, all modified sector buffers belonging to that file are written to the disk. Both the FAT and directory entries on the disk are updated. The sector buffers belonging to that file are then released for further use.

QBASIC Sequential Files

QBASIC sequential files consist of variable-length *logical* records, each terminated by the <CR><LF> end-of-record symbol. The physical record size is determined by the LEN clause in the OPEN statement. If the LEN clause is omitted, the default physical record size is 512 bytes (one sector). When a sequential file is OPENed, the run-time heap manager creates a buffer area in upper string space containing approximately 40 bytes more than the physical record length. The extra bytes contain QBASIC's bookkeeping data for the file.

When you OPEN an INPUT file, QBASIC requests the DOS file manager to open the specified file as "read only." (If DOS cannot find the file, it returns a DOS critical error message, which QBASIC translates to its corresponding error message.) QBASIC then requests DOS to read the first physical record into QBASIC's file transfer space, thereby initiating a "disk read." As information is read from the QBASIC transfer space with INPUT# or LINE INPUT# statements, QBASIC's file pointer is updated to indicate the next position to be read. After the last byte of the record has been read, QBASIC requests DOS to read the next record.

Sequential reading can continue until either an end-of-file mark (<Ctrl-Z>) is found or the physical end of file (as indicated in the directory entry) is reached. At end of file, the corresponding QBASIC EOF flag is set to -1.

You can OPEN the same actual file as several INPUT file numbers simultaneously, limited only by the DOS handle limit. However, this is usually unnecessary, as you can reread the same INPUT file as many times as you wish by rewinding with a "SEEK #<filenum>,0" statement.

When you OPEN an OUTPUT file, DOS is first asked to delete any existing file having the same <filespec> before creating and opening a write-only file. (If such an existing file has the read-only attribute bit set, a DOS "access denied" critical error message will be generated; the equivalent BASIC error interrupt will be "Path/file access error.") PRINT# or WRITE# statements load bytes into QBASIC's file transfer space, moving QBASIC's file pointer accordingly. When the physical record is full, DOS is requested to "write" the record, and the QBASIC file pointer is returned to the beginning of the transfer space.

APPEND files are opened as DOS read/write files. If the <filespec> does not exist, DOS is asked to create it. If it does exist, its contents are read into the QBASIC file buffer and scanned for an end-of-file mark, or until the physical end of file is reached. The QBASIC file pointer is set to this end-of-file position, after which the operation proceeds as with an OUTPUT file.

If you attempt to OPEN an OUTPUT or APPEND file for a <filespec> that is already OPEN as a QBASIC file, you will get the "File already open" error interrupt.

When a CLOSE statement is executed for an OUTPUT or APPEND file, no end-of-file mark is written to the current pointer location in the QBASIC file buffer. DOS will be given a record length equal to the byte count between the start of the record buffer and the current pointer position to write to the disk. Executing CLOSE also requests DOS to close the file, writing all modified buffers to the file and updating the FAT and directory sectors.

QBASIC executes an implicit CLOSE statement on all its OPEN files when it executes an explicit or implicit END statement. Thus, it is not always necessary, although it is good programming practice, to program a CLOSE statement when you are through with a QBASIC file.

You *must* execute an explicit CLOSE statement for any OPEN file that might have written to a diskette, before the program requests the user to remove that diskette from a drive and insert another. Otherwise, DOS may write the updated sectors belonging to the old diskette at the corresponding locations on the new diskette.

A CLOSE statement frees the corresponding file buffer for further use, but its space is still under the control of the run-time heap manager. If you later OPEN another sequential file (either under the same file number or a different one), the space may be reused, depending on the record lengths of the two files. Or it can be reclaimed for the string- space manager by using the FRE function to force garbage collection.

QBASIC Random Files

If no "FOR <mode>" is specified in an OPEN statement, or if the specification is "FOR RANDOM," QBASIC sets up a file buffer for a random file and asks DOS to open the file in read/write mode. If the specified directory does not contain a file of that name, DOS will be asked to create it.

Random files are treated by BASIC as fixed record length files; the logical and physical records are identical. The record length is specified by the optional "LEN=" clause in the OPEN statement. If no LEN= is given, the default record length is 128 bytes. Any record length from 1 byte to 32,767 bytes can be specified.

Although BASIC allows you to have several random files referring to the same actual file OPEN simultaneously, subject to the maximum handle rule, *don't*! QBASIC doesn't tell DOS when two or more file buffers (each asking DOS to open a file and assign it a handle) belong to the same actual file, so DOS keeps separate books on each of them. Writing to one such random file does not update sector buffers belonging to the others.

Since BASIC keeps a random-record write pointer similar in function to that used with OUTPUT sequential files, you can load information into random-record transfer space with PRINT# and WRITE# statements. But you must keep track of the number of bytes transferred to the buffer. All characters in the PRINT# string will be loaded into the transfer space, plus the line-end <CR><LF> bytes if the statement doesn't end with a semicolon. If you attempt to write off the end, you will produce a run-time "Field overflow" error interrupt. The transfer-space pointer is reset to its origin with any GET or PUT statement.

The FIELD Statement

The nomenclature for random-file usage stems from punch-card accounting usage. The 80-column punch cards were known as "unit records." Each "record" was divided into "fields." Each field contained data pertaining to a single item in the record, and was of a length sufficient to accommodate the longest value that might appear therein.

The traditional way to establish fields for BASIC random records is by using a statement of the form

```
FIELD #<filenum>, <width> AS <stringvar> [,...]
```

where <filenum> is the file identity number of an open random file. All <width>s should be integers and all <stringvar>s must be the names of *string* variables. The sum of all the <width>s used in a single FIELD statement must be less than or equal to the record length of the file.

N.B.   The compiler will not find any error with a FIELD statement specifying an improper <filenum>, but the run-time support will produce a "Bad file mode" (error 54) interrupt when the statement is executed. Nor will the compiler check for the sum of the <width>s exceeding the record length. The run-time error is "Field overflow" (error 50).[2]

After a FIELD statement is executed, each <stringvar> descriptor will have its length word equal to the <width> integer and its second word pointing to the offset of the proper location in the transfer area of the random-file buffer. You can execute as many FIELD statements for valid

<filenum>s as you wish, but each must use different <stringvar>s to prevent resetting previous string descriptors.

<Filenum>s (for both sequential and random files) have "universal" scope; they are valid anywhere in the program, irrespective of which module contained the OPEN statement. But <stringvar>s follow the normal QBASIC scope rules. You can avoid trouble due to this inconsistency by declaring all <stringvar>s with "DIM [SHARED]" statements at the beginning of the main module of your program. (Use "COMMON SHARED /<name>/" in both modules if the same field variable is to be used in a called subroutine in a different module.) Keep all FIELD statements in the program segment that OPENs the file, either in the main segment or in a single called subroutine.

When you CLOSE a random file, all <stringvar> descriptors associated with that file are set to null.

LSET and RSET Statements

As far as BASIC is concerned, the <stringvar>s defined in FIELD statements are treated in the same manner as any other string variable. If you were to assign a new value to a field variable with a LET or INPUT statement, the QBASIC support system would write the new value in "normal" string space and update the string variable descriptor accordingly; you would have lost access to the file field in the process.

LSET and RSET "assignment" statements avoid the problem. A statement of the form

```
LSET <stringvar> = <stringexpression>
```

replaces the value of <stringvar> with the value of <stringexpression>, *in situ*, leaving the string descriptor unchanged. If <stringexpression> is longer than <stringvar>, the low-order (right-end) bytes are truncated to fit. If <stringexpression> is shorter than <stringvar>, <stringexpression> is left-justified in <stringvar> and the balance is padded with <SP> bytes.

RSET works in a similar manner, except that short <stringexpression>s are right-justified in <stringvar> before the balance is padded with <SP> bytes.

The TYPE Statement

As an alternate to the traditional method of establishing record fields in random files, QBASIC 4.0 introduced the record-defining TYPE block. "TYPE <type>" is the header statement for a TYPE block defining a structure having type <type> containing one or more members, each having a defined type. A record-structure variable is declared in a statement equivalent to

```
DIM <recname> AS <type>
```

where <recname> is the variable name of a record structure having the <type> defined in a structure TYPE block. The <recname> of the structure itself is used only in [file] GET and PUT statements. The individual members of each structure are accessed by their compound names: the declared name of the structure and the defined name of the member, joined by a period. For examples, see the declared record-structure variables HEAD and REC, having defined types HEADER and RECORD, in RECORD88.BAS (Listing 10-2).

Member names follow the rules for BASIC variable names; use of keywords (or declared procedure names) is prohibited. Thus, the necessity for the structure-member name MARK.ENDD in VARCHK (Listing 9-3). However, a record-structure <type> can have members with names also used as simple variable names or as member names within other <type>s. As with FIELD# statements, record structures used to field random-file records cannot be longer than the file record; the error produces the same run-time "Field overflow" interruption.

Since the record-structure type was designed for fielding random records, the only string members allowed are fixed-length strings. All LET or INPUT assignments to fixed-length strings operate as though they were LSET statements. If you want to right-justify the value in the fixed-length string, use an RSET statement to make the assignment.

The major advantage of record structures over FIELD# statements in performing what is otherwise the same task is that you can make direct assignments to the members of a declared structure, usually reducing the number of variables required to implement the file-using function and the complexity of the source code.

GET and PUT

There are no end-of-record or end-of-file marks in random files. The record length is determined by the program. The file length in the directory entry is the product of the record length multiplied by the highest record number ever written to that file.[3]

Random records are read from a file with the text mode GET statement, and written to the file with the PUT statement. The form of either statement when using a FIELDed file is

```
GET/PUT #<filenum>,<recnum>
```

where <recnum> is a numeric expression giving the number of the record requested. Record numbers are counted starting from one; the practical upper limit is when the file runs out of space on the disk.[4] If <recnum> is omitted, BASIC will increment the last <recnum> it has seen (for that file identity number) and use that — usually with unexpected results if you are alternately reading and writing records.

When using record-type structures to "field" the file, the equivalent statement is

```
GET/PUT #<filenum>,<recnum>,<recname>
```

where <recname> is the *declared* name of the record- type structure.

When you GET a record, BASIC requests DOS to read the appropriate sector into one of its sector buffers and transfer the current contents of the requested record into either the FIELDed record buffer in string space or the requested record variable in data space. If the requested record is *beyond* the current end of file, the transferred-into space will be loaded with all <NUL>s [CHR$(0)] and the file's EOF flag will be turned on (set to -1).

When you PUT a record, the current contents of the transfer space are written to the file starting at the byte location corresponding to the file record number. If you PUT a record beyond the current end of file, the current end of file will be established at the end of the newly written record, and the EOF flag will be turned off (set to 0). Any intervening records between the previous end of file and the new record are now part of the file, but the contents of those unwritten records are indeterminate.

BUFFIN.BAS

Random files consist of a set of fixed-length records, each of which is made up of specified-length fields. If any of those fields contain strings entered from the keyboard, the maximum acceptable string length is established by the <width> of its field variable. Although LSET and RSET "assignment" statements will truncate overlong strings, it is more user friendly to limit keyboard input to the string length allocated for the data. This function is provided by the compiled library subroutine BUFFIN.BAS, shown in Listing 10-1.

BUFFIN(<prompt>,<text>) accepts string input of any length up to that established by the length of the <text> string argument, and will BEEP to warn the user if an attempt is made to enter more. The maximum length <text> that BUFFIN will accept is governed by the necessity to contain the <prompt> string, the <text> string, and the two displayed delimiter symbols on a single display line. Since meeting this limitation is under the control of the programmer, not of the user, violation will produce a nonrecoverable "error 255" during program implementation (lines 27–29).

The major complexities of BUFFIN stem from the desire to provide the BASIC input line editing functions. I left out the "word" editing functions requiring the Ctrl key. You may wish to supply them.

RECORD88.BAS

RECORD88.BAS (Listing 10-2) is the latest of a series of programs I have used to keep my nonwage income and expense records for income tax purposes. As shown, it keeps its menu and data files in the ACCT_88 subdirectory on my hard disk. (The modifications necessary to use RECORD88 on a diskette-only system are given in Listing 10-3.) Since these records must withstand a tax audit, no data is ever deleted; the only way to correct erroneous data in a record is to write another record making the correction a part of the file itself. This lack of "update in place" also simplifies file backup. If any files have been modified during a session, they will be copied (automatically) to a backup diskette having the volume label ACCT_88_BAK at session end.

```
 1:  '****************************************************************************
 2:  '                         BUFFIN.BAS                                      *
 3:  '     BUFFIN(<prompt>,<text>) is a compiled QBASIC subroutine for         *
 4:  ' limiting the length of a single keyed input string.  BUFFIN operates    *
 5:  ' in a manner similar to the DOS "Buffered Keyboard Input" while using    *
 6:  ' those BASIC line-editing functions not requiring the Ctrl key.          *
 7:  '     <prompt> is a string variable or expression giving the prompt to    *
 8:  ' be displayed.  It can be the null string.                               *
 9:  '     <text> must be a string variable.  The length of the keyed input    *
10:  ' string cannot exceed len(<text>), and the input will be returned in     *
11:  ' <text>.  If <text> is a null string, only the <CR> will be accepted.    *
12:  '     The initial display consists of the <prompt>, followed by a         *
13:  ' string of <SP> characters having the length of <text> and surrounded    *
14:  ' by the pair of large arrowheads (CHR$(16) and CHR$(17)).  Display of    *
15:  ' the prompt starts at the BASIC cursor location at the time the          *
16:  ' subroutine is called, and the entire display must fit on one row.       *
17:  ' Cursor location in the row is indeterminate on return.                  *
18:  '                  Written by M. L. Lesser, April 9, 1987                 *
19:  '            Modified for Microsoft BC version 4.0, 12/24/87              *
20:  '****************************************************************************
21:      DEFSTR B,P,T
22:      DEFINT C,F,L
23:      DIM SHARED BUFFER, COL, COLUMN, FLAG.INS, LENGTH, T
24:  '    $INCLUDE: 'PQB.BI'
25:
26:  SUB BUFFIN(PROMPT,TEXT) STATIC
27:      LET LENGTH = LEN(TEXT)                            'Buffer length
28:      LET BUFFER = PROMPT + CHR$(16) + SPACE$(LENGTH) + CHR$(17)
29:      IF POS(0) + LEN(BUFFER) > 81 THEN ERROR 255    'Row overflow error
30:      LET COL = POS(0) + INSTR(BUFFER,CHR$(16))    'Start of buffer display
31:      PRINT BUFFER;                                 'Display prompt
32:  ' Initialize input text string:
33:      LET TEXT= ""
34:      LET COLUMN = 1                                 'Current cursor position
35:      LET FLAG.INS = 0                               'Insert mode off
36:
37:  ENTRY:            'Start of input infinite loop
38:      LOCATE ,COL+COLUMN-1,1                         'Turn on visible cursor
39:      SELECT CASE KBPEEK
40:         CASE -1                                     'Nothing pending
41:            GOTO ENTRY
42:         CASE  0                                     'Ctrl-Break
43:            END
44:         CASE 71                                     'Home key
45:            LET COLUMN = 1
46:         CASE 75                                     'Cursor left key
47:            IF COLUMN > 1 THEN LET COLUMN = COLUMN - 1
48:         CASE 77                                     'Cursor right key
49:            IF COLUMN <= LEN(TEXT) THEN LET COLUMN = COLUMN + 1
50:         CASE 79                                     'End key
51:            LET COLUMN = LEN(TEXT) + 1
52:         CASE 82                                     'Insert key
53:            IF NOT FLAG.INS THEN                '    If not already on,
54:               LET FLAG.INS = -1                '       turn it on
55:               IF ISCOLOR THEN LOCATE ,,,3,7 ELSE LOCATE ,,,6,13
56:               GOTO ENTRY
```

Listing 10 - 1 (continued)

```
57:                END IF
58:             CASE 83                               'Delete key
59:                GOSUB WIPE.OUT
60:                GOTO REFRESH
61:             CASE 256                              'ASCII symbol pending
62:                GOTO ASCII
63:             CASE ELSE
64:          END SELECT
65:          GOSUB INSERT.OFF          'Turn off insert flag if get this far
66:          GOTO ENTRY
67:
68:   ASCII:                           'Extended ASCII symbol pending
69:          LET T = INPUT$(1)                  'Read next keyed input
70:          LOCATE ,,0                          'Turn off visible cursor
71:          IF T = CHR$(3) THEN END             'Ctrl-C
72:          IF T = CHR$(27) THEN                'Escape clears buffer
73:             LET TEXT = ""
74:             LET COLUMN = 1
75:             GOSUB INSERT.OFF
76:          ELSEIF T = CHR$(8) THEN                  'Backspace
77:             IF COLUMN > 1 THEN
78:                LET COLUMN = COLUMN - 1
79:                GOSUB WIPE.OUT
80:             END IF
81:          ELSEIF T <> CHR$(13) THEN               'Not <CR>
82:             IF (FLAG.INS AND LEN(TEXT) = LENGTH) OR (COLUMN > LENGTH) THEN
83:                BEEP                     'Full buffer, don't accept any
84:                GOSUB INSERT.OFF         '  symbol other than <CR>
85:                GOTO ENTRY
86:             ELSEIF FLAG.INS THEN                'Insert the symbol
87:                LET TEXT = LEFT$(TEXT,COLUMN-1) + T + MID$(TEXT,COLUMN)
88:             ELSE                                'Not insert mode
89:                LET TEXT = LEFT$(TEXT,COLUMN-1) + T + MID$(TEXT,COLUMN+1)
90:             END IF
91:             LET COLUMN = COLUMN + 1
92:          ELSE                                 'Enter key pressed
93:             GOSUB INSERT.OFF
94:             EXIT SUB                          'Normal exit from subroutine
95:          END IF
96:
97:   REFRESH:          'Redisplay amended text
98:          LOCATE ,COL
99:          PRINT TEXT SPACE$(LENGTH - LEN(TEXT));
100:         GOTO ENTRY
101:
102:  INSERT.OFF:       'GOSUB subroutine to turn off insert mode
103:         LET FLAG.INS = 0
104:         IF ISCOLOR THEN LOCATE ,,,7,7 ELSE LOCATE ,,,12,13
105:  RETURN
106:
107:  WIPE.OUT:         'GOSUB subroutine to delete byte at cursor location
108:         LET TEXT = LEFT$(TEXT,COLUMN-1) + MID$(TEXT,COLUMN+1)
109:  RETURN
110:  END SUB                 'End of BUFFIN definition, end of source code
```

Listing 10 - 1

```
1:  '***********************************************************************
2:  '                         RECORD88.BAS                                *
3:  '        RECORD88 is a record-keeping program maintaining accounts of non- *
4:  ' wage income and expense items for income tax purposes.  Access to an *
5:  ' account is by menu, keeping the menus in two levels of extendible   *
6:  ' sequential files.  There can be up to 22 categories of accounts     *
7:  ' (MENU.CAT), and each category can contain up to 22 accounts         *
8:  ' (MENU.ACCT).  The account data records are kept in random files with *
9:  ' 64-byte records.  All files used by the program are kept in the     *
10: ' subdirectory C:\ACCT_88.                                            *
11: '        Once an entry has been made to an account file, it cannot be *
12: ' modified except by addition.  If any file is written to during a    *
13: ' session, it will be backed up to a diskette with the label          *
14: ' "ACCT_88_BAK" in the A: drive before the program terminates.        *
15: '        To modify RECORD88 for other tax years:  Copy RECORD88.BAS to *
16: ' RECORDyy.BAS, where the "yy" are the last two digits of the new     *
17: ' year.  Use the "find and replace" function in a text editor to      *
18: ' replace all occurrences of "88" in RECORDyy.BAS with "yy".   Format *
19: ' a new backup diskette with the label, "ACCT_yy_BAK."                *
20: '                  Written by M. L. Lesser, April 15, 1987            *
21: '            Modified for Microsoft BC version 4.0, 12/27/87          *
22: '                  Compiled with the /O/E switches                    *
23: '***********************************************************************
24:
25:      DEFSTR A-Z
26:      DEFINT C,D,I,R,W
27:      DEFLNG S
28: '    $INCLUDE: 'PQB.BI'
29:
30:      TYPE HEADER
31:          FILENAME AS STRING*35        'Name of account
32:          TOTAL    AS LONG             'Total value of account
33:          CREATE   AS INTEGER          'Date file created
34:          NUMREC   AS INTEGER          'Number records in file
35:          DUMMY    AS STRING*21        'Filler
36:      END TYPE
37:
38:      TYPE RECORD
39:          DESCRIPT AS STRING*44        'Transaction description
40:          AMOUNT   AS LONG             'Transaction amount
41:          DATE     AS INTEGER          'Transaction date
42:          POST     AS INTEGER          'Date transaction posted
43:          VOUCHER  AS STRING*8         'Transaction voucher
44:          DUMMY    AS STRING*4         'Filler
45:      END TYPE
46:
47: ' Integer variables:
48:      DIM COUNT, I, ITEM.ACCT, ITEM.CAT, ITEM.PROC, WRITE.FLAG
49: ' String variables:
50:      DIM FILE, FILE.ACCT, FILE.CAT, FIRSTLINE, LABEL, MENU.ACCT(25)
51:      DIM MENU.CAT(25), MENU.PROC(5), NAME.ACCT, NAME.CAT, SWITCH, TEXT
52: ' Typed variables (random record fields):
53:      DIM HEAD AS HEADER, REC AS RECORD
54: ' Long variable:
55:      DIM SUM
56: ' Common variables:
```

Listing 10 - 2 (continued)

```
57:        COMMON /CURSOR/ ROW.T, COL.T, ROW.B, COL.B, ROW, COL
58:        COMMON /COLORS/ CBG, CFG
59:
60:   ' Function definition - Converts system date to mmyy integer:
61:        DEF FNDATE = VAL(LEFT$(DATE$,2) + MID$(DATE$,4,2))
62:
63:   DEF FNFILE.NO(ITEM)      'Converts ITEM.<menu> to file number
64:        LET FILE = MID$(STR$(ITEM-2),2)            'Delete leading blank
65:        IF LEN(FILE) = 1 THEN LET FILE = "0" + FILE
66:        LET FNFILE.NO = FILE
67:   END DEF
68:
69:   ' Program starts here:
70:        CALL COLORIT           'Get display colors from SYSTEM.PRO file:
71:   ' Set up MENU.PROC entries:
72:        LET MENU.PROC(0) = MKI$(4)
73:        LET MENU.PROC(1) = "Processing Options"
74:        LET MENU.PROC(2) = "QUIT This Account"
75:        LET MENU.PROC(3) = "ENTER A New Record"
76:        LET MENU.PROC(4) = "DISPLAY This Account"
77:        LET MENU.PROC(5) = "EMERGENCY EXIT"
78:
79:   CAT.SETUP:              'Loads MENU.CAT array from ACCT.88 file
80:        ERASE MENU.CAT
81:   ' Read file ACCT.88
82:        ON ERROR GOTO TRAP                          'Trap error on first run
83:        OPEN "C:\ACCT_88\ACCT.88" FOR INPUT AS #1
84:        ON ERROR GOTO 0
85:        INPUT# 1, MENU.CAT(1)
86:        LET MENU.CAT(2) = "QUIT This Session"     'Standard entries in
87:        LET MENU.CAT(3) = "OPEN A New Category"   '  menu (not in file)
88:        LET ITEM.CAT = 2
89:        WHILE NOT EOF(1)                          'Read the remaining file
90:            LET ITEM.CAT = ITEM.CAT + 1
91:            INPUT #1, MENU.CAT(ITEM.CAT + 1)
92:        WEND
93:        CLOSE #1
94:        LET MENU.CAT(0) = MKI$(ITEM.CAT)
95:
96:   CAT.STATE:       'Selects category of accounts to process
97:        LET FILE.CAT = ""                         'Delete any previous menu
98:        ERASE MENU.ACCT                           ' of accounts
99:        COLOR CFG,CBG                             'Reset entire display
100:       CLS
101:       PRINT "1988 Tax Record Program"
102:       PRINT STRING$(80,"-");
103:  ' Select category of accounts:
104:       LET COL = 10: ROW = 3: ROW.T = 3: COL.T = 1: ROW.B = 25: COL.B = 80
105:       CALL DWINDOW("Category selection: ")
106:       LET ITEM.CAT = MENU(MENU.CAT())
107:       PRINT MENU.CAT(ITEM.CAT+1);
108:       IF ITEM.CAT = 1 THEN                      'Session ended
109:           IF WRITE.FLAG THEN GOSUB BACKUP       'Back up new files
110:           END                                   'Normal program end
111:       ELSEIF ITEM.CAT = 2 THEN                  'Initiate new category
112:           GOTO NEW.CAT
```

Listing 10 - 2 (continued)

```
113:     ELSE                                    'Category was selected
114:         GOTO ACCT.SETUP
115:     END IF
116:
117: NEW.CAT:          'Opens a new account category
118: ' ITEM.CAT will be changed to next available entry in the MENU.CAT
119: '  array.  The new account category name will have the string
120: '  " Accounts" appended to it and will be assigned to NAME.CAT.  The
121: '  ACCT.88 file will be updated, and a new menu file of accounts in this
122: '  category will be created with <filename> being the value of FILE.CAT.
123:     IF CVI(MENU.CAT(0)) = 24 THEN           'Menu of categories full
124:         CALL CWINDOW("Menu full - Cannot accept any more categories.")
125:         CALL CWINDOW("--Press any key to continue--")
126:         WHILE INKEY$ = "": WEND
127:         GOTO CAT.STATE
128:     END IF
129:     CALL DWINDOW("")                        'Move down one row
130:     LET NAME.CAT = SPACE$(26)
131:     CALL BUFFIN("Enter new account category ",NAME.CAT)
132:     IF LEN(NAME.CAT) = 0 THEN               'If no entry
133:         GOTO CAT.STATE                      '  restart selection
134:     ELSE
135: ' Update the category menu file:
136:         LET NAME.CAT = NAME.CAT + " Accounts"
137:         LET ITEM.CAT = CVI(MENU.CAT(0)) + 1
138:         LET MENU.CAT(0) = MKI$(ITEM.CAT)
139:         LET MENU.CAT(ITEM.CAT + 1) = NAME.CAT
140:         CALL WRITE.FILE("ACCT",MENU.CAT())
141: ' Write new account menu file for this category:
142:         LET FILE.CAT = "ACCT" + FNFILE.NO(ITEM.CAT)
143:         LET MENU.ACCT(0) = MKI$(2)          'Only standard entries
144:         LET MENU.ACCT(1) = NAME.CAT
145:         CALL WRITE.FILE(FILE.CAT,MENU.ACCT())
146:     END IF
147:
148: ACCT.SETUP:     'Reads FILE.CAT into MENU.ACCT array
149:     ERASE MENU.ACCT
150:     LET FILE.CAT = "ACCT" + FNFILE.NO(ITEM.CAT)
151:     OPEN "C:\ACCT_88\" + FILE.CAT + ".88" FOR INPUT AS #1
152:     INPUT# 1, MENU.ACCT(1)
153:     LET NAME.CAT = MENU.ACCT(1)
154:     LET MENU.ACCT(2) = "QUIT This Category"   'Standard entries in
155:     LET MENU.ACCT(3) = "OPEN A New Account"   '  menu (not in file)
156:     LET ITEM.ACCT = 2
157:     WHILE NOT EOF(1)                          'Read the remaining file
158:         LET ITEM.ACCT = ITEM.ACCT + 1
159:         INPUT #1, MENU.ACCT(ITEM.ACCT + 1)
160:     WEND
161:     CLOSE #1
162:     LET MENU.ACCT(0) = MKI$(ITEM.ACCT)
163:
164: ACCT.STATE:       'Selects category of accounts to process
165:     LET FILE.ACCT = ""                      'Delete previous data file name
166:     LOCATE 1,1
167:     PRINT SPACE$(80)
168:     LET FIRSTLINE = "1988 " + NAME.CAT + ":  "
```

Listing 10 - 2 (continued)

```
169:        LOCATE 1,1
170:        PRINT FIRSTLINE
171:        CALL DWINDOW("Account selection: ")
172:        LET ITEM.ACCT = MENU(MENU.ACCT())
173:        PRINT MENU.ACCT(ITEM.ACCT+1);
174:        IF ITEM.ACCT = 1 THEN
175:            GOTO CAT.STATE
176:        ELSEIF ITEM.ACCT = 2 THEN
177:            GOTO NEW.ACCT
178:        ELSE                            'Account was selected
179:            GOTO PROC.SETUP
180:        END IF
181:
182:   NEW.ACCT:          'Opens a new account in this category
183:   ' ITEM.ACCT will be changed to next available entry in the MENU.ACCT
184:   '  array.  The new account name will be assigned to NAME.ACCT.  The
185:   '  Account menu file (FILE.CAT) will be updated, and a new account
186:   '  data (random) file will be created with <filename> being the value
187:   '  of FILE.ACCT.
188:        CALL DWINDOW("")
189:        IF CVI(MENU.ACCT(0)) = 24 THEN            'Menu of accounts full
190:            CALL CWINDOW("--Menu full--")
191:            CALL CWINDOW("Cannot accept new accounts in this category.")
192:            CALL CWINDOW("--Press any key to continue--")
193:            WHILE INKEY$ = "": WEND
194:            GOTO CAT.STATE
195:        END IF
196:        LET NAME.ACCT = SPACE$(35)
197:        CALL BUFFIN("Enter new account name ",NAME.ACCT)
198:        IF LEN(NAME.ACCT) = 0 THEN            'If no entry
199:            GOTO ACCT.STATE                  '  restart selection
200:        ELSE
201:   ' Update the Account menu file:
202:            LET ITEM.ACCT = CVI(MENU.ACCT(0)) + 1
203:            LET MENU.ACCT(0) = MKI$(ITEM.ACCT)
204:            LET MENU.ACCT(ITEM.ACCT + 1) = NAME.ACCT
205:            CALL WRITE.FILE(FILE.CAT,MENU.ACCT())
206:   ' Write new account file (header record only):
207:            LET FILE.ACCT = FILE.CAT + FNFILE.NO(ITEM.ACCT)
208:            OPEN "C:\ACCT_88\" + FILE.ACCT + ".88" AS #1 LEN = 64
209:            LET HEAD.FILENAME = NAME.ACCT
210:            LET HEAD.TOTAL = 0
211:            LET HEAD.CREATE = FNDATE            'Created today
212:            LET HEAD.NUMREC = 1
213:            PUT #1,1,HEAD                        'File header record only
214:            CLOSE #1
215:        END IF
216:
217:   PROC.SETUP:
218:   ' Open account file:
219:        LET FILE.ACCT = FILE.CAT + FNFILE.NO(ITEM.ACCT)
220:        OPEN "C:\ACCT_88\" + FILE.ACCT + ".88" AS #1 LEN = 64
221:        GET #1, 1, HEAD
222:   ' File identification message sign-on:
223:        LET FIRSTLINE = FIRSTLINE + HEAD.FILENAME
224:        LOCATE 1,1: PRINT FIRSTLINE;
```

Listing 10 - 2 (continued)

```
225:        LET TEXT = STR$(HEAD.CREATE)                    'File creation
226:        IF LEN(TEXT) = 4 THEN LET TEXT = " " + TEXT     ' date shown at
227:        PRINT TAB(76) TEXT;                             ' upper right
228:
229: PROC.STATE:                    'Processes account data file
230:        CALL DWINDOW("Processing Option: ")
231:        LET ITEM.PROC = MENU(MENU.PROC())
232:        PRINT MENU.PROC(ITEM.PROC+1);
233:        IF ITEM.PROC = 1 THEN                    'Return to Account menu
234:            CLOSE #1
235:            GOTO ACCT.STATE
236:        ELSEIF ITEM.PROC = 2 THEN           'Write a new record to the file
237:            GOSUB ENTRY
238:            GOTO PROC.STATE
239:        ELSEIF ITEM.PROC = 3 THEN            'Display the account file
240:            GOSUB SHOW.FILE
241:            GOTO PROC.STATE
242:        ELSE
243: ' Emergency exit terminates program without backing up any files:
244:            CALL DWINDOW("")
245:            CALL CWINDOW("--Program Terminated by User--")
246:        END IF
247:
248: ENDIT:            'Terminates program without backing up files
249: ' When program ends, first row of display will show account category and
250: '  name.  Lowest rows of remaining display will give sign-off message
251: '  and show <filespec> of account file that was active at the time.
252:        CALL CWINDOW("Program terminated while writing to file:  " _
253:                        + FILE.ACCT + ".88")
254:        CALL CWINDOW("Files written to during this session have not been " _
255:                        + "backed up.")
256:        IF ROW > 24 THEN
257:            CALL SCROLLIT                           'Assures row 25 clear
258:            LOCATE 24,1                             'Prevents scroll on END
259:        END IF
260: END                 'End of main portion
261:
262:
263: ' GOSUB subroutines in alphabetic order:
264: BACKUP:            'Backs up any files written to during this session
265:        CLS
266:        LET ROW = 1: ROW.B = 25
267:        CALL PWINDOW("Backing Up 1988 Tax Records:")
268:        LET LABEL = "ACCT_88_BAK"
269: ' Check label in A: drive:
270: DOIT:
271:        LET TEXT = "Insert diskette with label " + CHR$(34) _
272:                      +  LABEL + CHR$(34) + " in A: drive."
273:        CALL CWINDOW(TEXT)
274:        CALL CWINDOW("--Press <ENTER> when ready--")
275:        WHILE INKEY$ <> CHR$(13): WEND              'Wait loop for <ENTER>
276:        LET TEXT = "A:" + SPACE$(9)                 'Input string for VLABEL
277:        ON ERROR GOTO TRAP.LABEL                    'May have
278:            CALL VLABEL(TEXT)                       '   "Disk not ready"
279:        ON ERROR GOTO 0                             '   error
280: ' Test for results:
```

Listing 10 - 2 (continued)

```
281:        IF LEFT$(TEXT,1) = CHR$(255) THEN              'No label on diskette
282:            CALL CWINDOW("Diskette in drive A: has no label.")
283:            GOTO DOIT
284:        ELSEIF TEXT <> LABEL THEN                     'Wrong label on diskette
285:            CALL CWINDOW("Label on diskette in drive A: is:  " + TEXT)
286:            GOTO DOIT                                 'Try again
287:        END IF
288: ' Use SHELL to run XCOPY:
289:        SHELL "XCOPY C:\ACCT_88\*.88 A:/M"
290:        LET ROW = CSRLIN                             'Sets ROW to current cursor row
291:        CALL CWINDOW("All 1988 Tax Files have been backed up")
292:        IF ROW > 24 THEN
293:            CALL SCROLLIT                            'Assures row 25 clear
294:            LOCATE 24,1                              'Prevents scroll on END
295:        END IF
296: RETURN                    'End of BACKUP
297:
298: ENTRY:              'Writes a new record in account file
299:        CALL PWINDOW("Enter the following transaction data:")
300:        LET COL = 10
301: ' Date:
302:        LET TEXT = SPACE$(4)
303:        CALL DWINDOW("")
304:        CALL BUFFIN("Transaction date (mmyy) ",TEXT)
305:        LET REC.DATE = VAL(TEXT)
306: ' Voucher:
307:        CALL DWINDOW("")
308:        CALL BUFFIN("Transaction voucher      ",REC.VOUCHER)
309: ' Amount (AMOUNT is stored in a long integer, in pennies, to avoid
310: '   binary/decimal fraction conversion errors):
311:        LET TEXT = SPACE$(9)
312:        CALL DWINDOW("")
313:        CALL BUFFIN("Transaction amount       ",TEXT)
314:        LET REC.AMOUNT = 100 * VAL(TEXT)
315: ' Description:
316:        CALL DWINDOW("")
317:        CALL BUFFIN("Transaction Description ",REC.DESCRIPT)
318: ' Verification:
319:        LET REC.POST = FNDATE
320:        GOSUB SHOW.HEADING
321:        GOSUB SHOW.RECORD
322:        CALL PWINDOW(STRING$(80,"-"))
323:        LET COL = 10
324:        CALL DWINDOW("Is this OK to file (y/n): ")
325:        LET TEXT = UCASE$(INPUT$(1))
326:        IF TEXT = "Y" OR TEXT = " " THEN             'File record
327:            PRINT "Yes";
328:            LET WRITE.FLAG = -1
329:            LET HEAD.NUMREC = HEAD.NUMREC + 1
330:            LET HEAD.TOTAL = HEAD.TOTAL + REC.AMOUNT
331:            PUT #1, HEAD.NUMREC, REC
332:            PUT #1, 1, HEAD
333:        ELSE
334:            PRINT "No";
335:        END IF
336: RETURN                    'End of ENTRY
```

Listing 10 - 2 *(continued)*

```
337:
338:    PAUSE:                  'Display pause legend in row 25 and wait
339:        LOCATE 25,57
340:        COLOR 0,7
341:        PRINT "Press ENTER to Continue";
342:        WHILE INKEY$ <> CHR$(13): WEND
343:        LOCATE 25,1
344:        COLOR CFG,CBG
345:        PRINT SPACE$(80);
346:    RETURN                          'End of PAUSE
347:
348:    SHOW.FILE:          'Displays entire account file
349:        CALL CLEARIT
350:        LET ROW = 0
351:        LET SUM = HEAD.TOTAL
352:        GOSUB SHOW.HEADING
353:        LET ROW.T = 5: ROW.B = 24                   'Limit window size
354:        LET COUNT = 0                               ' to 20 records
355:        FOR I = 2 TO HEAD.NUMREC                     'All data records
356:            GET #1,I, REC
357:            GOSUB SHOW.RECORD
358:            LET SUM = SUM - REC.AMOUNT
359:            LET COUNT = COUNT + 1
360:            IF COUNT = 20 THEN                       'Full window
361:                GOSUB PAUSE
362: ' After initial window full, successive windows scroll up maximum of 19
363: '   rows to retain previous bottom record in window:
364:                LET COUNT = 1
365:            END IF
366:        NEXT I
367: ' When entire file has been displayed:
368:        LET ROW.B = 25
369:        IF SUM <> 0 THEN                            'Account doesn't balance
370:            CALL DWINDOW("")
371:            CALL CWINDOW("--File Damaged!  Account Does Not Balance--")
372:            CALL CWINDOW("Reconstruct from backup file.")
373:            GOTO ENDIT                              'Abnormal termination
374:        END IF
375: ' Display file total:
376:        CALL PWINDOW(SPACE$(15) + STRING$(13,"-"))
377:        CALL PWINDOW("Account Total: ")
378:        PRINT USING "$$,#######.##"; HEAD.TOTAL/100;
379:        GOSUB PAUSE
380:        LET ROW.T = 3: ROW = 3
381:        CALL CLEARIT
382:    RETURN                          'End of SHOW.FILE
383:
384:    SHOW.HEADING:    'Displays header for data file records
385:        CALL PWINDOW("")                    'Cursor at beginning of next row
386:        PRINT "DATE";
387:        PRINT TAB(8) "VOUCHER";
388:        PRINT TAB(19) "AMOUNT";
389:        PRINT TAB(41) "DESCRIPTION";
390:        PRINT TAB(75) "POSTED";
391:        CALL PWINDOW("")
392:        PRINT STRING$(4,"-") TAB(7) STRING$(8,"-") TAB(16) STRING$(13,"-");
```

Listing 10 - 2 (continued)

```
393:        PRINT TAB(31) STRING$(44,"-") TAB(77) STRING$(4,"-");
394: RETURN                      'End of SHOW.HEADING
395:
396: SHOW.RECORD:     'Displays data file record
397:        CALL PWINDOW("")
398:        PRINT USING "####"; REC.DATE;
399:        PRINT TAB(7) REC.VOUCHER; TAB(16);
400:        PRINT USING "$$,#######.##"; REC.AMOUNT/100;
401:        PRINT TAB(31) REC.DESCRIPT; TAB(77);
402:        PRINT USING "####"; REC.POST;
403: RETURN                      'End of SHOW.RECORD
404:
405: ' Called subroutine:
406: SUB WRITE.FILE(FILE,ARRAY()) STATIC          'Update menu file
407: SHARED WRITE.FLAG
408:        LET WRITE.FLAG = -1                   'Enable BACKUP routine
409:        OPEN  "C:\ACCT_88\" + FILE + ".88" FOR OUTPUT AS #1
410:        WRITE #1, ARRAY(1)
411:        FOR I = 4 TO CVI(ARRAY(0)) + 1
412:            WRITE #1, ARRAY(I)
413:        NEXT I
414:        CLOSE #1
415: END SUB              'End of WRITE.FILE definition
416:
417: 'Error traps:
418: TRAP:               'Error trap for initializing ACCT.88 file
419:        IF ERR = 76 THEN                     'No subdirectory
420:            MKDIR "C:\ACCT_88"
421:        END IF                               'Initialize file:
422:        OPEN "C:\ACCT_88\ACCT.88" FOR OUTPUT AS #1
423:        WRITE #1, "Available Account Categories"
424:        CLOSE #1
425:        RESUME CAT.SETUP
426:
427: TRAP.LABEL:         'Error trap if "disk not ready" when reading LABEL
428:        CALL CWINDOW("Cannot read diskette in A drive.  Check door")
429:        RESUME DOIT
430: ' End of source Code
```

Listing 10 - 2

The program is menu-driven, there being three levels of menus: Category, Account, and Process. The Category menu selects the category of accounts to be viewed, an Account menu selects the particular account out of that category to be processed, and the Process menu selects the process to be performed on that account. All menus are similar in that the first menu entry is a "QUIT" that returns control to the previous level ("QUIT" from the Category menu ends the session). The second entry in each menu adds information obtained from keyed input: a new category, a new account in that category, or a new record in the account data file, respectively.

```
 1: !-----------------------------------------------------------------!
 2: !                        RECORD88.INS                             !
 3: !    RECORD88.INS provides a modification procedure to convert the !
 4: ! record-keeping program RECORD88.BAS (Listing 10-2) for use with a !
 5: ! diskette-only system.  In this pseudo listing, lines beginning with !
 6: ! an exclamation mark are modification instructions.  All other lines !
 7: ! are code to be inserted into, or to replace existing code within, !
 8: ! Listing 10-2.                                                   !
 9: !    To modify the hard disk source code in Listing 10-2:          !
10: !       1.  Change all occurrences of "C:\ACCT_88" to "B:".        !
11: !       2.  Insert the following block of code between lines 77 and 78 !
12: !           of Listing 10-2:                                       !
13: !-----------------------------------------------------------------!
14: ' Check for proper data diskette in drive B:
15:     LET ROW.T = 3: COL.T = 1: ROW.B = 25: COL.B = 80
16:     LET LABEL = "ACCT_88_DAT"
17: DOIT.DAT:
18:     LET TEXT = "Insert diskette with label " + CHR$(34) _
19:                    + LABEL + CHR$(34) + " in B: drive."
20:     CALL CWINDOW(TEXT)
21:     CALL CWINDOW("--Press <ENTER> when ready--")
22:     WHILE INKEY$ <> CHR$(13): WEND               'Wait loop for <ENTER>
23:     LET TEXT = "B:" + SPACE$(9)        'Input string for VLABEL
24: 100 ON ERROR GOTO TRAP.LABEL               'May have
25:         CALL VLABEL(TEXT)                  '   "Disk not ready"
26: 200 ON ERROR GOTO 0                        '   error
27: ' Test for results:
28:     IF LEFT$(TEXT,1) = CHR$(255) THEN          'No label on diskette
29:         CALL CWINDOW("Diskette in drive B: has no label.")
30:         GOTO DOIT.DAT
31:     ELSEIF TEXT <> LABEL THEN                   'Wrong label on diskette
32:         CALL CWINDOW("Label on diskette in drive B: is:  " + TEXT)
33:         GOTO DOIT.DAT                           'Try again
34:     END IF
35: !-----------------------------------------------------------------!
36: !       3.  Delete the IF-block in the TRAP error trap (lines      !
37: !           419-421 of Listing 10-2).                              !
38: !       4.  Replace the TRAP.LABEL error trap (lines 427-430 of    !
39: !           Listing 10-2) with the following block of source code: !
40: !-----------------------------------------------------------------!
41: TRAP.LABEL:        'Error trap if "disk not ready" when reading LABEL
42:     CALL CWINDOW("Cannot read diskette.  Check drive door")
43:     IF ERL = 100 THEN
44:         RESUME DOIT.DAT
45:     ELSE
46:         RESUME DOIT
47:     END IF
48: !-----------------------------------------------------------------!
49: !       5.  Modify the prologue to Listing 10-2 accordingly.       !
50: !-----------------------------------------------------------------!
```

Listing 10 - 3

The Category and Account menus are carried as sequential files. The data for each account is carried in a random file having 64-byte records. Although the only record in a data file that is "updated in place" is the header record (carrying the number of records in the file and the total of the individual amount entries), using random files for the account data has the following advantages:

- Updating is faster, since random files can be added to without reading and rewriting unchanged data.
- The files are shorter. All numeric data is carried in fixed-length internal form, displayed with "PRINT USING" statements.

RECORD88.BAS is designed so the source code can be updated easily for any other year, as described in the prologue to the listing. It is designed as a "state" machine for ease in implementation, with the major states corresponding to the menu levels.

Record Design Considerations

The most important design problem in programs using random files is to lay out the fields in the file. This task is simplified if you remember that the only function fulfilled by an automatic computing engine is to reformat input information, using data either contained within the program itself or in files available to the program, to produce the desired output information. The formats of both the input and output information must be pleasing to the user. Thus, the solution to designing the record layouts starts with designing the input format and/or the output format, and going from there.

In the case of RECORD88, the output format controlled the record layout. I wanted all the data from one record to be displayed in a single row on the screen, thereby limiting the total displayed record to 80 characters (including spacing between displayed fields). This screen layout established the field widths for the RECORD structure (lines 38–45). Since no interfield spacing is required in the file record and the numeric data takes up less room than does the same information displayed on the screen, I could use a record length of 64 bytes.

Initialization Code

As with all programs, there is a certain amount of initialization code required before anything pertaining to the application itself happens. This is given in lines 25–77 of Listing 10-2.

All money amounts are carried in pennies, as LONG (4-byte) integers (lines 32, 40, and 55). Since BASIC does its arithmetic in binary, and it is impossible to translate all fractional values *exactly* between decimal and binary notations, this is the best way to keep the books balanced "to the penny."

The COLORS common segment (line 58) is to allow the COLORIT library subroutine to "return" the foreground and background text colors specified by the SYSTEM.PRO file.

The defined function FNFILE.NO (lines 63–67) is used to create the directory <filename>s of the Account menu and account data files. Since each menu contains the first two "standard" entries, FNFILE.NO(<item>) converts the "item number" returned by MENU() to a two-digit string having a value two less than the integer <item>, adding a leading zero if necessary. This two-digit string is appended to the directory <filename> of its "parent" file to produce the new <filename>. For example, the first Account menu file created will have the <filename> ACCT01. The second account data file created from that Account menu will have the <filename> ACCT0102. All file extensions will be .88, showing the accounting year.

The Category State

The category state is really made up of three substates: CAT.SETUP (lines 79–94), CAT.STATE (lines 96–115) and NEW.CAT (lines 117–146). CAT.SETUP could be considered a portion of the initializing code, since it is executed only once per session. The first time the program is run, there will be an error interrupt when attempting to open the Category menu file ACCT.88 in subdirectory ACCT_88, because neither the subdirectory nor the file will exist. This omission is taken care of in the initializing code in TRAP (lines 418–425). TRAP establishes the subdirectory and writes the menu title record to the file, before trying again by a RESUME to CAT.SETUP.

During the remainder of the session, the Category menu will be contained in the array MENU.CAT, as read from ACCT.88 (lines 85–94). The two "standard" entries are inserted into the array in lines 86–87. The file is closed after it is read; there is never more than one file open at a time during program execution. The total number of entries in the menu is inserted as a pseudo string integer into MENU.CAT(0), as required by the MENU() library function.

The menu choice is made while in CAT.STATE. Since the CAT.STATE label is the return point for a "QUIT" command from the Account menu level, CAT.STATE must first clean up the debris left from processing previous accounts. The value of the string variable FILE.CAT is the directory <filename> of the file containing the menu for the accounts in the category selected on the previous cycle; the corresponding menu is in the string array MENU.ACCT. These variables are cleared to null values before selecting a new category of accounts to process (lines 97–98). The screen is cleared and a new title line is written (lines 99–102), after which the menu of category choices is displayed (lines 106–107).

The MENU() return corresponding to the menu entry selected is assigned to ITEM.CAT (line 106), which is evaluated in the abbreviated IF-block in lines 108–115. Unless one of the first two entries is selected, control passes to ACCT.SETUP to read the menu file for the newly selected account category.

If the "QUIT" choice (first entry) is made, the session is ended, performing an automatic backup if WRITE.FLAG indicates that any file was updated. The GOSUB subroutine BACKUP (lines 264–296) is edited from the DOBACK.BAS (Listing 8-4) source code.

If "OPEN A New Category" (second entry) is selected, control passes to NEW.CAT. Unless the Category menu is full, NEW.CAT (lines 117–146) prompts for keyed input giving the name of the new category. (The program as written allows a maximum of twenty-two categories, limited by the MENU() function.) Entering a null string will return control to CAT.STATE for another selection. A nonnull input string will have the word "Accounts" appended to it and will become the next entry in the Category menu, with the corresponding item number assigned to ITEM.CAT.

The Category menu file will be updated by calling the WRITE.FILE called subroutine (lines 406–415) to open, write, and close a new ACCT.88 file. A called subroutine is used to allow different file and array names to be passed as arguments. WRITE.FILE uses the WRITE# statement, rather than PRINT#, in the event a menu entry includes a comma or semicolon. Figure 10-1 shows a copy of my 1987 Category menu file, as produced on my display with the DOS built-in TYPE utility.[5]

NEW.CAT initializes the new Account menu file, writing only the menu name, by another call to WRITE.FILE. Control then passes to ACCT.SETUP, which will now read the newly written Account menu file for further selection.

```
"Available Account Categories"
"Business Income Accounts"
"Business Expense Accounts"
"Other Income Accounts"
"General Deduction Accounts"
"Miscellaneous Accounts"
```

Figure 10 - 1
Category menu sequential file

The Account State

Figure 10-2 is a copy of the menu display showing the 1987 accounts in my "Business Expense Accounts" category.

Most of the code for the account state (lines 148–215) was written by editing the equivalent code in the category state. Only the portion of NEW.ACCT dealing with initializing an account data random file (lines 206–214) is completely new code.

Each account file starts with a header record, defined as type HEADER (lines 30–36) giving summary data for the complete file. Only

```
---Business Expense Accounts--
A. QUIT This Category
B. OPEN A New Account
C. Postage
D. Supplies
E. Telephone Calls
F. Automobile Mileage
G. Publications
H. Computer Software
I. Professional Society Dues
```

Figure 10 - 2
Account menu display

this header record is written by the NEW.ACCT routine. Note that the WRITE.FLAG is not turned on, even though the PUT statement will turn on the "archive" file attribute bit in the file directory. The WRITE.FLAG was turned on by WRITE.FILE when the Account menu file was updated.

The Process State

The process state (lines 217–246) manipulates the data files. The Process menu is not in a file; its array is written as part of the initial program setup code (lines 71–77). PROC.SETUP (lines 217–227) opens the account data file and reads the header record. This will not be written back to the file unless new data are entered.

PROC.STATE (lines 229–246) evaluates the menu selection in an IF-block and calls on other routines to do most of the work. The GOSUB subroutine ENTRY (lines 298–336) collects the data for a new record to be added to the account data file, requesting each required input with a BUF-FIN() prompt and delimiter string. (The "voucher" field contains my audit trail to the transaction's original paper; it is usually a check number, but can be a disk-file reference or merely "receipt.") After all input requests are completed, the user is shown the entire record in its normal display format, with a choice of either filing it or ignoring it. The "Y" choice (lines 326–333) will PUT the new record to the file, update the header record, and turn on WRITE.FLAG.

The GOSUB subroutine SHOW.FILE (lines 348–382) displays the file in a twenty-record window, requiring the Enter key to be pressed after every twenty records to continue scrolling the display. SHOW.FILE also makes a file integrity check by assuring that the sum of all the data record amount entries agrees with the total given in the header record. If these are not identical, an error message is printed and control is passed to the error exit routine ENDIT (lines 248–260). ENDIT terminates the program without an automatic backup, displaying the directory <filename> of the data file in use at the time of termination for ease in reconstructing that file from the backup diskette.

I have never had this error interrupt occur except in testing. It is tested by using SYMDEB (or DEBUG) to rewrite the value of HEAD.TOTAL in a test account data file. Figure 10-3 shows a SYMDEB display of the header and first two data records of my test Postage file. You will note that the file name is the first 35 bytes in the header record, while the item description is the first 44 bytes of each data record. Since

```
4278:0100  50 6F 73 74 61 67 65 20-20 20 20 20 20 20 20 20   Postage
4278:0110  20 20 20 20 20 20 20 20-20 20 20 20 20 20 20 20
4278:0120  20 20 20 48 08 00 00 A5-01 3A 00 00 00 00 00 00      H...%.:......
4278:0130  00 00 00 00 00 00 00 00-00 00 00 00 00 00 00 00   ................
4278:0140  4F 72 64 65 72 20 49 52-53 20 70 75 62 73 20 20   Order IRS pubs
4278:0150  20 20 20 20 20 20 20 20-20 20 20 20 20 20 20 20
4278:0160  20 20 20 20 20 20 20 20-20 20 20 20 16 00 00 00               ....
4278:0170  69 00 A5 01 20 20 20 20-20 20 20 20 00 00 00 00   i.%.          ....
4278:0180  4F 72 64 65 72 20 4E 59-53 20 49 54 20 66 6F 72   Order NYS IT for
4278:0190  6D 73 20 20 20 20 20 20-20 20 20 20 20 20 20 20   ms
4278:01A0  20 20 20 20 20 20 20 20-20 20 20 20 16 00 00 00               ....
4278:01B0  70 00 A5 01 20 20 20 20-20 20 20 20 00 00 00 00   p.%.          ....
```

Figure 10 - 3
Account data random file (SYMDEB display)

these are in string format, they are directly readable from the ASCII portion of the display. The value (in hex) of HEAD.TOTAL is in the 4 bytes starting at displayed offset 0123H. I tested the error exit by increasing the low-order (leftmost) byte of this value by 1, thereby making the file total one cent off of the summed amounts from the data records.

The final PROC.MENU selection is "Emergency exit" (lines 242 – 245). Selecting this menu entry will force termination with no backup. If you have written absolute nonsense to an account data file (in spite of the validation aids), you can reconstitute the data file from the backup diskette and start over.

A Diskette-Only Version

Since my backup system does not have a hard disk, I needed a version of RECORD88 that would run on a diskette-only system. The necessary changes to the Listing 10-2 source code are given in the pseudo listing RECORD88.INS (Listing 10-3). All files used by the diskette-only version are kept on a diskette in the B drive, rather than in a subdirectory on the C hard disk.

A volume label check is inserted to make sure that the proper data diskette is installed in drive B (lines 14–34 of Listing 10-3) to prevent initializing a new set of records on some strange diskette. This code is edited from the BACKUP subroutine, with a few changes. Note, especially, the

ERL identification by using two BASIC line numbers (lines 24 and 26). ERL will be 100 only if the error occurs during the VLABEL call in line 25. The modified TRAP.LABEL routine (lines 41–47) uses ERL to display the appropriate message and to RESUME at the appropriate label.

If you use the diskette-only version of RECORD88, you will have to format your data diskette with the label ACCT_88_DAT before you try to run the program. Also, your backup diskette must now contain copies of COMMAND.COM and XCOPY.EXE for the SHELL statement in the back-up routine to work.

I tested the diskette-only version of RECORD88 on a minimal DOS 3.3 configuration as described in the next chapter. Diskette-only RECORD88 will run in a system with only 192K of installed memory.

PRINT88.BAS

Since the IRS probably would not be happy to be given a diskette in case of audit, and since I find it easier to fill out form 1040 and its siblings from a printed record than from a display screen, I needed a program to list my tax record files on demand. That program is PRINT88.BAS (Listing 10-4).

PRINT88.BAS is largely edited from RECORD88.BAS. The parsing code to obtain the display colors and printer "normal" characteristics from the SYSTEM.PRO file (lines 55–96) is a modified version of that used in Listing 7-3.

PRINT88 is set up to list the files from my backup diskette in the A drive. I list those files quarterly, both to satisfy the IRS there has been a legitimate attempt to keep "current" records, and to satisfy myself that the files on the backup diskette are alive and well. I carry the (packed) stand-alone PRINT*yy*.EXE file on that year's backup diskette, so the single diskette is a sufficient archive record after the books for the accounting period are closed. At that time, I delete all the files (and the subdirectory) for the previous year's accounts from my hard disk, leaving only the new year's active files in its own subdirectory.

Notes

1. A disk *access* consists of reading or writing a single disk sector. A disk *seek* requires moving the drive read/write head arm.

```
 1:  '***********************************************************************
 2:  '                          PRINT88.BAS                                *
 3:  '     PRINT88 lists the backed-up account files written by RECORD88.  *
 4:  ' To use: the files must be in the root directory on drive A:         *
 5:  '     To modify PRINT88 for other tax years:  Copy PRINT88.BAS to     *
 6:  ' PRINTyy.BAS, where the "yy" are the last two digits of the new      *
 7:  ' year.  Use the "find and replace" function in a text editor to      *
 8:  ' replace all occurrences of "88" in PRINTyy.BAS with "yy".           *
 9:  '                 Written by M. L. Lesser, April 16, 1987             *
10:  '              Modified for Microsoft BC version 4.0, 12/30/87        *
11:  '***********************************************************************
12:
13:        DEFINT A-Z
14:        DEFSTR F,M,S,T
15:        DEFLNG A
16:  '     $INCLUDE: 'PQB.BI'
17:
18:        TYPE HEADER
19:            FILENAME AS STRING*35              'Name of account
20:            TOTAL    AS LONG                    'Total value of account
21:            CREATE   AS INTEGER                 'Date file created
22:            NUMREC   AS INTEGER                 'Number records in file
23:            DUMMY    AS STRING*21               'Filler
24:        END TYPE
25:
26:        TYPE RECORD
27:            DESCRIPT AS STRING*44               'Transaction description
28:            AMOUNT   AS LONG                     'Transaction amount
29:            DATE     AS INTEGER                  'Transaction date
30:            POST     AS INTEGER                  'Date transaction posted
31:            VOUCHER  AS STRING*8                 'Transaction voucher
32:            DUMMY    AS STRING*4                 'Filler
33:        END TYPE
34:
35:  ' Integer variables:
36:        DIM CBG, CFG, COUNT, I, ITEM, ITEM.ACCT, ITEM.CAT, J, OFFSET
37:        DIM N.PAGE, WID.M, WID.N
38:  ' String variables:
39:        DIM FILE, FILE.ACCT, FILE.CAT, MENU.ACCT(25), MENU.CAT(25)
40:        DIM S.INIT, S.NORM, SWITCH, TEXT
41:  ' Typed variables:
42:        DIM HEAD AS HEADER, REC AS RECORD
43:  ' Long variable:
44:        DIM AMOUNT
45:  ' Common variables:
46:        COMMON /CURSOR/ ROW.T, COL.T, ROW.B, COL.B, ROW, COL
47:
48:  ' Function definition:
49:  DEF FNFILE.NO(ITEM)        'Converts ITEM.<menu> to file number
50:        LET FILE = MID$(STR$(ITEM),2)              'Delete leading blank
51:        IF LEN(FILE) = 1 THEN LET FILE = "0" + FILE
52:        LET FNFILE.NO = FILE
53:  END DEF
54:
55:  'Read SYSTEM.PRO file for display colors and printer characteristics:
56:        LET FILE = "SYSTEM.PRO"
```

Listing 10 - 4 (continued)

```
57:        CALL FINDFILE(FILE)
58:        IF LEN(FILE) = 0 THEN              'If no SYSTEM.PRO file, use
59:           LET CFG = 7                     '  BASIC's default display mode
60:           LET CBG = 0
61:           WID.N = 80
62:           OFFSET = 0
63:           S.INIT = ""
64:           S.NORM = ""
65:           GOTO START
66:        END IF
67:        OPEN FILE FOR INPUT AS #255
68:        INPUT #255, TEXT
69:        CLOSE #255
70:  ' Check for display color and normal print switches:
71:        WHILE LEN(TEXT)                    'As long as any left:
72:           LET I = INSTR(2,TEXT,"/")       'Check for more switches
73:           IF I THEN                       'If more
74:              LET SWITCH = LEFT$(TEXT,I-1)  ' separate off first
75:              LET TEXT = MID$(TEXT,I)
76:           ELSE
77:              LET SWITCH = TEXT
78:              LET TEXT = ""
79:           END IF
80:  ' Find switch setting used:
81:           IF LEFT$(SWITCH,4) = "/CFG" THEN        'Set foreground flag
82:              LET CFG = VAL(MID$(SWITCH,6))
83:           ELSEIF LEFT$(SWITCH,4) = "/CBG" THEN    'Set background flag
84:              LET CBG = VAL(MID$(SWITCH,6))
85:           ELSEIF LEFT$(SWITCH,7) = "/WID.N=" THEN 'Normal print line
86:              LET WID.N = VAL(MID$(SWITCH,8))
87:           ELSEIF LEFT$(SWITCH,6) = "/POFF=" THEN  'Initial page offset
88:              LET OFFSET = VAL(MID$(SWITCH,7))
89:           ELSEIF LEFT$(SWITCH,6) = "/INIT=" THEN  'Control string for
90:              LET S.INIT = MID$(SWITCH,7)          '   initialization
91:           ELSEIF LEFT$(SWITCH,6) = "/NORM=" THEN  'Control string for
92:              LET S.NORM = MID$(SWITCH,7)          '   normal print
93:           END IF
94:        WEND
95:        COLOR CFG,CBG
96:        CLS
97:
98:  START:              'Start of main listing program
99:  ' Load MENU.CAT array from file A:ACCT.88:
100:       OPEN "A:ACCT.88" FOR INPUT AS #1
101:       LET ITEM.CAT = 0
102:       WHILE NOT EOF(1)                         'Read the file
103:          LET ITEM.CAT = ITEM.CAT + 1
104:          INPUT #1, MENU.CAT(ITEM.CAT)
105:       WEND
106:       CLOSE #1
107:       LET MENU.CAT(0) = MKI$(ITEM.CAT - 1)
108:  ' Sign-on messages:
109:       LET ROW = 1: ROW.T = 1: COL.T = 1: ROW.B = 25: COL.B = 80
110:       CALL PWINDOW("Listing 1988 Tax Records")
111:       CALL PWINDOW(STRING$(80,"-"))
112:       CALL PWINDOW("Do you want to list all records (y/n)?   ")
```

Listing 10 - 4 (continued)

```
113:       LET TEXT = UCASE$(INPUT$(1))
114:       IF TEXT = "Y" OR TEXT = " " THEN
115:           PRINT "Yes";
116:           LET ITEM.CAT = 1: ITEM.ACCT = 1
117:           GOTO LIST.START
118:       ELSE
119:           PRINT "No";
120:       END IF
121:  ' Select starting category and account:
122:       CALL PWINDOW("Select starting category and account:")
123:       LET COL = 10
124:       CALL DWINDOW("Starting category: ")
125:       LET ITEM.CAT = MENU(MENU.CAT())
126:       PRINT MENU.CAT(ITEM.CAT+1);
127:       LET FILE.CAT = "ACCT" + FNFILE.NO(ITEM.CAT)
128:       GOSUB LOAD.ACCT                              'Load MENU.ACCT array
129:       CALL DWINDOW("Starting account: ")
130:       LET ITEM.ACCT = MENU(MENU.ACCT())
131:       PRINT MENU.ACCT(ITEM.ACCT+1);
132:
133:  LIST.START:
134:  ' Set up printer:
135:       WIDTH LPRINT 255                            'Bug killer
136:       CALL PCONTROL(S.INIT)
137:       CALL PCONTROL(S.NORM)
138:       LET WID.M = (WID.N - 80)/2                  'Left margin
139:       IF OFFSET THEN                              'If using IBM Graphics printer
140:           CALL PSKIP(OFFSET)                      '  set print line at top of page
141:           CALL PAGELEN(66)                        '  and reset form-feed point
142:       END IF
143:  ' List the account files:
144:       FOR I = ITEM.CAT TO CVI(MENU.CAT(0))                    'List categories
145:           CLS
146:           LET ROW = 0
147:           CALL PWINDOW("Listing 1988 " + MENU.CAT(I+1))
148:           CALL PWINDOW(STRING$(80,"-"))
149:           LET COL = 10
150:           LET FILE.CAT = "ACCT" + FNFILE.NO(I)
151:           GOSUB LOAD.ACCT
152:           FOR J = ITEM.ACCT TO CVI(MENU.ACCT(0))
153:               LET FILE.ACCT = FILE.CAT + FNFILE.NO(J)
154:               OPEN "A:" + FILE.ACCT + ".88" AS #1 LEN = 64
155:               GET #1,1,HEAD
156:               IF HEAD.NUMREC = 1 THEN              'Skip file with no data
157:               ELSE
158:                   CALL DWINDOW(HEAD.FILENAME)      'Display file name
159:                   GOSUB SHOW.FILE                  'List file
160:               END IF
161:               CLOSE #1
162:  ' Emergency exit active only after listing a complete file
163:               SELECT CASE KBPEEK
164:                   CASE 0                                      'Ctrl-Break
165:                       GOTO FINI
166:                   CASE 256
167:                       IF INKEY$ = CHR$(3) THEN GOTO FINI     'Ctrl-C
168:                   CASE ELSE
```

Listing 10 - 4 (continued)

```
169:            END SELECT
170:         NEXT J
171:         LET ITEM.ACCT = 1              'List all remaining accounts
172:      NEXT I
173: FINI:           'Restore initial paper offset, if any
174:      IF OFFSET THEN
175:         CALL PSKIP(66 - OFFSET)
176:         CALL PAGELEN(66)
177:      END IF
178: END              'End of main program
179:
180: ' GOSUB subroutines in alphabetic order:
181: LOAD.ACCT:      'Loads MENU.ACCT array from FILE.CAT file
182:      OPEN "A:" + FILE.CAT + ".88" FOR INPUT AS #1
183:      LET ITEM = 0
184:      WHILE NOT EOF(1)                  'Read the file
185:         LET ITEM = ITEM + 1
186:         INPUT #1, MENU.ACCT(ITEM)
187:      WEND
188:      CLOSE #1
189:      LET MENU.ACCT(0) = MKI$(ITEM - 1)
190: RETURN                   'End of LOAD.ACCT
191:
192: SHOW.FILE:      'Lists entire account file
193:      LET AMOUNT = HEAD.TOTAL
194:      LET N.PAGE = 1
195:      GOSUB SHOW.HEADING
196:      LET COUNT = 0
197:      FOR ITEM = 2 TO HEAD.NUMREC          'All data records
198:         GET #1,ITEM,REC
199:         GOSUB SHOW.RECORD
200:         LET AMOUNT = AMOUNT - REC.AMOUNT
201:         LET COUNT = COUNT + 1
202:         IF COUNT = 55 THEN               'Full page
203:            LET N.PAGE = N.PAGE + 1
204:            CALL PFORM
205:            GOSUB SHOW.HEADING
206:            LET COUNT = 0
207:         END IF
208:      NEXT ITEM
209: ' When entire file has been displayed:
210:      IF AMOUNT <> 0 THEN                  'Account doesn't balance
211:         CALL DWINDOW("")
212:         CALL CWINDOW("--File A:" + FILE.ACCT + ".88 Damaged!   "_
213:                     + "Account Does Not Balance--")
214:         CALL CWINDOW("TERMINATING PROGRAM")
215:         CALL DWINDOW("")                  'Assure row 25 clear
216:         END                              'Abnormal termination
217:      END IF
218: ' List file total:
219:      LPRINT TAB(WID.M) SPACE$(15) STRING$(13,"-")
220:      LPRINT TAB(WID.M) "Account Total: "; TAB(WID.M+16);
221:      LPRINT USING "$$,#######.##"; HEAD.TOTAL/100;
222:      CALL PFORM
223: RETURN                   'End of SHOW.FILE
224:
```

Listing 10 - 4 (continued)

```
225:  SHOW.HEADING:    'Lists page header for account
226:      LPRINT
227:      LPRINT TAB(WID.M) "1988 "; MENU.ACCT(1) ":";
228:      LPRINT TAB(WID.M+71) DATE$
229:      LPRINT TAB(WID.M) MENU.ACCT(J+1);
230:      LPRINT TAB(WID.M+74) "page"; N.PAGE
231:      LPRINT: LPRINT
232:      LPRINT TAB(WID.M) "DATE";
233:      LPRINT TAB(WID.M+8) "VOUCHER";
234:      LPRINT TAB(WID.M+19) "AMOUNT";
235:      LPRINT TAB(WID.M+41) "DESCRIPTION";
236:      LPRINT TAB(WID.M+75) "POSTED";
237:      LPRINT TAB(WID.M) STRING$(4,"-") TAB(WID.M+7) STRING$(8,"-");
238:      LPRINT TAB(WID.M+16) STRING$(13,"-") TAB(WID.M+31);
239:      LPRINT STRING$(44,"-") TAB(WID.M+77) STRING$(4,"-")
240:  RETURN                      'End of SHOW.HEADING
241:
242:  SHOW.RECORD:     'Displays data file record
243:      LPRINT TAB(WID.M);
244:      LPRINT USING "####"; REC.DATE;
245:      LPRINT TAB(WID.M+7) REC.VOUCHER; TAB(WID.M+16);
246:      LPRINT USING "$$,#######.##"; REC.AMOUNT/100;
247:      LPRINT TAB(WID.M+31) REC.DESCRIPT TAB(WID.M+77);
248:      LPRINT USING "####"; REC.POST;
249:  RETURN                      'End of SHOW.RECORD
250:  '                     End of source code
```

Listing 10 - 4

2. The compiler cannot check improper FIELD statements because it allows <filenum> and <width> to be expressions, rather than requiring literals or symbolic constants.

3. The exception to the rule that the directory length of a random file is given by the record length times the number of records is when the record structure used to "field" the record is shorter than the declared record length. In that case, the length of file will be the product of the record length times one less than the number of records, plus the length of the record structure used for the last record.

4. According to its manual, the maximum record number that QBASIC 4.0 will allow is (2^{31} - 1). For 1-byte records, this would be a file length of 1 byte less than 2,048 megabytes!

5. I tested RECORD88 as it was implemented, state by state, using data files converted to RECORD88 file format from my 1987 tax record files. The original data files were written with a previous record-keeping program compiled with QBASIC version 3.0, which used the old-style double-precision floating point num-

bers to carry the pennies as "whole numbers." The conversion was made with a one-time utility (not shown) having a kernel similar to the sample shown in the Microsoft tutorial *Learning and Using Microsoft QuickBASIC*, section B.1.2.4. If you are implementing a similar program for the first time, you can test each state using dummy category, account, and data files "built" by the previous states.

Chapter 11

Putting the Program Together

Linking is the process of putting separately compiled and assembled modules together into a single file of executable code. Using QBASIC in development-environment mode shields the programmer from the linking process, although an explicit linking phase occurs when converting programs to executable form from within the development environment by using the "Make EXE File" menu option.

This final chapter is devoted to an overview of the linking process, providing background information to supplement the "cookbook" procedures for using LINK given in earlier chapters. Following the generalized discussion, there are descriptions of two specialized uses of LINK: for testing substitute library modules before replacing them in a searchable library, and for building a "Quick" library in order to use assembled procedures under the development environment.

The process of linking a program written entirely in assembly language and converting it to an executable COM file is illustrated by the short program MEMSET.ASM. MEMSET.COM is used in a procedure for determining the minimum installed memory required to run any program that will fit into the actual installed memory of your system.

The Linking Process

Linking involves several overlapping processes. The purpose of linking is to convert one or more object code files into a single relocatable executable file, suitable for DOS to load into memory and start execution of the program. The major task of the linker is to resolve the relative addressing established in each segment of each separate object module into the absolute addresses used in the final executable code file. Additional capabilities of LINK are: to rename the executable file if required; to produce a listing file showing the sequence and size of the linked segments; and to search library files and link only those modules required by the program.

Running LINK

LINK requires four file categories to be specified for it to operate, although some may be given by default. The four categories, in the order they must be specified, are:

1. The name(s) of the object module file(s) to link. There is no default; LINK must be given at least one <filename> to link or it will terminate with an error message. Additional object-file names are separated by either <SP> characters or by "plus" signs. The object files are linked in the order named.
2. The name of the executable file. The default is <filename>.EXE, where <filename> is that of the first object file named.[1]
3. The name of the listing file to be produced. The default is either <filename>.MAP when using LINK in command-line mode, or NUL.MAP (no file written) when using LINK in prompt mode.
4. The name(s) of any library file(s) to search for satisfying unresolved external labels. LINK has no default library; the QBASIC compiler inserts a special instruction into its object file, telling the linker to search the appropriate compiler-furnished library, BCOM40.LIB or BRUN40.LIB. This search will be made *after* LINK searches any library name(s) entered in the calling command.

The linking examples in previous chapters showed the file categories entered with the LINK call on the DOS command line. In command-line

```
DLINK

Microsoft (R) Overlay Linker  Version 3.61
Copyright (C) Microsoft Corp 1983-1987.  All rights reserved.

Object Modules [.OBJ]: RECORD88/E
Run File [RECORD88.EXE]:
List File [NUL.MAP]:
Libraries [.LIB]: PQB

D>
```

Figure 11 - 1
Linking in prompt mode

mode, each file category is separated from its neighbor by a comma. The
call can be terminated with a semicolon and the Enter key after any file
has been specified; LINK will use the default names for the remaining
categories. Defaults can also be specified by no entry between commas.

If there is no terminating semicolon when the Enter key is pressed,
LINK will default to its prompt mode (unless all four categories have been
specified), starting with the next category in the sequence. Entering LINK
on the command line with no following names will initiate prompt mode.
Figure 11-1 is a copy of my screen when so linking RECORD88, as compiled with the /o/e compiler switches. A null entry on a prompt line tells
the linker to use the default displayed by the prompt in square brackets.
This example is equivalent to the command-line entry

```
LINK RECORD88/E,,,PQB
```

except that no RECORD88.MAP file will be produced.

The /e linker switch tells LINK to "pack" the RECORD88.EXE file
by eliminating runs of identical symbols from the file. The DOS loader
will replace the eliminated material before the code is executed.

The other linker switches that may be useful when linking QBASIC
object files are:

/M   The /m switch forces a full listing file to be generated that includes all the public symbols as well as the segment list. Such a listing file is required if you wish to use a symbolic debugger, such as SYMDEB, in its intended mode.

/NOE The /noe link switch disables an "improved" linking process introduced with Microsoft LINK version 3.61. It is required when testing a "substitute" library module without replacing it in the library. It is neither available nor required when using earlier Microsoft linkers when performing the same function.[2]

/Q   The /q linker switch is used to build a "Quick" (<libname>.QLB) library, which is not a searchable library as are the libraries furnished with the compiler or built with the LIB utility. "Quick" libraries are private run-time modules usable only with the development environment.

Address Reconciliation

The feature of the 8086 family of microprocessor chips that complicates the linking process is the way the architect managed to squeeze a megabyte of address space into a chip architecture that has no registers longer than 16 bits.

Computer architects use a different metric system than do scientists and engineers. In computerese, one *kilobyte* is 2^{10} (1,024) bytes; one *megabyte* is 2^{20} (1,048,576) bytes. Since it takes an *n*-bit binary number to count 2^n objects the way computer architects do (starting with zero), a minimum register length of *n* bits is required to address a memory with 2^n locations — unless you cheat! The trick used by the 8086 architect to get 20-bit addressing with 16-bit registers was to use registers in pairs — segment:offset addressing. All members of the 8086 family (including the 80286 and 80386 when operating in what Intel calls "real mode") can address up to one megabyte of memory without resorting to "expanded memory" or other hardware means of rerouting the memory address signals.[3]

Four of the registers on the chip are dedicated "segment registers." These 16-bit registers carry the absolute (20-bit) memory address corresponding to the start of a 64K *segment* containing the memory byte being addressed. All individually addressable segments must begin on a *paragraph* boundary — a memory location with zero as the low-order hex digit of its address. Thus, the segment registers need hold only four hex digits (16 bits); the fifth (zero) digit is implied. The 16-bit *offset* locates the byte being addressed within that segment. The offset can have any value from 0 through FFFF (65,535) and may be carried in one of several remaining registers or as a literal in the instruction itself.

Two of the segment registers have special purposes: instructions are executable only from the segment addressed by the CS (Code Segment) register, and the stack operations take place only in the segment addressed by the SS (Stack Segment) register. All four segment registers can be used to address data, although the DS (Data Segment) register is the default.

While a program is running, the absolute address of the *next* instruction to be executed is given by the segment:offset pair in the CS and IP (Instruction Pointer) registers. Usually, this address is that of the following instruction. An exception occurs if the executing instruction is a call or a jump. In assembly-language terms, a CALL instruction to a NEAR procedure label (which must be in the same segment as the CALL instruction) first pushes the current contents of the IP register onto the stack, and then loads the offset of the label into the IP; the next instruction executed will be the first instruction in the subroutine. A NEAR return pops the stack into the IP register.

A CALL instruction to a FAR procedure label (which may be in another code segment) pushes the contents of both the CS and IP registers, before replacing them with the segment and offset of the called subroutine. The FAR return pops the two values off the stack into the IP and CS registers to return control to the calling sequence.

The QuickBASIC compiler uses FAR calls and returns to transfer control between separately compiled or assembled modules that may be in different segments. Thus, the only permitted intersegment control transfers are to and from called subroutines or declared functions, whether compiled or assembled. Each compiled procedure, even if in the main module, is coded as a FAR procedure.

The linker uses information coded into the object modules to determine where such intersegment reconciliation is required. The compiler codes the procedure labels appearing in FAR CALL statements as external in the calling module, and the corresponding labels as public in the procedure module. The programmer must provide similar information when writing assembled subroutines.

If the linker cannot match all the external requirements with public labels, it produces an appropriate error message.

N.B.   In spite of the error message, the linker will still write a <filename>.EXE file. Running such a file will produce unpredictable results.

Segment Ordering

A major task of the linker is to position the segments in the executable code. The assembler or compiler sends sequencing information to the linker by defining segments having the attributes: name, align type, combine type, and class. These attributes are passed to the linker.

The *align type* establishes the starting address requirements for each new segment: PARA (paragraph) is the default, but QBASIC uses WORD alignment for code and data segments.[4]

Portions of the same-name segment appearing in different object modules, with *combine type* PUBLIC and belonging to the same *class*, are concatenated into the same segment in the executable file. Portions of the same-name same-class segment with combine type COMMON are overlayed. All different-name segments belonging to the same class are linked contiguously. The segments within a class, and the classes themselves, are linked in the order first encountered in the set of object models being linked together.

Segments with combine type STACK are linked in a manner similar to segments with combine type PUBLIC, but addressed by the SS and SP (Stack Pointer) registers.

The compiler (or assembler) can also designate segments as belonging to a *group*. The group designation notifies the linker that any instructions that contain address references to any location within a segment in the group should be modified so the offsets are from the origin of the initial segment in the group, rather than from the origin of the individual segment. While this allows the entire group to be addressed without changing the contents of a segment register, it requires that the total size of the group not exceed 64K. In QBASIC, DGROUP, which contains all the data available to the program (except that in far object space), is such a group.

The QuickBASIC compiler defines a set of dummy segments, containing neither code nor data, at the beginning of each compiled object module. These dummy segments assure that all following segments are in the order required by the QBASIC support system. Although empty dummy segments will be shown in the linker list file, <filename>.MAP, they will not take up any space in the executable file.

All segments defined in assembled procedures must adhere to the class, align type, combine type, and group designations established by the compiler. In some cases, the name used for the segment must also agree with that used by the compiler. If you are using MASM 5.0 in its "simplified segment definition" mode, code and data segment definitions will be made for you, although you will still have to use the "detailed" segment definitions for COMMON segments — including defining DGROUP to contain them. If you are using an earlier version of MASM, you will have to make detailed segment and group definitions for all segments used and to supply the appropriate ASSUME directive. You will also have to declare the FAR procedures as such.

The rules for segment definitions in assembled procedure modules are:

- All code segments have segment name <filename>_TEXT, align type WORD, combine type PUBLIC, and class CODE. <Filename> is the name of the file containing the source-code module.
- All data segments have segment name _DATA, align type WORD, combine type PUBLIC, and class DATA.
- All named common segments have segment name <name>, align type WORD, combine type COMMON, and class BC_VARS.
- Blank common has segment name COMMON, align type WORD, combine type COMMON, and class BLANK.
- If you are using a version of MASM earlier than 5.0, DGROUP must be defined to include both data and common segments. If you are using MASM 5.0, the DGROUP definition should include only the COMMON segments.

Linking Library Modules

A searchable library, usually designated as <filename>.LIB, is a combination of independent object code modules, along with sufficient indexing information to allow the linker to find the public entries in each module.

The names of any library files to be searched are given to LINK as the fourth category of input file names. Rather than linking all the modules in the library, LINK searches the library, looking for public entries that will satisfy unresolved externals in the modules previously linked. As each one is found, the entire module containing that entry is linked to the previous ones.

LINK will make multiple searches of the library, if necessary, to satisfy any unresolved external that arose when linking a module from that library. Thus, the order in which the modules appear in the library is not important.

If multiple library names are specified to LINK, the searches will occur in the order the files are named. When linking to QBASIC object modules, the last search will be of the compiler-furnished library specified in the first compiler-generated object module in the list. Thus, any remaining unresolved externals in compiled subroutine modules linked from private libraries will be resolved in the search of the appropriate compiler-furnished library.

Testing Substitute Library Modules

As time passes, you will probably want to make changes in (enhance) the existing modules in your private subroutine library, such as when the PCONTR subroutine was inserted into the source code for the preexisting *print* module (Chapter 5). In general, it is safest to test the revised module for compatibility before replacing the old module in the library. Such testing is done by using existing programs (that used the module in its previous form) as drivers, substituting the revised module for the original library module while linking the remaining library.

Prior to the existence of LINK version 3.61, it was very easy to make this substitution. All that was required was a LINK command-line call of the form

```
LINK <progname> <subsmodname>,,,PQB
```

and the deed was done. The old <progname> would be linked to the substitute module, which resolved any external references to the procedures in that module before the library was searched, so those externals would not be linked from the library module. Unfortunately, those easy days are over.

Starting with LINK version 3.61, the substituting command call must be

```
LINK <progname> <subsmodname>/NOE,,,PQB
```

or you will get a flock of error messages telling you to use the /noe switch and relink your program. If you don't, *both* sets of modules will be contained in your executable file, although (usually) only the set from the substitute module will be linked to your compiled object code.

Building "Quick" Libraries

The only way you can coerce the development environment to recognize assembled or separately compiled procedures is to put those procedures into a "Quick" library. A Quick library is really a private run-time module for the development environment, just as the BRUN40.EXE file is a compiler-furnished run-time module for QBASIC programs compiled in the default mode. Since only one Quick library can be used with the development environment at a time, that library must contain all the preassembled (or precompiled) modules that will be used by the program being developed under the development environment.

You can build a Quick library, PQB.QLB, containing all the modules in your PQB.LIB file by using LINK in its least-efficient mode: linking in all the modules in a searchable library, whether they are needed or not. The linker command would be

```
LINK PQB.LIB/Q,,,BQLB40
```

where BQLB40 is a searchable library on one of the QBASIC 4.0 distribution diskettes. PQB.QLB would be "included" within the development environment by calling QB.EXE with a command line containing the /1 switch followed by the Quick library name, as in:

```
QB <progname>/LPQB
```

If a Quick library is not in the default directory, QB.EXE will look for it in those directories listed in the LIB environment string. After loading, the development environment will have access to all the modules in the Quick library, whether they are to be used or not.

This is fine if you wish to use the development environment for small one-shot programs that may or may not require any of your private library subroutines. However, if you then decide to build an executable file containing such a program, *do not* use the RUN menu option "Make EXE File" to do so. The development environment will load the entire PQB.LIB into your executable file, since its built- in "again.bat" file uses LINK's inefficient "full library" mode. Thus, all those unused modules will take up memory space, and loading time, every time you run the program so developed.

Things get somewhat worse if you are trying to develop a major program that requires an assembled module that isn't one of your "normal" private-library modules, say VARCHK.BAS (Listing 9-3). You first would have to build a Quick library containing CTYPE.OBJ plus all the PQB.LIB modules called by VARCHK. But you might not know which of the PQB.LIB modules will be used — before you start the development process. The easy way out is to build a special Quick library, say CTYPE.QLB, containing both CTYPE.OBJ and all the PQB.LIB modules, using the linker command:

```
LINK CTYPE/Q PQB.LIB,,,BQLB40
```

and live with the space problem.

Once you had VARCHK implemented and running under the development environment, if you wanted to compile and link it by using the "Make EXE File" option, you would also need a CTYPE.LIB private library containing all the same modules.

Program Size

When you write, compile, link, and test a program on your system, all you know about the memory-space requirements for performing those tasks is that the system you are running on has sufficient available memory. If you are going to share your programs with others, it might be helpful if you could tell them the minimum memory size in which the program will

```
 1:          PAGE   ,105
 2:          TITLE  MEMSET
 3: ;****************************************************************
 4: ;                      MEMSET.ASM                             *
 5: ;    MEMSET.COM resets the ROM BIOS "memory size" word and then boots  *
 6: ; the system by calling the ROM BIOS bootstrap loader.  Invoke MEMSET  *
 7: ; with the command-line call:                                 *
 8: ;                      MEMSET <nnn>                           *
 9: ; where <nnn> is a digit string representing the new "memory size"  *
10: ; (in K) to be loaded into the ROM BIOS data area.           *
11: ;    MEMSET will return an error message and terminate if <nnn> is  *
12: ; greater than the current value set in the "memory size" word, or is  *
13: ; less than 64.  (DOS may require more than 64K to boot.)     *
14: ;    WARNING:  Do not run MEMSET unless the system has been booted  *
15: ; from a DOS diskette in the A: drive.  Leave that diskette in place  *
16: ; until you are through using MEMSET.                         *
17: ;         Written by M. L. Lesser, February 6, 1987          *
18: ;         Reassembled with Microsoft MASM version 5.0        *
19: ;             Converted to MEMSET.COM with EXE2BIN           *
20: ;****************************************************************
21:
22: CODE     SEGMENT PARA PUBLIC 'CODE'
23:          ASSUME CS:CODE, DS:CODE
24:          ORG    100H
25:
26: MEMSET   PROC NEAR
27:          JMP SHORT START
28:
29: SIGNOFF DB      13,10,13,10,'Improper input - Terminating program'
30:          DB      13,10,'$'
31:
32: START:   MOV    SI,80H                ;Command-line-buffer count byte
33:          LODSB                        ;Put count in AL
34:          OR     AL,AL                 ;Anything there?
35:          JZ     ERROR                 ;If not, error exit
36:          CBW                          ;If so, convert byte to word
37:          MOV    CX,AX                 ;  and put value in CX
38: DESPACE:               ;Remove leading <SP> bytes
39:          LODSB                        ;Next byte from buffer
40:          CMP    AL,20H                ;Is it a <SP>
41:          JNZ    OK                    ;If not, continue
42:          LOOP   DESPACE               ;Else go around again
43: OK:      OR     CX,CX                 ;Any more in command buffer?
44:          JZ     ERROR
45:          CMP    CX,03                 ;More than three bytes?
46:          JA     ERROR
47:          DEC    SI                    ;Reset source to first digit
48:          XOR    AX,AX                 ;Collect hex word here
49:          MOV    BX,10                 ;Digit multiplier
50: ; Convert ASCII string to binary integer word:
51: ATOI:    IMUL   BX                    ;Multiply previous value by 10
52:          MOV    DX,AX                 ;Save it
53:          LODSB                        ;Load next ASCII digit
54:          CMP    AL,'0'                ;Range check
55:          JB     ERROR
56:          CMP    AL,'9'
```

Listing 11 - 1 (continued)

```
57:             JA      ERROR
58:             AND     AX,0FH                  ;Convert to hex integer word
59:             ADD     AX,DX                   ;Value to this point
60:             LOOP    ATOI                    ;Repeat until finished
61: ; Set ES addressability to ROM BIOS absolute segment:
62:             XOR     DX,DX
63:             MOV     ES,DX
64:             MOV     DI,0413H                ;Address of "memory size" word
65: ; Check that new size not greater than old size:
66:             CMP     ES:[DI],AX
67:             JL      ERROR
68: ; Check that new size is at least 64K:
69:             CMP     AX,64
70:             JL      ERROR
71:             STOSW                           ;Load new memory size
72:             INT     19H                     ;Call ROM BIOS bootstrap loader
73:
74: ERROR:      LEA     DX,SIGNOFF              ;Display error sign off message
75:             MOV     AH,09H
76:             INT     21H
77:             INT     20H                     ;Terminate program
78:
79: MEMSET      ENDP
80: CODE        ENDS
81:             END     MEMSET
```

Listing 11 - 1

operate. MEMSET.ASM (Listing 11-1) is a short assembly-language program that can be used to make such a determination.

MEMSET.ASM is written to be converted to a COM file. When you link it (there is nothing to link it to), you will get the "no stack segment" warning message. You can convert the MEMSET.EXE file to MEM-SET.COM with the command:[5]

```
EXE2BIN MEMSET MEMSET.COM
```

MEMSET resets the word in the BIOS data area that holds the installed memory size, changing it to the value given on the calling command line, and then forces a warm boot with a ROM BIOS interrupt 19H. After the warm boot, CHKDSK will inform you that the "total memory" is the amount specified in the MEMSET call. MEMSET operates correctly only if the system was booted originally from a diskette in the A drive; using MEMSET after a boot from a hard disk will lock up your system.

I usually test for program memory requirements with a special "boot" diskette carrying a minimum DOS 3.3 system and MEMSET.COM. The CONFIG.SYS file has only the BUFFERS=4 command, and the only command in the AUTOEXEC.BAT file is "MODE MONO." The diskette also has a copy of CHKDSK.COM and any program I am testing. I prefer to test on my two-diskette IBM PC, as this minimizes the size of resident DOS that is loaded. Since memory for the PC can be purchased only in 64K increments, I use MEMSET to decrease the apparent memory size by 64K at a time until the tested program will no longer run.

For example, the diskette-only version of RECORD88 will not run in 128K of installed memory — the source of the 192K requirement mentioned in the last chapter. A further test showed that it will not compile in 192K. Thus, 256K is the minimum practical memory size for using QBASIC in separately compiled mode for programs as large as RECORD88.BAS.

Although one would never run (or even develop) a program such as RECORD88 under the development environment, I tried running it just to get an idea of the costs. I used the /l switch to load a PQB.QLB file containing all my PQB.LIB modules except COMMAND.OBJ. The program would compile and run with 384K memory, but QB.EXE couldn't load itself and PQB.QLB into a 320K memory.

Concluding Remarks

This book has been devoted to the mechanics of extending the QuickBASIC language, along with excursions into the language-system architecture. The following observations summarize my approach to using the compiler:

- QuickBASIC is neither a "portable" nor a "device independent" language. The programs run only on members of the IBM PC family and compatible copies, and the dialect is designed to take advantage of that hardware. The programmer who understands the underlying language-system architecture can write code that maximizes performance while minimizing wear and tear on the hardware.
- All nontrivial programs have a vanishingly small probability of being bug free as first written. The only valid approach to this unsolvable problem is to assume that a newly written program will always contain errors, and to design, implement, and test it in-

crementally — building each stage on the scaffold of previously tested code. I find it more convenient to use BC.EXE, the separate compiler, for this purpose than to struggle with the poor editing and linking facilities of QB.EXE, the development environment.

- While the compiler contains bugs, as do all other large system programs, these are surprisingly few. I consider that I have found a compiler bug *only* if I can reduce the offending source code to a few lines that demonstrate the problem, such as the example shown in Figure 6-1. Otherwise, I keep hunting until I find the source of my own bug. I have never found any "debugger" to be helpful in this exercise.

Notes

1. Many language compilers (particularly those that allow the user a choice of memory model) require a module of initializing code to be linked ahead of the first module of compiled code. The LINK renaming facility allows the resulting executable file to have the name of the main module of compiled code, rather than the name of the initializing module. An example of linker renaming is shown in Chapter 2.

2. Small tests I have run indicated that using LINK 3.60 (distributed with MASM 5.0) for substituting a library module with no /noe switch produced the same executable file as did using LINK 3.61 (distributed with QBASIC 4.0) when used with the /noe switch. Be that as it may, you are probably better off using the later version of the linker.

3. The 8086 family includes the 8086, 8088, 80186, 80286, and 80386 microprocessors. While the 80286 and 80386 have additional memory addressability capabilities when operating in "protected mode," QBASIC programs (and DOS) will run only in "real mode," where addressability is limited to the one megabyte address space. The 640K "user memory" limitation of the IBM PC (and compatibles) is built into the PC system architecture, which reserves the upper 340K of the first megabyte of address space for ROM BIOS and other hardware uses.

4. Previous versions of the QBASIC compiler used BYTE alignment for code segments. Segments with BYTE alignment may start at any memory address. Segments with WORD alignment must start on a word boundary (absolute address an even number). The actual code for segments with align types BYTE and WORD do not necessarily start on a paragraph boundary. The linker adjusts any instruction that contains segment and offset values that refer to locations within such segments to force the effective segment starting address to a paragraph boundary.

5. EXE2BIN.EXE is not furnished with PC-DOS 3.3; it is distributed on the "DOS Utilities" diskette furnished with the version 3.3 *DOS Technical Reference* manual.

Appendix A

Driving a Serial Printer

The PC architects expected that any printer being used would be connected to a parallel port, so they provided excellent parallel printer support in ROM BIOS. Both the DOS standard printer device driver (PRN/LPT1) and the printer-control extensions shown in this book make direct calls on that parallel printer support.

If you want to drive a serial printer from programs intended to drive a parallel printer, you must intercept all calls being sent to the parallel port support, translate the control sequences to those required by the ROM BIOS serial (asynchronous communications adapter) support, and then call on the communications support to drive your printer.

The simplest way to perform this task is to use the DOS utility MODE. For example, to drive my Qume printer at 1,200 baud, 7 data bits, don't-care parity, and 2 stop bits, with wait cycles if the Qume's buffer is full, the COM1 port is initialized with the command:

```
MODE COM1:12,N,8,2,P
```

This actually sets COM1 to 8 data bits and no parity, but since the ANSI serial data transmission standard is to ship data bits low-order first, it is equivalent to sending the necessary 7 low-order data bits and substituting the eighth data bit for the don't-care parity bit. Once the COM1 port has been initialized, a second MODE command:

```
MODE LPT1:=COM1
```

reroutes any output intended for LPT1 to COM1. If used, these two MODE commands are usually run from the AUTOEXEC.BAT file.

However, when used for printer control, MODE is a "terminate and stay resident" (TSR) program, leaving its residue sitting above the resident portion of the command processor. Since I prefer not to use TSR programs — not even those that come with DOS — I wrote SERIAL.ASM (Listing A-1), an installable device driver. SERIAL performs the equivalent of the two MODE commands in AUTOEXEC.BAT with one "DEVICE=SERIAL.SYS" command in the CONFIG.SYS file. Since SERIAL becomes an integral part of the DOS configuration, its resident space is buried below the command processor, where it is unlikely to interfere with other programs.

To generate SERIAL.SYS from SERIAL.ASM: assemble the source code and link it in the normal fashion. Then, convert the resulting SERIAL.EXE to SERIAL.SYS with the command:

```
EXE2BIN SERIAL SERIAL.SYS
```

Copy SERIAL.SYS to your boot disk where CONFIG.SYS can find it.

SERIAL is not as flexible as MODE; its COM1 initialization is built into its source code (line 160). Values of this constant for other parameters are given in any IBM "system" edition of the *Technical Reference* manual (except those for the Personal System/2 machines) or in the *Personal System/2 and Personal Computer BIOS Interface Technical Reference* (for all members of the IBM PC and PS/2 families).

The driver loaded by SERIAL.SYS has the device name "SDRIVER." Since SDRIVER is now the name of a device, it cannot be used for the name of a file. However, you can open the device SDRIVER to change its routing back and forth between the serial and parallel ports, using a DOS IOCTL call. This switching is done by the program PSWITCH.ASM (Listing A-2), to be assembled, linked, and converted to PSWITCH.COM with EXE2BIN. The PSWITCH calling conventions are given in the listing prologue.

```
 1:          PAGE    ,105
 2:          TITLE   SERIAL
 3:  ;*******************************************************************
 4:  ;                          SERIAL.ASM                            *
 5:  ;    SERIAL.SYS is an add-on special device driver which sets COM1 to  *
 6:  ; 1200 baud, no parity, 8 data bits and 2 stop bits, installs an  *
 7:  ; intercept to INT 14H to wait on COM1 if a time-out occurs, and then  *
 8:  ; reroutes LPT1 output to COM1.                                   *
 9:  ;    Using SERIAL.SYS in the CONFIG.SYS file is the equivalent of  *
10:  ; using AUTOEXEC.BAT to call "MODE COM1:12,N,8,2,P" followed by   *
11:  ; "MODE LPT1:=COM1" but is a little faster on boot and does not load  *
12:  ; memory above resident DOS with "terminate and stay resident" code.  *
13:  ;    NOTE:  Due to RS-232C characteristics, the LPT1 "initialize"  *
14:  ; will return "OK" response if the printer has ever been turned on  *
15:  ; since system power-on.                                          *
16:  ;    After boot, output can be switched between LPT1 and COM1 with the  *
17:  ; utility program PSWITCH.COM.                                    *
18:  ;*******************************************************************
19:
20:  ;          Written by M. L. Lesser, July 23, 1986
21:  ;          Modified 9-17-86 to revise "Initialize LPT1"
22:  ;          Reassembled with Microsoft MASM v 5.0
23:  ;          Converted to memory-image format with EXE2BIN after linking
24:
25:  CSEG      SEGMENT PARA PUBLIC 'CODE'
26:
27:  ; Static Request Header Assignments:
28:  SRH          EQU 0                 ;Static Request Header start
29:  SRH_LEN      EQU 13                ;    "       "       "    length
30:  SRH_CCD_FLD  EQU SRH+2             ;    "       "       "    comm'nd code fld
31:  SRH_STA_FLD  EQU SRH+3             ;    "       "       "    status field
32:  BRK_ADD      EQU SRH+SRH_LEN + 1   ;Pointer to INIT cutoff address
33:  TRAN_ADD     EQU SRH+SRH_LEN + 1   ;Pointer to IOCTL buffer address
34:
35:  ; Status code returns:
36:  DONE    EQU    0080H
37:  ERROR   EQU    8083H                 ;"Unknown command" error
38:
39:  SERIAL  PROC FAR
40:          ASSUME CS:CSEG,DS:CSEG
41:
42:  ; Device header:
43:  NEXT_DEV   DD   -1                    ;Only header in this driver
44:  ATTRIBUTE  DW   0C000H                ;Char. device, IOCTL permitted
45:  STRATEGY   DW   DEV_STRATEGY          ;Pointer to device strategy
46:  INTERRUPT  DW   DEV_INT               ;Pointer to device interrupt
47:  DEV_NAME   DB   'SDRIVER '            ;Driver name padded to 8 bytes
48:
49:  ; Local storage:
50:  DOSCOM     DD   ?                      ;Original INT 14 target address
51:  PRINTER    DD   ?                      ;Original INT 17 target address
52:
53:  DEV_STRATEGY:                     ;Dummy, not used in this driver
54:          RET
55:
56:  DEV_INT:                          ;Perform device command
```

Listing A - 1 (continued)

```
57:         PUSH    DS                          ;Save registers used
58:         PUSH    AX
59:         PUSH    CX
60:         PUSH    DX
61:  ;  Branch according to command passed
62:         MOV     AL,ES:[BX]+2                ;Function command byte
63:         CMP     AL,12                       ;IOCTL output command
64:         JZ      IOCTL_OUT
65:         OR      AL,AL
66:         JNZ     NOPE                        ;INIT too far away for JZ
67:         JMP     INIT                        ;Initialize driver
68:  ;  NOTE:  Any other command will return error with no further action:
69: NOPE:   MOV     AX,ERROR
70: EXIT:   MOV     ES:SRH_STA_FLD[BX],AX       ;Set return status word
71:         POP     DX                          ;Restore remaining registers
72:         POP     CX
73:         POP     AX
74:         POP     DS
75:         RET
76:
77:  ;  New targets of output interrupts:
78: INT_14:                             ;New COM intercept
79:         OR      DX,DX                       ;Check if for COM1
80:         JNZ     OTHER                       ;If not, use normal driver
81:         CMP     AH,01                       ;Check if for "send character"
82:         JZ      WRITE                       ;If so, use "waiting" driver
83: OTHER:  JMP     CS:DOSCOM                   ;Else use normal DOSCOM driver
84:
85: WRITE:  MOV     AH,01                       ;Return point if time-out occurs
86:         PUSHF                               ;Simulated interrupt to
87:         CLI                                 ;  original INT 14
88:         CALL    CS:DOSCOM                   ;  target address
89:         TEST    AH,80H                      ;Test for serial time-out
90:         JNZ     WRITE                       ;If time-out, try again
91:         IRET                                ;Else return from interrupt
92:
93: INT_17:                             ;New parallel printer intercept:
94:         OR      DX,DX                       ;Check for LPT1 command
95:         JZ      DOIT                        ;If for LPT1, send via COM1
96:         JMP     CS:PRINTER                  ;Else, execute on LPT requested
97: DOIT:   STI                                 ;Enable external interrupts
98:         PUSH    AX                          ;Will need to recover AL
99:         CMP     AH,01                       ;Request to initialize printer?
100:        JNZ     NEXT                        ;If not, try next LPT1 command
101:        MOV     AH,03                       ;Get COM1 status
102:        INT     14H                         ;Status will return AL = 0 if
103:        OR      AL,AL                       ;printer has never been on
104:        POP     AX
105:        MOV     AH,0A8H                     ;Response for printer not on
106:        JNZ     PRIN                        ;If printer is on
107:        IRET
108: PRIN:  MOV     AH,0                        ;Response for printer on
109:        IRET                                ; and return to DOS
110: NEXT:  OR      AH,AH                       ;Request to print character?
111:        JNZ     STATUS                      ;If not, must be status request
112:        MOV     AH,1                        ;ROM BIOS RS232 "send" command
```

Listing A - 1 (continued)

```
113:           INT     14H
114:           POP     AX
115: OK:       MOV     AH,90H              ;Send INT 17 "not busy"
116:           IRET                        ; and return to DOS
117: STATUS: MOV       AH,03              ;Request COM1 status
118:           INT     14H
119:           AND     AL,30H             ;Mask all except DSR and CTS
120:           CMP     AL,30H             ;Are both bits "on"?
121:           POP     AX                 ;Restore AL (will throw AH away)
122:           JZ      OK                 ;If DRS and CTS ready, "OK"
123:           MOV     AH,10H             ;Else send "selected" (busy)
124:           IRET
125:
126: ;   Driver operations:
127: IOCTL_OUT:                           ;Switch printers
128:           MOV     CX,ES:TRAN_ADD[BX]     ;IOCTL command character in CL
129:           CMP     CL,'p'             ;Test for  switch to parallel
130:           LDS     DX,CS:PRINTER      ;Setup for switch to parallel
131:           JZ      SWITCH             ;Note: Any other command letter will
132:           PUSH    CS                 ;    reset to serial.  Input error
133:           POP     DS                 ;    check must be made in program
134:           LEA     DX,INT_17          ;    making IOCTL call.
135: SWITCH: MOV       AX,2517H
136:           INT     21H
137: ;  Print output message:
138:           PUSH    CS                 ;Reset DS addressability to
139:           POP     DS                 ;    Code Segment
140:           LEA     DX,MESGE_2         ;Parallel output message
141:           CMP     CL,'p'
142:           JZ      SHOW
143:           LEA     DX,MESGE_3         ;Serial output message
144: SHOW:     MOV     AH,09H
145:           INT     21H
146:           MOV     AX,DONE
147:           JMP     EXIT
148: MESGE_2 DB        9,'LPT1 output returned to LPT1$'
149: MESGE_3 DB        9,'LPT1 output routed to COM1$'
150:
151: INIT:                                ;Initialize the driver
152:           PUSH    ES                 ;Save request-header address
153:           PUSH    BX
154:           LEA     DX,INIT            ;Set Break-off address in
155:           MOV     ES:BRK_ADD[BX],DX  ;request header
156:           MOV     ES:BRK_ADD+2[BX],CS
157: ;  Set COM1 transmit characteristics:
158: ;   (1200 baud, no parity, 8 data bits, 2 stop bits):
159:           XOR     AH,AH              ;AH = 0 initializes RS232 port
160:           MOV     AL,10000111B       ; to characteristics in AL
161:      ;NOTE:  See Technical Reference manual for AL values for bit codes
162:      ;          corresponding to other transmission  characteristics.
163:           XOR     DX,DX              ;COM1
164:           INT     14H                ;Call ROM BIOS
165: ;  Get target address of INT 14
166:           MOV     AX,3514H
167:           INT     21H
168:           MOV     CS:WORD PTR DOSCOM,BX
```

Listing A - 1 (continued)

```
169:         MOV     CS:WORD PTR DOSCOM+2,ES
170:  ;  Install new interrupt vector:
171:         MOV     AX,CS                    ;Set DS addressability to
172:         MOV     DS,AX                    ;  to CODE SEGMENT
173:         LEA     DX,INT_14
174:         MOV     AX,2514H
175:         INT     21H
176:  ;  Get target address of INT 17
177:         MOV     AX,3517H
178:         INT     21H
179:         MOV     CS:WORD PTR PRINTER,BX
180:         MOV     CS:WORD PTR PRINTER+2,ES
181:  ;  Install new interrupt vector:
182:         LEA     DX,INT_17
183:         MOV     AX,2517H
184:         INT     21H
185:  ;  Display setup message:
186:         LEA     DX,MESGE_1
187:         MOV     AH,09H
188:         INT     21H
189:  ;  Restore request-header address:
190:         POP     BX
191:         POP     ES
192:         MOV     AX,DONE                  ;Set status code
193:         JMP     EXIT
194:  MESGE_1 DB      13,10,'COM1 set at 1200 baud, 8 data bits, '
195:         DB      'no parity bit, 2 stop bits, waiting',13,10
196:         DB      9,'LPT1 output routed to COM1',13,10,10,'$'
197:  SERIAL  ENDP
198:  CSEG    ENDS
199:         END     SERIAL
```

Listing A - 1

One caveat: the IBM version of MODE checks the Ctrl-Break data byte in low memory during every "wait" cycle while the printer is hung up, say while you are changing the ribbon. If you want to get control of your system back without restoring the printer to service, pressing Ctrl-Break will break the loop and force a "device not ready" error interrupt. SERIAL.SYS does not include this feature; you can stop the wait loop by turning off the system printer before pressing Ctrl-Break.

A second caveat: serial printers requiring "software" handshaking, rather than the "hardware" (DSR-CTS) handshaking built into the ROM BIOS support for the asynchronous communication adapters, may not be able to use SERIAL. Such printers require a special driver, either in the form of an installable device driver or a TSR program, intercepting the "normal" calls to COM1 and substituting the software handshaking protocol. If the special printer driver includes the rerouting from LPT1, neither MODE nor SERIAL.SYS is needed. If the special driver does not

```
 1:          PAGE      ,105
 2:          TITLE     PSWITCH
 3: ;******************************************************************
 4: ;                        PSWITCH.ASM                            *
 5: ;    PSWITCH.COM is a utility to switch the LPT1 output between the  *
 6: ; COM1 and LPT1 ports after the system has been booted with SERIAL.SYS *
 7: ; specified in the CONFIG.SYS file.                            *
 8: ;    To use:  Command line is "PSWITCH P" to switch to parallel port  *
 9: ;                             "PSWITCH S" to switch to serial port   *
10: ;    Any other usage will produce an error message return but no other  *
11: ; action.                                                      *
12: ;******************************************************************
13:
14: ;            Written by M. L. Lesser, July 24, 1986
15: ;            Reassembled with Microsoft MASM v 5.0
16: ;            Converted to PSWITCH.COM with EXE2BIN after linking
17:
18:
19: CSEG     SEGMENT PARA PUBLIC 'CODE'
20:          ASSUME CS:CSEG,DS:CSEG
21:          ORG       100H
22:
23: PSWITCH PROC NEAR
24:          MOV       AX,3D00H        ;Open SDRIVER device
25:          LEA       DX,FILE
26:          INT       21H
27:          JC        ERROR_1         ;SDRIVER device not installed
28:          PUSH      AX              ;Save handle for SDRIVER
29:          MOV       SI,80H          ;Start of command-line echo
30:          LODSB                     ;Count in AL
31:          OR        AL,AL           ;Anything there?
32:          JZ        ERROR_2         ;If not, command-line error
33: SPACER:                           ;Eliminate leading spaces
34:          LODSB                     ;Next character on command line
35:          CMP       AL,20H          ;Is it a space?
36:          JZ        SPACER          ;Skip intervening spaces
37:          OR        AL,20H          ;Convert to lowercase
38:          CMP       AL,'p'          ;Character must be 'p' or 's'
39:          JZ        DOIT
40:          CMP       AL,'s'
41:          JNZ       ERROR_2
42: DOIT:    XOR       AH,AH           ;Put command character in
43:          MOV       DX,AX           ;  IOCTL offset address register
44:          POP       BX              ;SDRIVER's handle
45:          MOV       CX,1            ;Not used or checked
46:          MOV       AX,4403H        ;IOCTL write call
47:          INT       21H
48:          MOV       AH,3EH          ;Close device file
49:          INT       21H
50:          MOV       AX,4C00H        ;Normal exit, errorlevel 0
51:          INT       21H
52: ERROR_1:                          ;SDRIVER not installed
53:          LEA       DX,ERMES_1
54:          JMP SHORT FINI
55: ERROR_2:                          ;Improper command line
56:          LEA       DX,ERMES_2
```

Listing A - 2 (continued)

```
57:  FINI:    MOV     AH,09H
58:           INT     21H
59:           MOV     AX,4C01H                ;Error exit, errorlevel 1
60:           INT     21H
61:
62:  ;  Local data:
63:  ERMES_1 DB       13,10,'SDRIVER not installed at boot'
64:          DB       13,10,9,'Cannot switch outputs',13,10,'$'
65:  ERMES_2 DB       13,10,'Improper input values'
66:          DB       13,10,9,'Usage for parallel output:  PSWITCH P'
67:          DB       13,10,9,'Usage for serial output:    PSWITCH S'
68:          DB       13,10,'$'
69:  FILE    DB       'SDRIVER',0
70:
71:  PSWITCH ENDP
72:  CSEG    ENDS
73:          END      PSWITCH
```

Listing A - 2

include the rerouting, and is an installable device driver that can be used with MODE, it may be possible to use it with SERIAL.SYS if the special driver is installed first. Device drivers are installed in the order named in the CONFIG.SYS command list.

Writing installable device drivers is not a game for the novice assembly-language programmer. The only complete source of information is the rather terse prose in the relevant chapter of the *DOS Technical Reference* manual. While there are several books for the "advanced" assembly-language programmer dealing (in whole or in part) with the subject of installable device drivers, those I have read do not add much information to that given in the manual. The best is in *MS-DOS Developer's Guide* by John Angermeyer and Kevin Jaeger (H. W. Sams & Co., Indianapolis, 1986).

According to all of these texts (including the manual), the driver shown in Listing A-1 should not work. It uses DOS functions 25H and 35H, neither of which are in the published lists of DOS functions available at boot time.

Appendix B

The IBM Extended Codes

IBM uses "extended codes" to identify the function and cursor keys not having extended ASCII code values. These extended codes are associated with function rather than with key position as are the keyboard *scan* codes shown in the QBASIC manual for use with keystroke trapping. For example, the extended codes of the duplicated cursor control keys on the "enhanced" (101-key) IBM keyboard are the same as for the numeric keypad cursor control keys. Some keys have additional extended codes when pressed simultaneously with a Shift, Ctrl, or Alt key.

The assembled function KBPEEK (Listing 5-2) returns the extended codes given in the following table. Keystroke combinations that have neither extended ASCII codes nor extended codes are discarded from the type-ahead buffer by KBPEEK (and by DOS). Discarded keys include those keys on the enhanced keyboard that do not have 83-key keyboard equivalents, such as the F11 and F12 keys.

The INKEY$ function returns extended codes (*except* that for Ctrl-Break) as 2-byte strings: the first byte will be a <NUL> [CHR$(0)] and the second byte will have the ASC() value corresponding to the extended code. INKEY$ removes any pending keystroke from the type-ahead buffer.

INPUT$ does not return extended codes; it returns only the leading <NUL> of the "2-byte" code and discards the information byte.

Neither INKEY$ nor INPUT$ will return Ctrl-Break to the program. For programs compiled without the /d switch, Ctrl-Break is ignored by all QBASIC statements except INPUT and LINE INPUT. For programs compiled with that switch, Ctrl-Break causes an immediate "Break" interrupt.

It is impossible to encode an ASCII <NUL> [Ctrl-@ or CHR$(0)] directly from the PC keyboard, as the PC does not conform to the ANSI keyboard standard. Among other idiosyncracies making an ANSI keyboard difficult for a skilled typist to use, "@" is specified in the standard as a lowercase character. On the PC and typewriter keyboards, "@" is the upper case value of the "2" key. So the PC equivalent of the ASCII <NUL> is Ctrl-2. If you need a keystroke <NUL> entry, your program must translate it from the extended code for Ctrl-2 [3].

The following table gives the extended codes returned by KBPEEK:

Code(s)	Keystroke(s)
0	Ctrl-break
3	Ctrl-2 (Ctrl-@, ASCII <NUL> substitute)
15	Back Tab (Shift-Tab)
16-25	Alt- Q,W,E,R,T,Y,U,I,O,P
30-38	Alt- A,S,D,F,G,H,J,K,L
44-50	Alt- Z,X,C,V,B,N,M
59-69	Function keys F1 through F10
71	Home
72	Cursor Up
73	PgUp
75	Cursor Left
77	Cursor Right
79	End
80	Cursor Down
81	PgDn
82	Ins (Insert)
83	Del (Delete)
84-93	F11 through F20 (Shift- F1 through F10)
94-103	F21 through F30 (Ctrl- F1 through F10)
104-113	F31 through F40 (Alt- F1 through F10)

114	Ctrl-PrtSc (DOS "Echo to printer")
115	Ctrl-Cursor Left
116	Ctrl-Cursor Right
117	Ctrl-End
118	Ctrl-PgDn
119	Ctrl-Home
120-131	Alt- 1,2,3,4,5,6,7,8,9,0,-,=
132	Ctrl-PgUp

Index

Special Software Offer!

Get a running start on QuickBASIC 4.0 software development with the example programs from this book!

The library and utility software featured in *Advanced QuickBASIC 4.0* is available for only $9.95, plus $3.00 for shipping and handling.

Why spend hours typing it in yourself? Send us your check, or call us at our 800 number, and we'll send you a 5 $\frac{1}{4}$" or 3 $\frac{1}{2}$" diskette with all the source code from the library and utility programs in the book.

This disk is not available in stores; it can only be purchased directly from the publisher.

Use this coupon to order, or call 1-800-223-6834, ext. 479, and have your credit card information handy.

Mail to: Bantam Books, Inc., Dept. QB4
666 Fifth Avenue
New York, NY 10103

Yes! Send me the *Advanced QuickBASIC 4.0 Program Disk* (50054-6) for only $12.95 ($9.95 plus $3.00 for shipping and handling.)

I need the   ☐ 5 $\frac{1}{4}$"   ☐ 3 $\frac{1}{2}$" disk format. (Check one)

Name _____

Address _____

City _____ State _____ Zip _____

My check or money order for $12.95 is enclosed. (Please make check payable to Bantam Books, Inc.)

Charge my ☐ Visa ☐ MasterCard ☐ American Express
Acct. # _____ Exp. Date _____
Signature _____